*Reading Revelation Missiologically* is a rare gem that focuses on the contribution of the book of Revelation to the mission of God. The authors, drawn from different theological commitments and ecclesial traditions, challenge the readers to utilize the book of Revelation for life, ministry, and mission. This is a timely, well-researched, and inspiring call to see Revelation not merely as prophecy, and certainly not as that book we fear to read, but as an inspiration for how we live, worship, and expect the return of our Lord and Savior Jesus Christ. Take it. Read it. Let it propel you to serve faithfully in and for God's mission.

**David Tarus**, PhD
Executive Director, Association for Christian Theological Education in Africa (ACTEA)

This edited volume provides a contextual understanding of the book of Revelation in relation to mission, engaging scholars from diverse backgrounds. It addresses relevant issues concerning both the text and the contemporary context, making it a valuable addition for biblical and missiological students.

**Nebeyou A. Tefere**, PhD
Bible Translation Consultant, Wycliffe Ethiopia

## Other Books in the Reading Missiologically Series

*Reading Hebrews Missiologically* (2023)
Abeneazer G. Urga, Edward L. Smither, and Linda P. Saunders, Editors

*Reading 1 Peter Missiologically* (2024)
Abeneazer G. Urga, Jessica A. Udall, and Edward L. Smither, Editors

*Reading James Missiologically* (2025)
Abeneazer G. Urga, Jessica A. Udall, and Edward L. Smither, Editors

*Reading 2 Peter and Jude Missiologically* (forthcoming)
Abeneazer G. Urga, Jessica A. Udall, and Edward L. Smither, Editors

## About the Cover Artwork

"Procession to the King"
(1 Thessalonians 4:17)
Acrylic on canvas 11 x 13 in.

"Then we which are alive and remain shall be caught up together with them in the clouds, to meet the Lord in the air: and so shall we ever be with the Lord." (1 Thess 4:17 KJV)

I was inspired by the words of a song I love that tells of the great catching away of the saints up to our King Jesus. My painting depicts every race, tongue, and tribe throughout all the ages being caught up into that great event which ends this present age and ushers in the manifest kingdom of God. I can only imagine the total awe and delight we will experience in that twinkling of an eye! I particularly wanted to portray the message that disunity will be no more. We will see each other as He sees us. At long last, we will be one in Christ together. Glory!

Used with permission by Victoria Mundy.

Few would think to turn to the book of Revelation when it comes to the topic of missiology and missions in the New Testament, but they would perhaps miss one of the most profoundly visionary missional texts of the Bible. This is something robustly demonstrated in *Reading Revelation Missiologically*, edited by Abeneazer G. Urga, Michael P. Naylor, and Edward L. Smither. This volume contains stimulating and insightful essays written by first-rate biblical and missiological scholars. The essays are grouped according to the missionary motivation, message, and methods found within John's Apocalypse. While I have long believed Revelation has a missiological thrust, these essays explore and argue for it with extensive and profound depth beyond anything I've ever seen before. This book examines missiology in Revelation with scholarly acumen, methodological rigor, and vibrant faithfulness. I highly recommend this book and believe it is an excellent contribution to scholarship in the fields of Revelation and missiology studies.

**Alan S. Bandy**, PhD
Professor of New Testament & Greek and Robert L. Hamblin Chair of New Testament Exposition, New Orleans Baptist Theological Seminary

All of the writings that make up the New Testament were produced in the context of the missiological engagement between the followers of Jesus and the surrounding culture of the ancient Roman world. Sadly, these texts, and especially Revelation, have frequently not been read with this missional purpose in mind, leading to conclusions that are often at odds with the mission of God in the world. The essays in this volume seek to recover the missional intent and purpose of Revelation, and in so doing provide fresh insights into the most misunderstood text of the New Testament.

**John R. Franke**, DPhil
Affiliate Professor of Theology, Fuller Theological Seminary
Coauthor, *Liberating Scripture: An Invitation to Missional Hermeneutics*

The biblical canon has a missional trajectory that moves from one nation to all nations. Therefore, reading any part of the scriptural canon faithfully must align with this missional direction. Our blindness to this in the past is being overcome today by a growing number of publications that engage various parts of the canon with a missional hermeneutic. In this book, a fine group of international scholars helps us see the missional orientation of the book of Revelation. Revelation perhaps contains the richest theology of any New Testament book and has mission at the core of its message. I am delighted to see this book come into print and to see such good scholarship put to the task of examining various dimensions of the unfolding message of Revelation for the sake of the church's mission today.

**Michael W. Goheen**, PhD
Professor of Missional Theology, Calvin Theological Seminary

I have long argued that Revelation is a missional text for a missional people in a challenging, even dangerous context. The scholarly but readable—and timely—chapters in this book confirm, expand, and deepen that view of Revelation from diverse perspectives. Every student and teacher of the Bible's last book will benefit immensely from this volume.

**Michael J. Gorman**, PhD
Raymond E. Brown Professor of Biblical Studies and Theology,
St. Mary's Seminary & University

In all my years of life and service in the church, no other part of the Bible has sparked half as much misunderstanding, anxiety, and genuine fear in myself and my fellow Christ-followers as John's Apocalypse. Helpfully, the cure for such maladies lies right in this volume's title. *Reading Revelation Missiologically* (another formidable volume in a landmark series) unveils one of the most mysterious books in Christian Scripture by inviting us to place the book within the context of God's unfolding mission to reconcile the whole cosmos to himself. The authors expertly unpack the final words of the Bible, examining what mission means in Revelation, how it functions in the book, and how it forms the church to understand itself and its work in the world. This volume belongs on the shelves of missiologists, practical theologians, and pastors alike. Anyone who wants to better understand why God sent this Revelation to his beloved churches will be greatly edified by *Reading Revelation Missiologically*. I plan to do so from now on.

**Danny Hunter**, PhD
Director of the Ralph D. Winter Research Center,
William Carey International University

*Reading Revelation Missiologically* is a timely and incisive contribution to contemporary biblical and missiological scholarship. For too long, Revelation has been marginalized by both scholars and church practitioners, often dismissed for its dense symbolism and apocalyptic imagery. Yet in the wake of the COVID-19 pandemic and amid ongoing global disruption, apocalyptic language has resurfaced as a vital existential discourse that offers not only hope but also profound insight into what it means to be human in a world marked by uncertainty and upheaval.

In this context, an evangelical missiological reading of Revelation is both urgent and indispensable. This volume boldly reclaims Revelation's theological and missional dimensions, unveiling a compelling portrait of a missionary God actively engaged in history's unfolding drama. It is a significant, courageous, and necessary work—one that should command the attention of biblical scholars, theologians, missiologists, and mission practitioners alike.

**Chammah J. Kaunda**, PhD
Academic Dean, Oxford Centre for Mission Studies

# Reading Revelation Missiologically

## The Missionary Motive, Message, and Methods of Revelation

Abeneazer G. Urga,
Michael P. Naylor
Edward L. Smither,
Editors

*Reading Revelation Missiologically: The Missionary Motive, Message, and Methods of Revelation*



Published by William Carey Publishing
10 W. Dry Creek Cir.
Littleton, CO 80120 | www.missionbooks.org

William Carey Publishing is a ministry of Frontier Ventures
Pasadena, CA | www.frontierventures.org

Cover and Interior Designer: Mike Riester

ISBNs: 978-1-64508-680-2 (paperback)
978-1-64508-682-6 (epub)

Printed Worldwide

29 28 27 26 25 1 2 3 4 5 IN

Library of Congress Control Number: 2025946510

# Contents

# Preface

Only a few works on Revelation have shown that it is a missionary document. For the most part, works on New Testament theology of mission have zeroed in on the Gospels, Acts, and Pauline Epistles while often ignoring the contributions of the General Epistles and Revelation. The recent exceptions are Michael J. Gorman's *Reading Revelation Responsibly* (Cascade Books, 2011), and Dean Flemming's *Foretaste of the Future: Reading Revelation in Light of God's Mission* (IVP Academic, 2022). Flemming particularly provides a book-length discussion on the motif of mission in Revelation. *Reading Revelation Missiologically* is a sequel to *Reading Hebrews Missiologically* (2023), *Reading 1 Peter Missiologically* (2024), and *Reading James Missiologically* (2025) that aims to fill the gap by putting Revelation in the limelight. This volume explores Revelation's theology of mission and shows that Revelation is replete with the theme of God's mission and that God's people are called to participate in this missionary endeavor through witnessing, suffering, and worship until the consummation of the eschaton.

As the preceding volumes in this series have been structured, *Reading Revelation Missiologically* consists of three parts: the missionary motive of Revelation, the missionary message of Revelation, and the missionary methods of Revelation. The missionary motive addresses the "why" aspect of mission, the missionary message deals with the "what" (content) of mission, and missionary methods examine the "how" of mission and highlight the descriptive and prescriptive aspects of mission in Revelation.

Instead of putting forth a single definition of "mission" at the outset of the book, we have allowed each contributor to flesh out this complex concept in their own way as it relates to their topic. Thus, we believe this book makes the idea of mission shine, highlighting multifaceted aspects in unique and edifying ways. The contributors to this volume hail from a variety of ecclesial, cultural, theological, and ministerial backgrounds, all bringing their unique vantage points to Revelation, which will give readers enriching insights and perspectives on its missiological interpretation.

Part 1 deals with the missionary motive of Revelation—beginning with Alexander E. Stewart's evaluation of the foretaste of the future hermeneutic that denotes that the visions of the future in Revelation invite and motivate God's people to participate in God's mission. In chapter 2, Michael P. Naylor explores the Trinitarian theology of mission of Revelation and underscores the role of the Father, Son, and Spirit and the role of God's people in witnessing about God's redemptive salvation. In chapter 3, Cornelia van Deventer zooms in on the Third Person of the Trinity, the Spirit. Her chapter pays more attention to the much-sidelined role of the Spirit in mission in Revelation by fleshing out the speaking, seeing, and sending roles of the Spirit. In chapter 4, Sarah Lunsford challenges the common misconception in contemporary mission studies that the final goal of the *missio Dei* is that God will be glorified. Rather, Lunsford contends, the *telos* of God's mission is to share his glory with his peoples, and this glory-sharing mission is propelled by his love. In chapter 5, Alistair I. Wilson demonstrates that the vision of God's mission is to dwell among humanity.

Part 2 examines the missionary message of Revelation. Chapter 6 opens with John D. Harvey's examination of the motif of judgment and salvation in Revelation, both as a warning and encouragement. In chapter 7, Andrea L. Robinson underlines a vital fact that the church needs to heed: "Victory is attained through suffering and self-sacrifice." She points out this inevitable reality from the two faithful witnesses in Revelation 11. Jessica Janvier concludes this section in chapter 8 by fleshing out the missional political theology of Revelation, which critiques the idolatrous, violent, and oppressive empire of Rome. Janvier denotes that Revelation's missiological political theology invites (God's) peoples to emulate the Lamb rather than Rome.

Part 3 discusses the missionary methods of Revelation. Chapter 9 begins with Kwa Kiem-Kiok's chapter "Worship, Discipleship, and Politics in Revelation: Asian Perspectives." She proposes that Revelation clearly shows that God's people are to advance the cause of the kingdom through discipleship, worship, and Christians' involvement in the public square, particularly in politics. In chapter 10, Narry F. Santos overviews the role of God's people as witnesses by exploring the fourfold formula (i.e., nation, tribe, language, and people). In chapter 11, Sigurd Grindheim contends that the faithful witnessing of the suffering church is the primary means of bringing many peoples to repentance. Edward L. Smither ably demonstrates in chapter 12 that God's hospitality is both the outcome and the means of mission, which brings a "great multitude" to commune at the wedding supper of the Lamb and fellowship with God, and chapter 13 explicates Grant LeMarquand's discussion of the missiological aspect of worship. He insists that the faithful witness of God's people and their suffering for his sake will lead many to repentance and to worship the Lamb. In chapter 14, Michel

Kenmogne concludes part 3 with his examination of the implications of the all-inclusive worship in Revelation. He particularly points out the importance of language and Bible translation to make the all-inclusive worship a reality.

We hope that this volume fills the gap in the literature on New Testament theology of mission as we look forward to singing:

> Worthy are you to take the scroll
>     and to open its seals,
> for you were slain, and by your blood you ransomed people for God
>     from every tribe and language and people and nation,
> and you have made them a kingdom and priests to our God,
>     and they shall reign on the earth. (Rev 5:9–10 ESV)

Abeneazer G. Urga, Addis Ababa, Ethiopia
Michael P. Naylor, Columbia, South Carolina
Edward L. Smither, Columbia, South Carolina
May 2025

Part 1

# The Missionary Motive of Revelation

# Chapter 1

## Explicit Argumentation and a Foretaste of the Future Hermeneutic

*Alexander E. Stewart*

Dean Flemming recently produced a missional reading of Revelation that is accessible and often insightful.[1] He argues throughout his study of Revelation in light of God's mission that "Revelation seeks to shape and equip Christian communities to participate in God's saving purpose by living as a foretaste of God's coming new creation now, through their lips and through their lives."[2] Revelation does seek to shape and equip Christian communities, but Flemming's conclusion about the goal of this shaping and equipping ("to participate in God's saving purpose by living as a foretaste of God's coming new creation now") is less explicit in the book itself. I have elsewhere sought to argue something similar using the framework of social identity theory: Revelation's vision of the inclusive nature of new creation restoration (a saved humanity from every tribe, tongue, people, and nation and every economic level) both shaped the early Christians in their thinking about the composition of their communities and motivated them to make that vision of the future at least a partial reality in the present through mission and witness.[3] On this foretaste of the future reading, Revelation's vision of the future motivates its hearers to try to live out of and into that future vision in the present time. The visions in Revelation function as the ideal toward which we work in the less-than-ideal present.

The visions in Revelation can have this effect on motivated hearers, but it should also be acknowledged that such conclusions are not explicitly grounded in the text. To some degree, these conclusions must be inferred from the text using specific theoretical frameworks or reading strategies. That does not mean that such a foretaste of the future hermeneutic is a wrong way of thinking about how the text could function to inform and motivate mission, but rather it suggests that this was not how the first author and hearers were explicitly thinking about the impact of the text. Revelation is a challenging book, and we need to be careful that our missional readings do not domesticate it or make it more compelling to modern readers by

1 Flemming, *Foretaste of the Future.*

2 Flemming, 3.

3 Stewart, "Role of Fear and Hope," 85–97, 92–93.

emphasizing things that are not emphasized in the text or by failing to emphasize those that are.

This chapter will consider what Revelation explicitly shapes Christian communities to do by considering the explicit argumentation expressed through imperatives in the text. Such a study will keep our missional imagination carefully grounded in the exegetical details while considering the motive, message, and methods of mission in Revelation.

## Explicit Argumentation: Imperatives

There are 114 imperatives (both second and third person) in the Greek text of Revelation.[4] Of these, thirty-eight are directed toward the hearers of the book, eight of which stereotypically call upon the one who has ears to hear (Rev 2:7, 11, 17, 29; 3:6, 13, 22; 13:9).[5] That leaves thirty imperatives in fourteen verses to indicate the explicit motivational goals communicated by Revelation to its hearers.[6] Most of these hearers are assumed to belong to the seven addressed communities, and Revelation is primarily addressed to insiders of the Christian movement. However, 14:7 is addressed to any hearer, 22:11 includes hearers who were presumably not overcoming in its first two imperatives, and 22:17 seems to be addressed to any potential hearer.

---

4 For the purpose of this study, both second- and third-person imperatives are considered together as explicit indications of the author's rhetorical goals. Despite how they may sound in English, third-person imperatives do not communicate permission but instead make a volitional demand upon the hearer. See Wallace, *Greek Grammar*, 486.

5 The remaining imperatives fall into three categories. Twenty-eight are directed at John: Revelation 1:11 (two), 17, 19; 2:1, 8, 12, 18; 3:1, 7, 14; 4:1; 5:5; 10:4, 8 (two), 9 (two); 11:1 (two), 2; 14:13; 19:9, 10 (two); 21:5; 22:9 (two). Twenty-six are the rhetorically emphatic use of "behold" (Ἰδού): Revelation 1:7, 18; 2:10, 22; 3:8, 9 (two), 20; 4:1, 2; 5:5; 6:2, 5, 8; 7:9; 9:12; 11:14; 12:3; 14:1, 14; 16:15; 19:11; 21:3, 5; 22:7, 12. Twenty-two are directed at other characters in the visions: the four horsemen (6:1, 3, 5, 7), mountains and rocks (6:16 [two]), an angel (9:14), the two witnesses (11:12), the heavens and those dwelling in them (12:12), the one sitting on the cloud (14:15 [two]), to the angel with a sharp sickle (14:18 [two]), to the seven angels (16:1 [two]), unspecified punishing agents (18:6 [three]), heaven (18:20), birds (19:17), Jesus (22:20).

6 My earlier study of explicit argumentation in Revelation analyzed verbal indicators of logical relations to identify twelve instances of explicit motivational argumentation: Revelation 2:4–5, 10, 16, 25–26; 3:2, 3, 11, 18, 19; 14:7; 18:4, 20. The approach utilized here, of looking at imperatives directed at the hearers, leads to the removal of Revelation 2:4, 26; 3:18; 18:20 and the addition of 13:18; 19:5; 22:11, 17 to the list. See Stewart, *Soteriology as Motivation*, 215–24.

| Imperatives Directed Toward the Hearers of Revelation[7] | |
|---|---|
| Rev 2:5 | **Remember** then from what you have fallen; **repent**, and **do** the works you did at first. If not, I will come to you and remove your lampstand from its place, unless you repent. |
| Rev 2:10 | **Do not fear** what you are about to suffer. Beware, the devil is about to throw some of you into prison so that you may be tested, and for ten days you will have affliction. **Be faithful** until death, and I will give you the crown of life. |
| Rev 2:16 | **Repent** then. If not, I will come to you soon and make war against them with the sword of my mouth. |
| Rev 2:25 | . . . only **hold fast** to what you have until I come. |
| Rev 3:2 | **Wake up**, and **strengthen** what remains and is on the point of death, for I have not found your works perfect in the sight of my God. |
| Rev 3:3 | **Remember** then what you received and heard; **obey** it, and **repent**. If you do not wake up, I will come like a thief, and you will not know at what hour I will come to you. |
| Rev 3:11 | I am coming soon; **hold fast** to what you have, so that no one may seize your crown. |
| Rev 3:19 | I reprove and discipline those whom I love. **Be earnest**, therefore, and **repent**. |
| Rev 13:18 | This calls for wisdom: let anyone with understanding **calculate** the number of the beast, for it is the number of a person. Its number is six hundred sixty-six. |
| Rev 14:7 | He said in a loud voice, "**Fear** God and **give** him glory, for the hour of his judgment has come; and **worship** him who made heaven and earth, the sea and the springs of water." |
| Rev 18:4 | Then I heard another voice from heaven saying, "**Come out** of her, my people, so that you do not take part in her sins, and so that you do not share in her plagues." |
| Rev 19:5 | And from the throne came a voice saying, "**Praise** our God, all you his servants, and all who fear him, small and great." |
| Rev 22:11 | Let the evildoer still **do evil**, and the filthy still **be filthy**, and the righteous still **do right**, and the holy still **be holy**. |
| Rev 22:17 | The Spirit and the bride say, "**Come**." And let everyone who hears **say**, "**Come**." And let everyone who is thirsty **come**. Let anyone who wishes **take** the water of life as a gift. |

7 All English quotations are from the NRSV.

A survey of this list of imperatives leads to the following observations: All the imperatives directed toward the seven communities in Revelation 2–3 focus either on repentance or perseverance (in the order they occur in the text: remember, repent, do, do not fear, be faithful, repent, hold fast, wake up, strengthen, remember, obey, repent, hold fast, be earnest, repent).[8] All these imperatives are directed toward Jesus-followers with the goal of motivating them to overcome by repenting when necessary and persevering amid certain suffering and opposition. There is no obvious missional focus on outsiders in these imperatives, and the focus is instead on the preservation of the faithful community, which is in significant danger of extinction through religious syncretism and outright persecution. The call to repentance is generally linked to warnings and threats of judgment if the imperatives are not obeyed, while the focus on perseverance includes calls to obedience and faithfulness. These imperatives directed to the seven churches are the clearest indications in Revelation of the impact the book was intended to have on its hearers: Revelation seeks to motivate Christian hearers to repent and persevere in order to overcome.

The remaining imperatives directed at the hearers are more diverse in their scope. Revelation 13:18 invites hearers to engage in gematria to determine the meaning of the number of the beast; the number is likely a reference to Nero, but this is not the place to explore those implications in more detail.[9] Revelation 14:7 contains three imperatives that summarize the eternal gospel that is proclaimed to "those who live on the earth—to every nation and tribe and language and people" (v. 6). The eternal gospel calls upon every human being to fear God, give him glory, and worship him. This seems to summarize the saving human response to God in Revelation. It is a response to the gospel that directs worship and allegiance away from the beast to the creator and ruler of the universe.[10] Revelation does not speak about salvation by grace through faith. When "faith" is mentioned in Revelation it

---

8 Osborne, *Revelation*, 42–46, argues for "perseverance of the saints" as the overarching theme of Revelation that subsumes other concepts such as "endurance, faithfulness, witness, conquering, and obedience" (p. 42).

9 See Gumerlock, "Nero Antichrist," 347–60; Koester, "Number of the Beast," 1–21; Williams, "P115 and the Number," 151–53.

10 It is possible to read this announcement of the eternal gospel as primarily a message of judgment (Beale, *Revelation*, 748–50), but it seems better in line with the rhetorical nature of the book to see it as containing a genuine offer of salvation (Smalley, *Revelation to John*, 362–63; Osborne, *Revelation*, 534–36; Altink, "I Chronicles 16:8–36," 187–89; Michaels, *Revelation*, 173).

carries the idea of faithfulness or allegiance and not belief (2:13, 19; 13:10; 14:12), while the verb "believe" does not occur in the book. It is important not to draw the wrong conclusions from this observation, as if John and Paul were opposed to each other, since John likely assumes faith is included in allegiance expressed through worship.

Revelation 18:4 includes a command to God's people to come out of Babylon to avoid sharing in her sins and judgments.[11] Revelation 17–21 contains an explicit contrast between the Lamb's bride and the prostitute Babylon, and God's people (both Jew and gentile) are meant to identify with the bride and disassociate from the prostitute (18:4). This imperative is similar to the imperatives in the seven proclamations of Revelation 2–3 in how it is focused on the spiritual health and preservation of the Christian hearers. The call to come out of Babylon is a call to repentance and perseverance.

Revelation 19:1–8 describes future worship in heaven in response to God's judgment of Babylon, while 19:5 contains a command for God's people to join in this heavenly worship. This could be dismissed as a description of a future command, but it seems to function rhetorically in Revelation as an invitation to current hearers to participate preemptively in this heavenly worship. The scenes of heavenly worship throughout Revelation seem to function rhetorically this way, even though 19:5 is the only imperative directed to the hearers to participate in heavenly worship. Although implicit, this imperative linked to worship would support Flemming's foretaste of the future approach, noted in the introduction, of viewing the visions in Revelation as a call to God's people to live "as a foretaste of God's coming new creation now."[12] The hearers of Revelation are implicitly invited, by their worship in the present, to begin to engage in the praise and worship of God, which is already taking place in heaven and will continue into the new creation (22:3). The invitational nature of 19:5 is strengthened by the scenes

11 It is possible to connect this imperative with the imperatives calling for punishment in Revelation 18:6–8. It is true that in apocalyptic literature, the righteous do sometimes function as agents of divine judgment. Aune, *Revelation 17–22*, 994, notes 1 En. 90:19; 91:12; 95:3, 7; 96:1; 98:12; Jub. 23:30; Apoc. Ab. 29.17–20. The execution of judgment in Revelation, however, is consistently connected to God (Rev 18:8, 20; cf. 6:9–11; 8:2–5; 11:3–6, 18; 12:7–10; 14:8–20; 15:7; 16:5–7; 17:1, 17), and the command to "pay her back" in 18:6 does not naturally fit with the other imperatives directed toward the hearers in Revelation. It seems more natural to interpret it as an imperative toward angelic avenging divine agents. Koester notes that the imperatives in Revelation 18:6–8 are ambiguous, but that they are not likely directed at the saints because in Revelation "agents of evil destroy each other (Rev 17:16) or are destroyed by Christ (17:14; 19:11–21)." *Revelation*, 700.

12 Flemming, *Foretaste of the Future*, 3.

of worship and praise throughout the book, which seem to model for the hearers the proper saving response to God (4:1–11; 5:6–14; 7:9–17; 8:1–5; 11:15–19; 12:10–12; 14:1–5; 15:1–4; 16:1–7; 19:1–8).[13]

Revelation 22:11 is enigmatic and could be interpreted as promoting a form of determinism or fatalism that is entirely inimical to a missional reading of the book. The four third-person imperatives could be read that way, but in light of how all the other imperatives in Revelation call the hearer to respond and assume that the reader could and might respond in a saving manner, it is better to read the first two imperatives in Revelation 22:11 as a rhetorical strategy to motivate hearers to be the ones who respond properly and not the ones who respond negatively and are confirmed in their evil and filth.[14] Read this way, 22:11 is intended to motivate hearers to turn away from evil and choose righteousness and holiness.[15]

Revelation 22:17 contains five imperatives, which all seem to be directed toward hearers of Revelation in different ways and are quite important to any missional reading of Revelation. First, the Spirit and the bride call the hearer to "come."[16] Second, everyone who hears is commanded to invite others to "come." Third, everyone who is thirsty is invited to come. Fourth, anyone who wishes is invited to take the water of life as a gift. So the hearers are commanded to join in the invitation extended by the Spirit and bride to hearers to come, overcome in life, and enter the new Jerusalem. The invitation to take the water of life freely is extended to anyone who is thirsty

---

13 On worship in Revelation see Grabiner, *Revelation's Hymns*; Schedtler, *Heavenly Chorus*; Peterson, "Worship in the Revelation to John," 67–77; O'Rourke, "Hymns of the Apocalypse," 399–409; Kooy, "Apocalypse and Worship," 198–209; Barr, "Apocalypse of John as Oral Enactment," 243–56.

14 Ezekiel 3:27 contains a similar rhetorical move in how it uses third-person imperatives to call the hearer to hear and the one who refuses to refuse. The assumption in both Ezekiel and Revelation is that some indeed will refuse to respond to the call to repentance, but this does not happen in a deterministic manner. The stark reality that some will be confirmed in their rebellion is meant to motivate other hearers to hear and respond in a saving manner.

15 Cf. Koester, *Revelation*, 841.

16 The prayer to Jesus to come in Revelation 22:20 leads many interpreters to read these first imperatives in 22:17 as a prayer for Jesus to come (Koester, *Revelation*, 844), but in light of the following imperatives to the one who thirsts and the one who desires in the second half of 22:17, it seems preferable to read the imperatives in this verse as an invitation to the hearers to come to the new Jerusalem to drink from the living water. The clear allusion to Isaiah 55:1 would seem to confirm that the commands to come are an invitation to the hearer: "Ho, everyone who thirsts, come to the waters; and you that have no money, come, buy and eat! Come, buy wine and milk without money and without price." Beale, *Revelation*, 1149.

and anyone who desires to do so. This verse, which comes in the closing verses of the book, marks the entire book of Revelation with a stamp of invitation. The visions in Revelation do not describe a promised future reserved for a few exclusive communities or individuals. This future is open to anyone who would recognize their need, their thirst, and respond positively to the invitation from the Spirit and the community to join in God's promised future salvation, which was being partially realized and concretely embodied at the time by the existing Christian communities.

In addition to the main explicit persuasive and motivational goals of Revelation, evident by the use of imperatives, another theme related to mission must be noted. Revelation implicitly seeks to highlight the importance of active witness.[17] Jesus and Antipas are both described as faithful witnesses (1:5; 2:13; 3:14) in such a way as to invite emulation. The lampstand metaphor could suggest the idea of public witness (1:12, 13, 20; 11:4), and witnesses feature throughout the book as John himself bears witness (1:2, 9). The slain witnesses under the altar call out for justice and vindication (6:9–11); the two witnesses in 11:1–14 fulfill their mission, are killed, and are vindicated through resurrection. Victory over the dragon is attained through the blood of the Lamb and the word of witness in 12:10–12, and witnesses are shown as reigning in victory in 20:4–6. This focus on witness, however, needs to be understood from within the book itself, as Olutola K. Peters helpfully explains.

> It can be seen that "faithful witness" for the Church is a comprehensive mandate which implies maintaining authenticity and truthfulness (shunning all forms of falsehood and deception), hearing the voice of the Spirit, mediating the words of prophecy (especially as contained in the Apocalypse), showing patient endurance (especially in the midst of persecution), giving obedience to the commandments of God (especially those commanded by Christ—the sender of the letters and the revealer of the contents of the Apocalypse), being an overcomer, and expressing purity of devotion to Christ through worship, lifestyle, teachings and beliefs (especially in the midst of deception and perversion).[18]

17 The following examples are discussed at length in Peters, *Mandate of the Church*; Poythress, *Returning King*, 71; Blount, *Revelation*.

18 Peters, *Mandate of the Church*, 117–18.

Peters here fills in the content of "witness" from the explicit imperatives noted above.[19] The challenge remains, however, that no imperatives actually call upon God's people to engage in witness, and the promotion of witness as a missional goal of Revelation remains implicit.

In summary, the explicit imperatives in Revelation primarily focus on the spiritual health and preservation of the believing communities, as hearers are repeatedly called upon to repent and persevere in faithfulness and obedience. In the words of Revelation, the main goal of the book is to motivate hearers to be overcomers.[20] Three verses have a noticeably different focus. The imperatives contained in the eternal gospel in Revelation 14:7 uniquely call upon every human being to fear and worship God, the imperative in 19:5 calls upon hearers to participate in the worship of God, and the imperatives in 22:17 function to invite hearers to respond positively to the book's message by coming to drink from the water of life.

With the explicit emphasis of the imperatives in mind, we can tease out some further implications hinted at above, related to the church's posture toward outsiders. Based on 22:17, the Christian communities should adopt a posture of invitation to outsiders, to those who recognize their need and are thirsty. They should not be exclusive clubs but should indiscriminately invite anyone who wants to join the community and confidently embrace its hope for future access to the new Jerusalem. The churches should offer an invitation to repentance and the promise of water for thirsty souls, along with a great deal of suffering and the promise of increasing persecution until Jesus returns. This is an inclusive invitation in terms of ethnicity, language, and social and economic status, but it is not a theologically inclusive invitation, and respondents must submit to the rule and reign of Jesus as king.

The proclamation of the eternal gospel in 14:7 serves as a model, not just to invite people to come, but to proclaim God's truth to the entire world and to call anyone who might listen to respond to the message with allegiance expressed through worship. The theme of witness throughout Revelation supports this proclamation but also nuances it. Witness in Revelation is not just invitation and proclamation, but rather, the witness of God's people functions as negative evidence against those who reject God's rule

19 Flemming helpfully describes how witness in Revelation is verbal, embodied, public, and for the sake of the world. *Foretaste of the Future*, 110–15.

20 On overcoming in Revelation, see Shin, "More Than Conquerors"; Homcy, "To Him Who Overcomes," 193–201; den Dulk, "Promises to the Conquerors," 516–22; Aune, "Following the Lamb," 269–84.

in the final judgment; this is evident particularly in the visions of the slain witnesses under the altar in 6:9–11 and the opposed and killed witnesses of 11:1–14. Witnesses both bear witness of God's rule to the nations by way of proclamation and invitation and bear witness against oppressors and those who ally with the beasts against God's people.

## Conclusion

Revelation is a difficult book, and there have been no shortage of attempts to domesticate it or make it more serviceable to particular visions of Christian faith, practice, and mission through imposing various reading strategies or hermeneutical models. As noted in the introduction, it is tempting to employ a foretaste of the future approach to Revelation whereby the visions of the future invite and motivate participation and action in the present as a way to live into God's promised future. There is some indication, particularly in Revelation 19:5, that Revelation intended to have just this effect upon readers, at least in regard to worship. It would thus seem that a foretaste of the future approach is a legitimate reading strategy to seek to determine how Revelation might motivate and inform our participation in God's mission in the world.

It is also necessary, however, to keep in mind that such an approach is largely implicit, whereas Revelation provides explicit indications of how it sought to shape and equip Christian communities to be and to act in the world through the imperative mood. Revelation's main rhetorical goal for the Christian communities is to shape and equip them to be faithful and to persevere in the midst of intense pressure to compromise morally and religiously. Such compromise would cause the communities to lose their unique identities and dissolve into the surrounding syncretistic society. Based on the imperatives in Revelation, Christian communities first and foremost engage in God's mission in the world by surviving in faithfulness and obedience to Jesus alone. Such survival is victory over the forces of supernatural evil intent on the destruction of God's people.

It is tempting to skip past this goal as rudimentary or as something that can be assumed in order to focus on how a faithful and obedient community of faith could engage in God's mission to rescue and restore people and creation, but Revelation itself does not significantly move beyond this goal in an explicit way, and caution should be exercised when proposing missional readings that deviate from Revelation's explicit focus.

An example of this danger can be seen in using Revelation to argue for the inclusion of environmental action and advocacy within the scope of Christian mission. Flemming makes this argument by claiming that "Revelation calls us to engage in God's transforming purpose of 'making everything new' (Rev 21:5 NIV)."[21] This statement is wrong in that Revelation makes no such call upon Christians; in Revelation, God is the one who makes all things new. Flemming nuances the claim more carefully when he states, "Such care for the planet enables God's people to bear witness to God's commitment to make everything new, as a foretaste of the new creation to come."[22] This more nuanced claim seems logically appropriate in a foretaste of the future hermeneutical framework, but it also seems quite removed from what John actually and explicitly calls upon his hearers to do. This disconnect becomes more glaring when Flemming argues that Revelation "can help set an agenda for Christian environmental action and advocacy" that begins with repentance for the harm we have done to the environment.[23] Revelation does call God's people to repentance, but not for that reason and toward that end. The imperatives in Revelation make it explicitly clear that Revelation seeks to motivate and enable God's people to overcome in life through repentance and persevering faithfulness. The more a foretaste of the future reading deviates from the explicit emphasis of the text itself, the more doubtful it becomes.

In conclusion, this study of the imperatives in Revelation suggests that a foretaste of the future missional hermeneutic could be a legitimate means by which the visions in Revelation shape our understanding of the motive, message, and methods of Christian mission, but such a hermeneutic should not replace or overshadow clear statements from the text that call the hearer to action with hypothetical ideas about the effect the visions could or should have upon a hearer. When our reading strategies take priority over explicit statements, we run the danger of using the authority of Scripture to advocate for positions and causes that are far removed from the concerns and emphases of the original author and hearers.

---

21 Flemming, *Foretaste of the Future*, 42.

22 Flemming, 44.

23 Flemming, 219.

## Bibliography

Altink, William. "I Chronicles 16:8–36 as a Literary Source for Revelation 14:6–7." *Andrews University Seminary Studies* 22 (1984): 187–96.

Aune, David E. "Following the Lamb: Discipleship in the Apocalypse." In *Patterns of Discipleship in the New Testament*, edited by Richard N. Longenecker. Eerdmans, 1996.

Aune, David E. *Revelation 17–22*. Word Biblical Commentary 52C. Thomas Nelson, 1998.

Barr, David L. "The Apocalypse of John as Oral Enactment." *Interpretation* 40, no. 3 (1986): 243–56.

Beale, G. K. *The Book of Revelation*. New International Greek Testament Commentary. Eerdmans, 1999.

Blount, Brian K. *Revelation: A Commentary*. New Testament Library. Westminster John Knox, 2009.

den Dulk, Matthijs. "The Promises to the Conquerors in the Book of Revelation." *Biblica* 87, no. 4 (2006): 516–22.

Flemming, Dean. *Foretaste of the Future: Reading Revelation in Light of God's Mission*. IVP Academic, 2022.

Grabiner, Steven. *Revelation's Hymns: Commentary on the Cosmic Conflict*. Library of New Testament Studies 511. T&T Clark, 2015.

Gumerlock, F. X. "Nero Antichrist: Patristic Evidence for the Use of Nero's Name in Calculating the Number of the Beast (Rev 13:18)." *Westminster Theological Journal* 68, no. 2 (2006): 347–60.

Homcy, Stephen L. "'To Him Who Overcomes': A Fresh Look at What 'Victory' Means for the Believer According to the Book of Revelation." *Journal of the Evangelical Theological Society* 38, no. 2 (1995): 193–201.

Koester, Craig R. "The Number of the Beast in Revelation 13 in Light of Papyri, Graffiti, and Inscriptions." *Journal of Early Christian History* 6, no. 3 (2016): 1–21.

Koester, Craig R. *Revelation: A New Translation with Introduction and Commentary*. Anchor Yale Bible 38A. Yale University Press, 2014.

Kooy, Vernon H. "The Apocalypse and Worship—Some Preliminary Observations." *Review of Religion* 30 (1976): 198–209.

Michaels, J. Ramsey. *Revelation*. IVP New Testament Commentary 20. IVP Academic, 1997.

O'Rourke, John J. "The Hymns of the Apocalypse." *Catholic Biblical Quarterly* 30, no. 3 (1968): 399–409.

Osborne, Grant R. *Revelation*. Baker Exegetical Commentary on the New Testament. Baker Academic, 2002.

Peters, Olutola K. *The Mandate of the Church in the Apocalypse of John*. Studies in Biblical Literature 77. Peter Lang, 2005.

Peterson, David G. "Worship in the Revelation to John." *Reformed Theological Review* 47, no. 3 (1988): 67–77.

Poythress, Vern S. *The Returning King: A Guide to the Book of Revelation*. P&R, 2000.

Schedtler, Justin J. *A Heavenly Chorus: The Dramatic Function of Revelation's Hymns*. Wissenschaftliche Untersuchungen zum Neuen Testament 2/381. Mohr Siebeck, 2014.

Shin, Eun-Chul. "More Than Conquerors: The Conqueror (NIKΆΩ) Motif in the Book of Revelation." PhD diss., Pretoria University, 2006.

Smalley, Stephen S. *The Revelation to John: A Commentary on the Greek Text of the Apocalypse*. IVP Academic, 2005.

Stewart, Alexander E. "The Role of Fear and Hope in Drawing and Transcending Boundaries in the Apocalypse of John." In *Drawing and Transcending Boundaries in the New Testament and Early Christianity*, edited by Jacobus Kok, Martin Webber, and Jermo van Nes. Beiträge zum Verstehen der Bibel 38. LIT Verlag, 2019.

Stewart, Alexander E. *Soteriology as Motivation in the Apocalypse of John*. Gorgias Biblical Studies 61. Gorgias, 2015.

Wallace, Daniel B. *Greek Grammar Beyond the Basics: An Exegetical Syntax of the New Testament*. Zondervan, 1996.

Williams, Peter J. "P115 and the Number of the Beast." *Tyndale Bulletin* 58, no. 1 (2007): 151–53.

# Chapter 2

# Trinitarian Missiology in Revelation

*Michael P. Naylor*

Revelation is often treated as simply an esoteric text full of veiled predictions of the future or, less charitably, as inconsistent with New Testament convictions or with suspect Christology.[1] In such readings of the text, the rich theology and relevance for contemporary practice are missed. This chapter will explore John's depiction of the Father, Son, and Spirit in Revelation and will demonstrate the "triadic," or "Trinitarian," shape of the book's theology. Finally, implications for the mission of the church will be considered.

## Father, Son, and Spirit in Revelation

The term "Trinity," although coined later in church history, is helpful for describing the theological convictions expressed in Revelation concerning "Father," "Son," and "Spirit."[2] A comprehensive study of each is not possible due to space constraints, but this section will survey the references to the Father, Son, and Spirit as well as explore the "triadic" shape of the theology of Revelation.

### Father

References to God the Father appear from the very outset of the Revelation, as the "revelation" that John has received was ultimately given by God (1:1).[3] As God speaks, his people are identified as those who heed his word and obey what he commands, and the book itself offers a blessing on both those who read it and those who keep what is in it (1:3).[4] The greeting in 1:4 likewise speaks of the Father, this time related to the self-revelation of God in Exodus through the phrase "who is and who was and who is to come."[5] This phrase

---

1 Tertullian notes Marcion's rejection of Revelation (*Against Marcion* 4.5), and the rationale was likely due to the Jewish character of the book (Bandy, "Should John's Apocalypse Be," 15). Bultmann described the book as a "weakly Christianized Judaism." *Theologie des Neuen Testaments*, 518.

2 Tertullian (*Against Praxeas* 2; ca. 213) appears to be the first to use the Latin term *trinitas* to describe Father, Son, and Spirit. See Smith, *Trinity in the Book of Revelation*, 16–22; see also Swain, "To Him Who Sits," 4–22; Tabb, *All Things New*, 29–85; Paul, *Revelation*, 4.

3 Unless otherwise noted, Scripture quotations are from the ESV. On God in Revelation, see Karrer, "God in the Book of Revelation," 205–22; Tabb, *All Things New*, 29–45; Boring, "Theology of Revelation," 257–69.

4 On the "word of God," see Revelation 1:9; 6:9; 20:4. The "commands of God" (12:17; 14:12) should be understood as God's instruction in general rather than adherence specifically to the second half of the Decalogue (contra Aune, *Revelation 6–16*, 710–12).

5 The phrasing in Revelation 1:4 is a grammatical irregularity, as the ending used does not agree with the preposition "from" (ἀπό, which normally takes the genitive). The nominative

appears in full form in 1:8 and 4:8 in reference to the Father and in 11:16 and 16:5 with only the first two designations.[6] God is also "the Alpha and the Omega," a phrase likely drawn from Isaiah 44:6.[7]

One of the chief themes that emerges in Revelation concerning the Father is his sovereignty over creation and human history. As John is ushered into the heavens in Revelation 4, he describes the heavenly throne room in language drawn predominantly from Ezekiel 1, Isaiah 6, and Daniel 7.[8] This scene introduces one of the common titles for God in Revelation: "[the] one seated on the throne."[9] God is enthroned in the center of the heavenly sanctuary and receives worship from the heavenly host (see 4:8, 11; 7:12; 11:16–18; cf. 5:13). The one seated on the throne possesses the scroll in his right hand (5:1, 7). The heavenly throne room is also a place of permanence and stability (4:6; cf. 15:2). Despite the chaos present on earth, God remains seated on his throne and is the recipient of unending worship.

God's authority is likewise highlighted through the title "the Almighty" (1:8; 4:8; 11:17; 15:3; 16:7, 14; 19:6, 15; 21:22). The term used by John appears in the LXX in reference to God and is used to translate the Hebrew terms "of hosts" (צְבָאוֹת) and "almighty" (שַׁדַּי).[10] God's judgment on sin is just (11:18; 15:3; 16:5–7; 18:4–8; 19:2; the emphasis in the final judgment on "books" and "works" reinforces this assessment of God's justice). He is the Creator of all things (4:11), and God's redemptive work and eschatological actions, as highlighted by John, ultimately culminate in God dwelling in the new creation with his people (21:1–6; 21:22–22:5).

---

form that appears (ὁ ὤν) matches the form found in Exodus 3:14 (LXX). The grammatical irregularity helps identify this Old Testament allusion (see Beale, *Revelation*, 187–89; Tabb, *All Things New*, 31). Soulen also notes that the use of the nominative treats the phrase like an indeclinable name (*Distinguishing the Voices*, 178–79).

6 As Beale notes, these references anticipate the final kingdom in Revelation 11:16 and the final judgment in 16:5 (*Revelation*, 613; see also Boring, "Theology of Revelation," 259).

7 Revelation 1:8 and 21:6; see below on this shared title.

8 Through the imagery, titles, and descriptions drawn from these prophetic texts, John leaves little doubt that he speaks of the God of Israel. See Naylor, *Complexity and Creativity*, 122–30.

9 Revelation 4:2, 9, 10; 5:1, 7, 13; 6:16; 7:10, 15; 19:4; 21:5. The phrase also appears in 20:11 with the "great white throne." While this could be in reference to both God and Jesus (see Osborne, *Revelation*, 720), it is best understood as a reference to the Father (so Schreiner, *Revelation*, 700).

10 The former appears more commonly in the LXX, particularly in the historical (see 2 Sam 5:10; 7:8, 27; 1 Kgs 19:10, 14; 1 Chr 11:9; 17:24) and prophetic writings (e.g., Hos 12:6; Amos 3:13; 4:13; 5:14–16; 9:5; Mic 4:4; Hag 1:2, 5, 7, 9, 14; Zech 1:3, 4, 6; Mal 1:4, 6; Jer 5:14; 15:16; 23:16). The latter appears in Job (e.g., Job 5:17; 8:5; 11:7). On this language in Revelation, see Boring, "Theology of Revelation," 259–61.

## Son

Alongside the depiction of the "one seated on the throne," Jesus Christ receives prominent attention within Revelation.[11] First mentioned in chapter 1, Jesus is described with a number of titles and motifs within the book. These opening words, "the revelation of Jesus Christ," could identify Jesus as the source or the content of this revelation, and both aspects can be observed within the book as a whole.[12] Alongside the one "who is and who was and who is to come" and the "seven spirits," Jesus is identified in the epistolary opening with the threefold "faithful witness, the firstborn of the dead, and the ruler of kings on earth" (1:5).[13] These titles are typically seen as arising from Psalm 89:37 (88:38 LXX) and 89:27 (88:28 LXX).[14]

One of the chief images of Jesus used by John is that of the "Lamb."[15] This image is used in reference to Jesus twenty-eight times in the book.[16] Lamb imagery appears in a variety of New Testament texts, but different terms are used outside of Revelation.[17] The term used by John (ἀρνίον) does appear in John 21:15 but is used in reference to the people of God. The term appears infrequently in the LXX, and John's use of this term allows for broader Old Testament connections beyond any one particular text.[18] Jesus, as the Lamb, has been slain, and this sacrificial death is the means by which he has achieved victory and redeemed people from every tribe, tongue, people, and nation (5:9; cf. 1:7). By virtue of this

---

11 For a survey of studies of the Christology of Revelation, see Naylor, *Complexity and Creativity*, 2–16. Among these, see Slater, *Christ and Community*; Lioy, *Book of Revelation*; Hand, *Worthy Champion*; Johns, *Lamb Christology of the Apocalypse*; and Johns, "Jesus in the Book of Revelation," 223–39; Morton, *One upon the Throne*.

12 Wallace identifies Ἰησοῦ Χριστοῦ as a plenary genitive (*Greek Grammar*, 102–21). The genitive is more likely either subjective or objective, with the former more likely (so Beale, *Revelation*, 183; Mathewson, *Revelation*, 1).

13 As will be argued below, the phrase "seven spirits" is best understood as a reference to the Holy Spirit.

14 See Tabb, *All Things New*, 53; Charles, *Revelation of John*, 1:14.

15 Of note is Johns, *Lamb Christology*. See also Skaggs and Doyle, "Lion/Lamb in Revelation," 362–75; Charles, "Apocalyptic Tribute to the Lamb (Rev 5:1–14)," 461–73; van Unnik, "Worthy Is the Lamb," 445–61; Mounce, "Worthy Is the Lamb," 60–69; Fleming, *Foretaste of the Future*, 56–71.

16 Revelation 5:6, 8, 12, 13; 6:1, 16; 7:9, 10, 14, 17; 12:11; 13:8; 14:1, 4 (2x), 10; 15:3; 17:14 (2x); 19:7, 9; 21:9, 14, 22, 23, 27; 22:1, 3. The term is also used in reference to the beast from the land, who deceptively speaks like a lamb (13:11).

17 This includes the terms ἀμνός (John 1:29; Acts 8:32; 1 Pet 1:19) and πάσχα (1 Cor 5:7).

18 This included imagery of lambs offered in sacrifice (including the Passover; see Gen 22; Exod 12:1–30; 29:38–41, 43–46; Num 9:1–14; 28:1–10, 16–25, 26–31; 29:1–6, 7–11, 12–40; Deut 16:1–8; 2 Chr 30:1–27; Ezra 6:19–21) and depicted as a symbol of vulnerability (including the suffering servant; see Isa 53:7; Jer 11:19; Ps 114; Ps. Sol. 8; cf. Mic 5:6 LXX).

victory, the Lamb also possesses the authority to take the scroll and open it (5:5–6, 9). As the one who is worthy, the Lamb initiates the events of the end, which culminate in his return, reign, and the new heavens and new earth. In the intervening time, Jesus is present among the churches, calling them to faithful obedience. The people of God also look forward to his coming, depicted in chapter 19 as a rider on a white horse.[19]

Additionally, Jesus is identified with titles understood as messianic by Jews and early Christians. The title "Christ" appears four times in the book,[20] and Jesus is identified with the line of David.[21] He is also announced in 5:5 as "the Lion of the tribe of Judah."[22] The identification of Jesus as the "morning star" in 22:16 (cf. 2:28) is likely a reference to Numbers 24:17.[23]

John also utilizes divine motifs and titles throughout the book. Certain titles such as "the Alpha and the Omega" (22:13; cf. 1:8, 17; 2:8; 21:6; on these titles, see below) connect Jesus with God in Revelation, while other titles, such as "the Amen" (3:14; Isa 65:16), the one who "searches mind and heart,"[24] the "holy one, the true one,"[25] and the "Lord of lords and King of kings"[26] associate

19 On the language of this passage, see Naylor, *Complexity and Creativity*, 146–53; Thomas, *Revelation 19*.

20 Revelation 11:15; 12:10; 20:4, 6; cf. Psalm 2:2. On other early Christian expectations, see, for example, Matthew 24:30–31; Acts 1:11; 1 Thessalonians 4:13–18; Hebrews 9:28.

21 This includes the "root of David" (Rev 5:5) and the "root and offspring of David" (22:16). These expressions are drawn from Isaiah 11:1, 10 and follow the LXX reading most closely (see Naylor, *Complexity and Creativity*, 173). Other Jewish texts make the same messianic identification (see Pss. Sol. 17:21ff.; 4Q252 5:1–3; 4Q285 5:1–4; T. Jud. 24:4–6; Sir 47:22; 4 Ezra 12:32; Tg. Isa. 11:1, 10; on this, see Mounce "Worthy Is the Lamb," 68; and Mounce, *Revelation*, 131; Aune, *Revelation 1–5*, 350–51). The possession of the "keys of David" in Revelation 3:7 alludes to Eliakim in Isaiah 22:22. While Eliakim possessed the "keys" as a steward of the house, Jesus does so as the David heir (see Aune, *Revelation 1–5*, 1:235; Smith, *Trinity in the Book of Revelation*, 109; Fekkes, *Isaiah and Prophetic Traditions*, 130–32; Mathewson, "Isaiah in Revelation," 192–93). Murphy and Smalley connect this with the notion of "messianic authority" (see Murphy, *Fallen Is Babylon*, 151; and Smalley, *Revelation to John*, 88). On early Christian usage, see Romans 15:12; cf. Matthew 1:1, 6; 22:42–45; Mark 11:10; 12:35–37; Luke 1:32, 69; 3:31; 20:41–44; John 7:42; Acts 2:30–36; 13:22–23, 34; 15:16; Romans 1:1–4; 2 Timothy 2:8.

22 Genesis 49:9; see Testament of Judah 24; 4 Ezra 11:36–46 (interpreted in 12:31–34).

23 This text was understood messianically by other Second Temple Jewish writers (see T. Levi 18:3; T. Jud. 24:1; 1QM 11:6–7; 4QTest 9–13; CD 7:18–20; so Mounce, *Revelation*, 409; Aune, *Revelation 17–22*, 1226–27).

24 Revelation 2:23; cf. Psalm 7:10 (8:10 LXX); Jeremiah 11:20.

25 Revelation 3:7; cf. Isaiah 1:4; 5:19, 24; 10:20; 12:6; 17:7; 29:23; 30:11, 12, 15; 31:1; 37:23; 40:25; 41:20; 43:3, 14, 15; 45:11; 48:17; 49:7; 55:5 (cf. also 2 Kgs 19:22; Pss 16:10; 71:22; 78:41; Hab 3:3).

26 Revelation 17:14; 19:16. These titles appear together in Daniel 4:37 (LXX). The title "King of kings" is also used in reference to God in 2 Maccabees 13:4; 3 Maccabees 5:35. "Lord of lords" appears in Deuteronomy 10:17; Psalm 136:3 (135:3 LXX), 26 (135:26 LXX).

Jesus with key Old Testament texts. In chapter 1, John draws from several Old Testament texts in depicting the exalted Christ as the "one like a Son of Man," such as Daniel 7, 10, Ezekiel 1, and Isaiah 49, and the description both identifies Jesus with the glory of heaven and anticipates the messages that issue forth in Revelation 2–3. Jesus is also the one who has initiated the new creation (3:14) by virtue of his death and resurrection (1:5, 18).[27] He likewise possesses divine authority to pronounce judgment on the enemies of God.[28]

### Spirit

Although not referenced as frequently as the Father and Son in Revelation, the Spirit nevertheless plays an important role in the book.[29] The first potential reference to the Spirit is found in the epistolary opening in 1:4. After the reference to the "one who is, who was and who is to come," John refers to the "seven S/spirits before the throne." This plural reference could be understood as referring not to the Holy Spirit but instead to seven leading angels, such as the seven featured in Jewish tradition.[30] There is good reason, however, to understand this phrase as referring to the Holy Spirit.[31] The number "seven" may allude to the description of God's Spirit in Isaiah 11 that rests upon the anointed one. In this text, the Spirit is described with multiple characteristics, and the LXX formats this as a list of seven.[32] John elsewhere utilizes the language of Isaiah 11 in reference to Jesus, which serves to link the Spirit with John's identification of Jesus as the Davidic Messiah.[33] Additionally, Jesus is

---

27 See Tabb, *All Things New*, 63.

28 See the double-edged sword (Rev 1:16; 2:12, 16; 19:15, 21) and the pronouncement of judgment in 2:18 (cf. Ezek 33:27, 29 LXX). For Jesus as the divine eschatological judge, see Smith, *Trinity in the Book of Revelation*, 105–60.

29 See Waddell, *Spirit of the Book*; Thomas, "Spirit in the Book," 241–55; Smith, *Trinity in the Book of Revelation*, 138–72; Tabb, *All Things New*, 67–85; Bauckham, *Climax of Prophecy*, 150–73; de Smidt, "Hermeneutical Perspectives," 27–47; de Smidt, "Holy Spirit," 229–44; Kuykendall, "Expanded Role," 527–44; Smalley, "Pneumatology in the Johannine Gospel," 289–300.

30 See, for example, 1 Enoch 20:1–8. So Koester, *Revelation*, 216; Charles, *Revelation*, 1:11–13; Aune, *Revelation 1–5*, 34–35. Groups of seven angels also occur in Revelation (see Rev 8:2; cf. 15:1, 6–8).

31 So Bauckham, *Climax of Prophecy*, 162–66; Bruce, "Spirit in the Apocalypse," 333–37; Hultberg, "Origin and Function," 685–96; Beale, *Revelation*, 189–90.

32 The MT lists six attributes. The enumeration of the "seven" need not be seen as dependent solely on the LXX text, as John may have interpreted the Isaiah text in association with the seven eyes of Zechariah 3:9; 4:10 (so Hultberg, "Origin and Function," 696). This association of Revelation 1:4 with Isaiah 11:2 can be traced back to Victorinus (see Thomas, "Spirit in the Book," 243).

33 Connection with Isaiah 11 may be observed in Revelation 5:5 (cf. 11:1, 10), 1:16 (cf. 11:4), and 22:16 (11:1, 10).

described in 3:1 as "having the seven spirits of God." John later refers in 4:5 to the "seven spirits" appearing before the throne, this time appearing as seven fiery torches. Combined with the association of the "seven spirits" with the eyes of the Lamb sent out throughout the earth (5:6), this image likely alludes to the description of the Spirit of God in Zechariah 4:2–7.[34] In light of these considerations, the "seven Spirits" could be rendered as the "sevenfold Spirit" in order to stress the identity and perfection of the Spirit.

The involvement of the Spirit in the reception of this revelation from God may also be observed. On four occasions (1:10; 4:2; 17:3; 21:10), John speaks of being "in the Spirit."[35] The first occurrence describes John's circumstances when the exalted Christ appeared to him, and the latter three describe John's experience in viewing important scenes in the book as they unfold. The phrase is likely an allusion to Old Testament expressions, such as Ezekiel's experience in seeing the valley of the dry bones (Ezek 37:1; cf. 11:24; Zech 1:6; 4:6; 7:12; Mic 3:8; Neh 9:30).[36] These expressions in Revelation affirm the work of the Spirit of God in the inspiration of this book.

The Spirit is likewise associated with the people of God. In Revelation 2–3, the readers of the book are called to "hear what the Spirit says to the churches." This refrain, coupled with the words of the exalted Christ to these seven congregations, calls for a response to the message of the Spirit (see below).[37] In 14:13 the Spirit affirms divine comfort for those who "die in the Lord."[38] The Spirit also stands with the people of God (depicted as the bride) in the series of invitations ("Come!") in 22:17. The first of these invitations, issued together by the Spirit and the Bride, could be understood as a call for Jesus to come or as an evangelistic call to respond.[39] Although a call for Jesus

34 So Beale, *Revelation*, 355–56; Bauckham, *Theology of the Book*, 110–15; Tabb, *All Things New*, 70; Hultberg, "Origin and Function."

35 As Bauckham notes, the focus is more upon the source of the revelation than the nature of the experience (*Climax of Prophecy*, 158). The references in Revelation 1:10; 4:2; 17:3; 21:10 may serve as structural markers in the book as well (see Waddell, *Spirit of the Book*, 138–50). These concerns need not negate an actual visionary experience on the part of John (on the different approaches to this question, see de Smidt, "Holy Spirit," 233–41; the objections of Jeske ["Spirit and Community," 452–66] are unconvincing in light of Old Testament expressions).

36 The raising of the two witnesses in Revelation 11:11 may also be an allusion to the Spirit through the language of Ezekiel 37 (see Tabb, *All Things New*, 74–76; Kuykendall, "Expanded Role," 535–36).

37 See also Ezekiel 3:24–27; Tabb, *All Things New*, 80–81.

38 See Schreiner, *Revelation*, 515–18.

39 On the former, see Bruce, "Spirit in the Apocalypse," 343–44; Paul, *Revelation*, 370; Schreiner, *Revelation*, 765. On the latter, see Osborne, *Revelation*, 793–94; Mounce, *Revelation*, 409. As Beale notes, this statement represents the Spirit speaking through the entirety of the community, not just the prophets (*Revelation*, 1148).

to return appears just a few verses later in 22:20, the more immediate context suggests that this "come" is evangelistic in nature.[40]

**Triadic Shape**

Beyond the individual references to the Father, Son, and Spirit, the "triadic" shape of John's theology may be observed in the book. Father, Son, and Spirit all play an important role in the narrative, and John in no way suggests a view of three different gods or different modalities. Father, Son, and Spirit are all addressed in the epistolary opening,[41] and all three may be in view in the imagery of the new Jerusalem.[42] John also highlights Father, Son, and Spirit in the throne room scene in Revelation 4–5.[43] The Father is initially identified as the recipient of worship, and as the scene continues, the Lamb receives worship individually (5:12; cf. 4:11) and alongside the Father (5:13; cf. 7:10; 22:3). The identification of the Spirit with both Father and Son is notable in this scene of worship.

John also displays the relationships between Father, Son, and Spirit in the unfolding narrative in the book. The relationship highlighted most frequently in the book is that of the Father and Son. The title "Son of God" appears only in 2:18, but God is referred to as the "Father" with respect to the "Son" in 1:6, 2:28, 3:21, and 14:1. The relationship between Jesus and the Father, though, is addressed through a number of images and titles.[44] First, the titles "the Alpha and the Omega," "the first and the last," and "the beginning and the end" function synonymously in the book and identify both Father (1:8; 21:6) and Son (1:17; 2:8; 22:13). The "one seated on the throne" likewise shares his rule with the Lamb. This shared throne is introduced in 3:21, as Jesus is seated with his Father on his throne. The following scene depicts this heavenly throne, and Jesus, depicted as the Lamb, is celebrated as the one worthy to open the scroll at the right hand of God. The judgment depicted in chapter 6 is identified by the

---

40 So Osborne, *Revelation*, 793.

41 See above on the "sevenfold Spirit." Smith labels this as "incipient trinitarian discourse." *Trinity in the Book of Revelation*, 55.

42 Reference to the Father and Son (depicted as the "Lamb") can be clearly observed. References to "water" in the new Jerusalem (Rev 21:6; 22:1) may reflect the promise of the Spirit (see Schreiner, *Revelation*, 746; Beale, *Revelation*, 1104–5; Kuykendall, "Expanded Role," 537–39). As Mathewson demonstrates, John weaves together language from several Old Testament texts (Isa 55; Ezek 47; Zech 14) and draws from associations between "water" and the "Spirit" in Ezekiel 36 (cf. 1QS 3:7, 9; Odes Sol. 6:7–14; see Mathewson, "Holy Spirit in the New Creation," 113–24).

43 See Swain, "To Him Who Sits," 17–18.

44 Such a focus is unsurprising given broader New Testament interest in the identity of the Son and his relationship with God the Father. On the shape of early Christology more broadly, see Hurtado, *Lord Jesus Christ*. See also Hays, "Faithful Witness, Alpha and Omega," 70–77.

earth-dwellers as coming from both God and the Lamb (6:15–17), and God likewise exercises his kingly authority alongside Jesus in Revelation 11:15. The final vision of the new heavens and new earth features the climax of this scene, as the throne "of God and of the Lamb" will be accessible to the people of God in the new Jerusalem as they worship him and see his face (22:1).[45]

A close association can likewise be observed between the Spirit and the Son. If the above analysis is correct, the identification of the Spirit as "sevenfold" from imagery in Isaiah 11; 49:2; Zechariah 3:8–9; and 4:1–10, combined with the Davidic identification of the Son, stresses the unique relationship between Jesus (as Messiah) and the Holy Spirit, who rests upon him.[46] Next, Son and Spirit testify together to the churches. As John records the words of the exalted Christ to the seven churches, each message is reinforced with the call to "hear what the Spirit says to the churches."[47] Testimony about Jesus reflects the work of the Spirit (19:10). The Spirit is likewise present before the heavenly throne, depicted as seven fiery torches (4:5) and seven eyes (5:6), connecting the Spirit with both Father and Son.

## Church on Mission

In view of these theological convictions concerning the triune God, the people of God are called to respond and participate in the mission of God. This is articulated primarily in the tasks of bearing witness and faithfully enduring suffering. God's people serve an active role, empowered by the Spirit, in a world filled with evil and hostility.

### A Divine Commission

Revelation demonstrates a concern with the church's proclamation of the gospel through the theme of "witness."[48] The terminology is first employed in Revelation 1:2 concerning John's role in testifying to what has been conveyed to him in visionary form to convey to the churches (cf. Rev 22:16, 18). In the epistolary introduction that follows this prescript, Jesus is identified as the "faithful witness" (1:5), a title repeated in 3:14 in the message to Laodicea (cf. 22:20). Throughout the narrative, faithfully bearing witness to Christ is expressed as

---

45 This identification with the people of God can be seen in Revelation 14:1 with the name of Jesus and his Father's name on the foreheads of the 144,000.

46 See Hultberg, "Origin and Function," 691–96; Beale, *Revelation*, 355. Additionally, Thomas suggests that the Spirit is an implied recipient of the worship directed to the Lamb ("Spirit," 244).

47 See Schreiner, *Joy of Hearing*, 147; Bauckham, *Theology of the Book*, 117.

48 The terminology in Revelation consists of "witness" (*μάρτυς* [1:5; 2:13; 3:14; 11:3; 17:6]), "to bear witness" (*μαρτυρέω* [1:2; 22:16, 18, 20]), and "testimony" (*μαρτυρία* [1:2, 9; 6:9; 11:7; 12:11, 17; 19:10; 20:4]; *μαρτυρίον* [15:5]).

a major role of the people of God. John describes his own circumstances in Patmos as due to the "word of God and the testimony of Jesus."[49] Antipas, who apparently lost his life as a result of following Jesus, is identified by the exalted Christ as "my faithful witness," echoing the earlier identification of Jesus in 1:5. As the people of God look to Jesus as the "faithful witness," they hold to the word of God and bear witness to Jesus (6:9; 12:11, 17; 17:6; 19:10; 20:4).

The "two witnesses" of Revelation 11 serve as a unique instance of this theme. These two figures are introduced as "my two witnesses" in 11:3 (cf. 11:7) and offer bold proclamation and miraculous signs for the period designated by God. The imagery is drawn from Zechariah 4 and the miracles associated with Moses and Elijah. Some identify these two witnesses simply as a symbol for the church,[50] while others view them as eschatological figures.[51] Even if the latter view is taken, the witnesses should still be understood as representing the role of the church in the surrounding world.[52] The general pattern of bearing witness (11:3), facing opposition (11:7–10), and receiving divine vindication in the end (11:11–13; cf. 20:4) can be seen.

The ongoing witness of the church necessitates perseverance, as this mission faces internal and external threats. Ephesus is admonished for having forsaken her first love (2:4).[53] Laodicea (3:14–22) is rebuked for a spirit of self-sufficiency that fails to find true spiritual sustenance in Christ. Additionally, the churches face the challenge of false teachers who seek to lead the people of God away from fidelity to Christ. Addressed chiefly in Revelation 2, the false teachers are identified as "those who call themselves apostles and are not" (2:2), the "Nicolaitans" (2:6, 15), those who "hold to the teachings of Balaam" (2:14), and "Jezebel" (2:20–25). The issues associated with these false teachers, "idol foods" and "sexual immorality" (2:20), likely reflect participation in the wider culture in a way that compromises fidelity to Christ.[54]

---

49 Revelation 1:9. Some have suggested that John's presence on Patmos reflects a missionary endeavor (so Molony, *Apocalypse of John*, 51; Thompson, *Book of Revelation*, 172–73), but this is unlikely. With the explicit mention of John's participation in the "affliction" (θλίψις) experienced by the seven churches, John was more likely forced to leave the region due to a judicial decision or persecution. See Schreiner, *Revelation*, 96–97.

50 Bauckham, *Climax of Prophecy*, 168–73; Schreiner, *Revelation*, 388–409; Beale, *Revelation*, 573.

51 Ladd, *Commentary on the Revelation*, 154; Fanning, *Revelation*, 333.

52 So Osborne, *Revelation*, 418.

53 Some identify this primarily as love for others (Ladd, *Commentary on the Revelation*, 39; Koester, *Revelation*, 269; Beale, *Revelation*, 230–31 [expressed in witness to the world]) or love for God (Thomas and Macchia, *Revelation*, 89–90). Rather than focusing simply on one element, both may be in view (so Osborne, *Revelation*, 116; Schreiner, *Revelation*, 125).

54 See Naylor, "John and Dissenting Views," 116–22. The first of these terms (εἰδωλόθυτος) has been understood as any type of food associated with idols, including food sold in the

Threats external to the congregation are likewise addressed. Within the messages to the seven churches, the exalted Christ twice refers to those who "say that they are Jews and are not" (2:9; 3:9). Although it is difficult to determine the exact nature of this opposition, it likely reflects the hostility of some non-Christ-following Jewish people in these communities.[55] As the narrative continues, John depicts the hostility of the dragon, the beast from the sea, and the beast from the land against the followers of the Lamb. Those who follow the Lamb faithfully face economic ramifications (13:16–17) and the threat of death (12:17; 13:7, 10, 15; 16:6; 17:6; 20:4). Not all who follow the Lamb will die as a result of their faith, but Revelation depicts the reality of this threat and encourages believers that remaining faithful is worth it, no matter the cost.[56]

**Divine Empowerment**

Despite these challenges, the people of God are aided by the work of the Spirit. As addressed in chapters 2–3, the words of the exalted Christ to the churches are conveyed by the Spirit (2:7, 11, 17, 29; 3:6, 13, 22; cf. 13:9). These refrains recall the words of Jesus admonishing the people to heed his teaching (see Matt 11:15; 13:9, 43; Mark 4:9, 23; Luke 8:8; 14:35; cf. Mark 8:18), and the association of this "hearing" with the Spirit serves as both warning and encouragement to the congregations. The messages given to the seven churches are meant to be heard not only by the respective churches addressed but also by the wider community of faith. The Spirit continues to speak through the word, and believers of subsequent generations are called to heed these messages.

Additionally, John associates the Spirit with "prophecy" and the "testimony of Jesus" in 19:10. This statement has been subject to much debate concerning the meaning of "Spirit," "of Jesus," and the construction as a whole. Regarding the identification of the "Spirit," the reference could be understood in relation to the "spirit" of the prophet or to the Holy Spirit.

---

marketplace, but the term is better understood as referring to "sacral meals." The second term (πορνεύω) could refer to sexual practices. More likely, however, the term reflects spiritual unfaithfulness as expressed in similar sexual terms by the Old Testament prophets (see Isa 1:21–23; Jer 2:20, 23–25; 3:2; 13:27; Ezek 16:15–58; Hos 2:1–13; Nah 3:1–4).

55 John does not denounce these individuals simply because they are Jewish; rather, like the Old Testament prophets or John's Jewish contemporaries, these individuals are rebuked for their opposition to God and his work. See Dalrymple, "Was John Antisemitic?," 136; Friesen, "Sarcasm in Revelation 2–3," 127–44; Osborne, *Revelation*, 131.

56 The "witness" word family still retained a primary meaning derived from a legal context of observing and conveying information and had not yet acquired the later connotation of one who dies bearing witness to Christ (see Silva, *New International Dictionary*, 3:234–46).

Given the references to "prophecy" (1:3; 22:7, 10, 18, 19; cf. 10:11; 11:18; 16:6; 18:20, 24; 19:10; 22:6, 9, 16) and John being "in the Spirit" (1:10; 4:2; 17:3; 21:10), the reference in 19:10 is best understood as a reference to the Holy Spirit.[57] Next, "of Jesus" could refer to "testimony" that is given *by* Jesus or *about* Jesus. Although Jesus was identified earlier in the book as the "faithful witness" (1:5),[58] the phrase here is better understood in the latter sense as reflecting the testimony of the people of God, bearing witness to Jesus.[59] Taken as a whole, the phrase can be understood as conveying the relationship between the church bearing witness to Christ and the work of the Holy Spirit inspiring the prophets (including the text of Revelation). Such would then provide encouragement to the church as it carries out the mission of God, faithfully testifying to the world around. The same Spirit that inspired the prophets empowers the church to carry out this task.[60]

**Divine Sovereignty**

As this mission is carried forth, the people of God do so in light of the sovereignty of God in redemptive history, in the ongoing witness of the church, and in anticipation of the new heavens and new earth. The work of salvation is a divine act initiated by the Lamb as he purchases (5:9; cf. 1:7) and consecrates (1:5–6; 5:10; 20:6) his people. In this ongoing witness, God is in control despite the persecution of his people, as expressed in Revelation 6:9–11.[61] God will one day put an end to the suffering of his people and will raise them up (2:11; 20:6; cf. 20:14; 21:8). Believers are exhorted to remain faithful in the face of suffering (2:9–10, 13; 3:9) and false teaching (2:6, 14–16, 20–

---

57 See Schreiner, *Revelation*, 637–38; Fanning, *Revelation*, 484–85; contra Beale, *Revelation*, 947–48.

58 Additionally, the phrase could be understood as anticipating the pronouncement of judgment in 19:15, 21.

59 The preceding statement in Revelation 19:10 refers to that which believers "hold." Bruce also notes concern with the authenticity of witness and the role of the Spirit in 1 Corinthians 12:3 and 1 John 4:2–3 ("Spirit in the Apocalypse," 338).

60 The reference in Revelation 22:6 to the "spirits" of the prophets could be understood in terms of the human spirit of each prophet, but this also may be an allusion to the Holy Spirit. Waddell takes this as a reference to the Spirit in the hearts/minds of the prophets (*Spirit of the Book*, 190) and Mazzaferri relates the plural to the earlier "sevenfold Spirit" in Revelation (*Genre of the Book*, 301).

61 Koester argues that this is in reference to the "fullness" of the believers' witness about Christ (*Revelation*, 401). Despite the lack of explicit reference to a "number" here, it is plausible to conclude that John is envisioning a certain amount of suffering for the people associated with the Messiah, as depicted in other Jewish writings such as 1 Enoch 47:4; 4 Ezra 4:35–37; 2 Baruch 23:4–5 (so Bauckham, *Climax of Prophecy*, 48–56; Aune, *Revelation 6–16*, 412–13; Osborne, *Revelation*, 289; Schreiner, *Revelation*, 277–78).

23). Followers of the Lamb are marked by their fidelity in Revelation as they obey God's direction (1:9; 6:9; 12:17; 14:12; 20:4) and refuse to compromise with the world, even in the face of death (12:11). The promises given in chapters 2–3 and the blessing statements (1:3; 14:13; 16:15; 19:9; 20:6; 22:7, 14) encourage perseverance, and many of these promises are repeated later in the final vision of the book.[62] The people of God are likewise encouraged by God's sovereignty in the outworking of his divine plan, as no force of evil can oppose his power and authority.[63] The end promised and secured by God for his people provides an important motivation in the book. The experiences of suffering, death, and the curse present during this age will one day be no more. Those from the nations, redeemed by the blood of the Lamb, will dwell together in the new Jerusalem with Father, Son, and Holy Spirit.

## Conclusion

Revelation captures, with rich imagery, the mission of God in human history. Father, Son, and Spirit together play an important role in effecting the plan of salvation and its ultimate fulfillment in the new heavens and new earth. Believers, as those redeemed by the blood of the Lamb, play an important role as witnesses empowered by the Spirit.

## Bibliography

Aune, David E. *Revelation 1–5*. Word Biblical Commentary 52A. Nelson, 1997.

Aune, David E. *Revelation 6–16*. Word Biblical Commentary 52B. Nelson, 1998.

Aune, David E. *Revelation 17–22*. Word Biblical Commentary 52C. Nelson, 1998.

Bandy, Alan S. "Should John's Apocalypse Be in the Canon?" In *Apocalypse of John Among Its Critics*, edited by Alan S. Bandy and Alexander Stewart. Lexham Academic, 2023.

Bauckham, Richard. *The Climax of Prophecy: Studies on the Book of Revelation*. T&T Clark, 1993.

Bauckham, Richard. *The Theology of the Book of Revelation*. New Testament Theology. Cambridge University Press, 1993.

Beale, G. K. *The Book of Revelation*. New International Greek Testament Commentary. Eerdmans, 1999.

Boring, M. Eugene. "The Theology of Revelation: 'The Lord Our God the Almighty Reigns.'" *Interpretation* 40, no. 3 (1986): 257–69.

---

62 Revelation 21:7 identifies the fulfillment of the promises in the new Jerusalem. Individual correlations may likewise be seen in 2:7 (cf. 22:2); 2:11 (cf. 20:6; 21:8); 2:22–28; 3:5 (cf. 21:27); 3:12 (cf. 21:3–4, 7); 3:21 (cf. 20:4–6).

63 Fleming, *Foretaste of the Future*, 46.

Bruce, F. F. "The Spirit in the Apocalypse." In *Christ and Spirit in the New Testament: Studies in Honour of Charles Francis Digby Moule*, edited by Barnabas Lindars and Stephen S. Smalley. Cambridge University Press, 1973.

Bultmann, Rudolf K. *Theologie des Neuen Testaments*. Neue theologische Grundrisse. Mohr, 1953.

Charles, J. Daryl. "An Apocalyptic Tribute to the Lamb (Rev 5:1–14)." *Journal of the Evangelical Theological Society* 34, no. 4 (1991): 461–73.

Charles, R. H. *A Critical and Exegetical Commentary on the Revelation of John*. International Critical Commentary. 2 vols. T&T Clark, 1920.

Dalrymple, Rob. "Was John Antisemitic?" In Stewart and Bandy, *Apocalypse of John Among Its Critics*.

Fanning, Buist M. *Revelation*. Zondervan Exegetical Commentary on the New Testament. Zondervan, 2020.

Fekkes, Jan. *Isaiah and Prophetic Traditions in the Book of Revelation: Visionary Antecedents and Their Development*. Journal for the Study of the New Testament Supplement Series 93. Sheffield, 1994.

Fleming, Dean. *Foretaste of the Future: Reading Revelation in Light of God's Mission*. IVP Academic, 2022.

Friesen, Steve. "Sarcasm in Revelation 2–3: Churches, Christians, True Jews, and Satanic Synagogues." In *The Reality of Apocalypse: Rhetoric and Politics in the Book of Revelation*, edited by David L. Barr. Society of Biblical Literature Symposium Series 39. Brill, 2006.

Hand, Brian R. *The Worthy Champion: A Christology of the Book of Revelation Based on Elements of Its Literary Composition*. Bob Jones University Press, 2008.

Hays, Richard B. "Faithful Witness, Alpha and Omega: The Identity of Jesus in the Apocalypse of John." In *Revelation and the Politics of Apocalyptic Interpretation*, edited by Richard B. Hays and Stefan Alkier. Baylor University Press, 2012.

Hultberg, Alan D. "The Origin and Function of the Image of the Seven Spirits in Revelation." *Journal of the Evangelical Theological Society* 66, no. 4 (2023): 685–96.

Hurtado, Larry W. *Lord Jesus Christ: Devotion to Jesus in Earliest Christianity*. Eerdmans, 2003.

Jeske, Richard L. "Spirit and Community in the Johannine Apocalypse." *New Testament Studies* 31, no. 3 (1985): 452–66.

Johns, Loren L. "Jesus in the Book of Revelation." In Koester, *Oxford Handbook of the Book of Revelation*.

Johns, Loren L. *The Lamb Christology of the Apocalypse: An Investigation in Its Origins and Rhetorical Force*. Wissenschaftliche Untersuchungen zum Neuen Testament 2/167. Mohr, 2003.

Karrer, Martin. "God in the Book of Revelation." In Koester, *Oxford Handbook of the Book of Revelation*.

Koester, Craig R., ed. *The Oxford Handbook of the Book of Revelation*. Oxford University Press, 2020.

Koester, Craig R. *Revelation: A New Translation with Introduction and Commentary*. Anchor Bible Commentary 38A. Yale University Press, 2014.

Kuykendall, Michael. "An Expanded Role for the Spirit in the Book of Revelation." *Journal of the Evangelical Theological Society* 64, no. 3 (2021): 527–44.

Ladd, George Eldon. *A Commentary on the Revelation of John*. Eerdmans, 1972.

Lioy, Dan. *The Book of Revelation in Christological Focus*. Studies in Biblical Literature 58. Peter Lang, 2003.

Mathewson, David L. "The Holy Spirit in the New Creation of Revelation 21:1–22:5." *Journal of the Evangelical Theological Society* 67, no. 1 (2024): 113–24.

Mathewson, David L. "Isaiah in Revelation." In *Isaiah in the New Testament*, edited by Steve Moyise and Maarten J. J. Menke. T&T Clark, 2005.

Mathewson, David L. *Revelation: A Handbook on the Greek Text*. Baylor Handbook on the Greek New Testament. Baylor University Press, 2016.

Mazzaferri, Frederick David. *The Genre of the Book of Revelation from a Source-Critical Perspective*. Beihefte zur Zeitschrift für die neutestamentliche Wissenschaft 54. De Gruyter, 1989.

Molony, Francis J. *The Apocalypse of John: A Commentary*. Baker Academic, 2020.

Morton, Russell. *One upon the Throne and the Lamb: A Tradition Historical/Theological Analysis of Revelation 4–5*. Studies in Biblical Literature 110. Peter Lang, 2007.

Mounce, Robert H. *The Book of Revelation*. Rev. ed. New International Commentary on the New Testament. Eerdmans, 1998.

Mounce, Robert H. "Worthy Is the Lamb." In *Scripture, Tradition, and Interpretation: Essays Presented to Everett F. Harrison by His Students and Colleagues in Honor of His Seventy-Fifth Birthday*, edited by W. Ward Gasque and William Sanford LaSor. Eerdmans, 1978.

Murphy, Frederick J. *Fallen Is Babylon: The Revelation to John*. New Testament in Context. Trinity, 1998.

Naylor, Michael P. *Complexity and Creativity: John's Presentation of Jesus in the Book of Revelation*. Gorgias Biblical Studies 69. Piscataway, 2018.

Naylor, Michael P. "John and Dissenting Views: Was He Intolerant?" In Stewart and Bandy, *Apocalypse of John Among Its Critics*.

Osborne, Grant R. *Revelation*. Baker Exegetical Commentary on the New Testament. Baker Academic, 2002.

Paul, Ian. *Revelation*. Tyndale New Testament Commentaries 20. IVP Academic, 2018.

Schreiner, Thomas R. *The Joy of Hearing: A Theology of the Book of Revelation*. New Testament Theology. Crossway, 2021.

Schreiner, Thomas R. *Revelation*. Baker Exegetical Commentary on the New Testament. Baker Academic, 2023.

Silva, Moisés, ed. *New International Dictionary of New Testament Theology and Exegesis*. 2nd ed. 5 vols. Zondervan, 2014.

Skaggs, Rebecca, and Thomas Doyle. "Lion/Lamb in Revelation." *Currents in Biblical Research* 7, no. 3 (2009): 362–75.

Slater, Thomas B. *Christ and Community: A Socio-Historical Study of the Christology of Revelation*. Journal for the Study of the New Testament Supplement Series 178. Sheffield Academic Press, 1999.

Smalley, Stephen S. "Pneumatology in the Johannine Gospel and Apocalypse." In *Exploring the Gospel of John: In Honor of D. Moody Smith*, edited by R. Alan Culpepper and C. Clifton Black. Westminster John Knox, 1996.

Smalley, Stephen S. *The Revelation to John: A Commentary on the Greek Text of the Apocalypse*. SPCK, 2005.

de Smidt, Kobus. "Hermeneutical Perspectives on the Spirit in the Book of Revelation." *Journal of Pentecostal Studies* 14 (1999): 27–47.

de Smidt, J. C. "The Holy Spirit in the Book of Revelation—Nomenclature." *Neotestamentica* 28, no. 1 (1994): 229–44.

Smith, Brandon D. *The Trinity in the Book of Revelation: Seeing Father, Son, and Holy Spirit in John's Apocalypse*. Studies in Christian Doctrine and Scripture. IVP Academic, 2022.

Soulen, R. Kendall. *Distinguishing the Voices*. Vol. 1 of *The Divine Name(s) and the Holy Trinity*. Westminster John Knox, 2011.

Stewart, Alexander E., and Alan S. Bandy, eds. *The Apocalypse of John Among Its Critics: Questions and Controversies*. Lexham, 2023.

Swain, Scott R. "'To Him Who Sits on the Throne and to the Lamb': Hymning God's Triune Name in Revelation 4–5." *Reformed Faith & Practice* 4, no. 2 (2019): 4–22.

Tabb, Brian J. *All Things New: Revelation as Canonical Capstone*. New Studies in Biblical Theology 48. InterVarsity Press, 2019.

Thomas, David Andrew. *Revelation 19 in Historical and Mythological Context*. Studies in Biblical Literature 118. Peter Lang, 2008.

Thomas, John Christopher. "The Spirit in the Book of Revelation." In *The Oxford Handbook of the Book of Revelation*, edited by Craig Koester. Oxford University Press, 2020.

Thompson, Leonard L. *The Book of Revelation: Apocalypse and Empire*. Oxford University Press, 1990.

van Unnik, W. C. "'Worthy Is the Lamb': The Background of Apoc. 5." In *Melanges Bibliques En Hommage Au R. P. Beda Rigaux*, edited by Albert Descamps and R. P. André Halleux. Duculot, 1970.

Waddell, Robby. *The Spirit of the Book of Revelation*. Journal of Pentecostal Studies Supplement Series 30. Deo, 2006.

Wallace, Daniel B. *Greek Grammar Beyond the Basics: An Exegetical Syntax of the New Testament*. Zondervan, 1996.

# Chapter 3

## Speaking, Seeing, Sending

### The Missional Role of the Holy Spirit in Revelation

*Cornelia van Deventer*

From the first verse of the Apocalypse, the agency of God the Father and Jesus, the Son, is clear. John identifies what he receives as the revelation of Jesus Christ, given to him by God, to show his servants what must soon take place (1:1). Since John's missional mandate is to write what he sees and send it to the churches in Asia Minor (1:11), the missional roles of the Father and Son as revealers, speakers, and senders are clear from the book's opening. Seemingly sidelined in this opening verse is the Third Person of the Trinity—the Holy Spirit. Additionally, John identifies the content of his central message as τὸν λόγον τοῦ θεοῦ καὶ τὴν μαρτυρίαν'Ιησοῦ Χριστοῦ ("the Word of God and the testimony of Jesus Christ"; 1:2).[1] Again, the Holy Spirit shines in his absence here. Much ink has been spilled on the identities, roles, and significance of the aforementioned persons of the Trinity, including their respective and united roles in mission, while works on the Holy Spirit and mission in Revelation do not abound.

Many have commented on the difficulties of studying pneumatology in John's Apocalypse. This is because the noun πνεῦμα (Spirit) and adjective ἅγιον (holy) never occur together in Revelation.[2] Rather, references to the Spirit are obscure, unique, and often ambiguous. The study of pneumatology in Revelation therefore often leads to the multiplication of exegetical issues.[3] Even further uncertain is the role of the Holy Spirit in God's mission. In his recent book *Foretaste of the Future*, Dean Flemming explores the mission of God in Revelation. He argues that Revelation, like the whole Bible, serves to first tell us about the *missio Dei* and that it distinguishes itself as the book with the strongest emphasis on the divine mission.[4] He aptly discusses the

1 While, if taken as a plenary genitive, 'Ιησοῦ Χριστοῦ might also imply that the revelation is about Jesus, the identification of Jesus as *ὁ μάρτυς* in 1:5 supports the view that this is a subjective genitive. Unless otherwise stated, all translations from the Greek are my own.

2 This way of speaking about the Spirit is rare for John. In the Johannine corpus (Gospel of John; Johannine letters; Revelation), we only find three instances where he is called the Holy Spirit (John 1:33; 14:26; 20:22), each being a direct quotation from Jesus, demonstrating that this was not John's preferred epithet for the Spirit of God.

3 Smith, "Holy Spirit's Eternal Procession," 255.

4 Flemming, *Foretaste of the Future*, 35.

mission of the Father, the Lamb, and God's people, but he fails to engage the Third Person of the Trinity.

An underdeveloped pneumatology raises a particular concern for Christian Africans, where well-developed doctrines of spirits and demons often outweigh the understanding of the Holy Spirit,[5] frequently fueling fear and syncretistic practices in ministry and mission. If we hold that the triune God serves as the initiator and fulfiller of mission, understanding the Spirit's missional role is key. As he was indispensable in the birth of the ancient church (see Acts 1:8), his role in calling it to endure and be holy is likewise essential. In this chapter, I discuss the missional role of the Holy Spirit in Revelation along with references to him as τὰ ἑπτὰ πνεύματα (the seven spirits), τὸ πνεῦμα (the Spirit), πνεῦμα ζωῆς (the living Spirit), and ἐν πνεύματι (in [the] Spirit).[6] I endeavor to paint a mosaic of a seeing, speaking, and sending/sent Spirit who functions as missional agent alongside the Father, Son, and the church in Revelation.

## The Seven Spirits

The appellation τὰ ἑπτὰ πνεύματα (the seven spirits) is first used in the epistolary greeting (1:4–5). In typical fashion, John recounts χάρις ὑμῖν καὶ εἰρήνη (grace and peace to you) and names three parties as senders: the one who is, was, and is to come; the seven spirits before the throne; and Jesus Christ (1:4–5). While

5 Foday-Khabenje, *Byang Kato*, ch. 3, under "Kato's Theological Pitfalls." This is not unique to the study of Revelation. Even the African father of evangelicalism, Byang Kato, has been criticized for an underdeveloped pneumatology in his theology of the *missio Dei*.

6 There are also a few implicit references to the Spirit in Revelation, including 13:9 (Εἴ τις ἔχει οὖς ἀκουσάτω; cf. 2:7, 11, 17, 29; 3:6, 13, 22). The allusion back to the phraseology used in Revelation 2–3 could be indicative of the agency of the Holy Spirit in John's vision of the rise of evil on the earth. Additionally, in continuity with the Lamb's eyes being identified at the Spirit (5:6), there is good reason to believe that Jesus's eyes, described as φλὸξ πυρός (blazing fire; 1:14; 19:2) could refer to the Holy Spirit. Building on the language of the seven burning torches of fire (4:5), Lee argues that the fire from the altar, which is thrown onto the earth in judgment in Revelation 8:5, marks a reference to the "fire of the Divine Spirit." See Lee, *Dynamic Reading of the Holy Spirit*, 99–102. Mathewson argues that the water imagery in 21:6 and 22:1 metaphorically refers to the Holy Spirit. He points to the inclusio formed by Revelation 4–5 and 21:1–22:5; the connection between [τοῦ] ὕδατος [τῆς] ζωῆς (21:6) and πνεῦμα ζωῆς (11:11); the interpretive note in John 7:39, which explains the shared allusions to Isaiah 55:1, Ezekiel 47:1–12, and Zechariah 14:8 as a reference to the Holy Spirit; and the positions of the Spirit (Rev 4–5) and living water (22:1) vis-à-vis the throne. See Mathewson, "Holy Spirit in the New Creation," 113–24. Other possible implicit references to the Holy Spirit include the cloud mentioned in the harvest of the righteous in 14:14–16 and the smoke from God's glory and power in 15:8. See Wilson, "Spirit in Revelation," 89–96.

some hold that the seven spirits here are angels,[7] the arguments in favor of them referring to the Holy Spirit are more persuasive. First, in the immediate context (1:4), the seven spirits are included in the doxological formula and identified as a party who, together with the Father and Son, sends grace and peace—a common literary feature in New Testament letters that always proceeds from a divine party (Rom 1:7; 1 Cor 1:3; 2 Cor 1:2; Gal 1:3; Eph 1:2; 2 Pet 1:2).[8] All three parties are preceded by the preposition ἀπό, identifying them as three agents equally involved in the greeting. It would be highly unlikely for angels to be wedged between the Father and Son in this bestowal of grace and peace. In a book so concerned with idolatry and false worship—including the worship of angels (Rev 19:10; 22:9)—it would be unthinkable for an unworthy party to be included in a doxological formula, which Smith classifies as "worship language."[9] Finally, there are significant differences between the roles of the seven spirits and the seven angels in John's vision, most notably that the seven spirits never worship God.[10]

While confusing to the contemporary reader, John's use of the appellation τὰ ἑπτὰ πνεύματα makes good sense when one appreciates Revelation as apocalyptic literature, where numbers carry specific significance. The number seven is not only tied to the Spirit's name, but he speaks seven times to seven churches (Rev 2–3). This marks the Spirit as divine, whole, and perfect—characteristics represented by the number seven. This is further bolstered by a glance back at Isaiah 11:2–3 (LXX). In this messianic prophecy, the prophet describes the Davidic leader as one on whom the πνεῦμα τοῦ θεοῦ (Spirit of God) will rest (v. 2). He then elaborates on seven characteristics of this Spirit, namely, that he is the Spirit of wisdom (σοφίας), understanding (συνέσεως), determination (βουλῆς), might (ἰσχύος), knowledge (γνώσεως), piety (εὐσεβείας), and the fear of God (φόβου θεοῦ).[11] One might venture to say that "the seven spirits" is an apocalyptic synonym for "the Holy Spirit," and

---

7 This is not far-fetched, as writings like Tobit 12:15 and 1 Enoch 20:1–7 mention seven angels, and the association of angels and fire can be found in 2 Baruch 21:6, 4 Ezra 8:20–22, and Psalm 104:4. See Hultberg, "Origin and Function," 685–87, for a discussion of the emergence of this view.

8 See Smith, "Holy Spirit's Eternal Procession," 258.

9 Smith, 257.

10 We also find explanations for other images like the seven stars (the seven angels of the seven churches) and seven lampstands (the seven churches) in 1:20, but none for the seven spirits, implying that they are not representative of something else.

11 Hultberg, "Origin and Function," argues that the references to Isaiah 11, Zechariah 3, and Zechariah 4 culminate in a Christology of Jesus as the Branch and Servant, endowed with the Spirit of God (see esp. Isa 11:2 and Zech 3:8–9).

a worthy match for the exquisite descriptors used for the Father and Son in Revelation's doxology.

The epithet τὰ ἑπτὰ πνεύματα is again used in 3:1 as Jesus introduces himself to the church in Sardis as the one who holds the seven spirits of God and the seven stars. This holding marks Jesus as the sender of the Spirit—akin to the Father as sender of the Son.[12] Here the seven spirits are further defined by the genitive τοῦ θεοῦ (of God). As in the epistolary greeting, John again describes the Trinity in a masterful way, with all three persons involved in one short description, demonstrating their interwovenness and cooperation in revealing the true spiritual state of a dead church (3:1–4).

The last two references to τὰ ἑπτὰ πνεύματα are found in the throne room (Rev 4–5). In 4:5, John clarifies that the seven lamps burning with fire before the throne are the seven spirits of God. Ezekiel 1:13 provides important context here. The prophet describes the four living creatures following the Spirit (v. 12), with fire (God's presence) moving back and forth between them, giving them the appearance of torches (v. 13). The lamps thus represent God's presence, embodied in the Holy Spirit.[13] In Revelation 5:6, the Lamb is described as having seven horns (κέρατα ἑπτά) and seven eyes (ὀφθαλμοὺς ἑπτά). Similar to 4:5, the latter[14] are identified as the seven spirits of God (τὰ [ἑπτὰ] πνεύματα τοῦ θεοῦ).[15] The reference to the seven eyes is an anthropomorphism—a description of the divine using human characteristics—which harkens back to Zechariah 4 in the vision of the golden lampstand and the two olive trees. Here, the angel confirms that Zerubbabel will complete the temple, followed by the assertion that the seven eyes of the Lord are those who look attentively on/over the whole earth (ἐπὶ πᾶσαν τὴν γῆν; Zech 4:10 LXX). In context, this expression affirms the all-knowing nature of the Lord. This again attributes a divine characteristic to the Holy Spirit, underlying his rightful equality as part of the Godhead. Moreover, contrary to objections that the Spirit does not sit enthroned in Revelation, he is essentially proceeding from the throne in this image.[16] Additionally, he is described as ἀπεσταλμένοι εἰς πᾶσαν τὴν γῆν (sent into all the earth; Rev 5:6), emphasizing his heavenly *and* earthly activity.

12 Osborne, *Revelation*, 84.

13 Osborne, 101.

14 The masculine relative pronoun οἵ marks ὀφθαλμούς as the referent instead of κέρατα.

15 While there is uncertainty about the inclusion of the adjective seven (ἑπτά) in the original manuscripts (see Metzger, *Textual Commentary*, 666), the meaning remains relatively stable. Whether John is referring to seven spirits or just spirits, the seven eyes signal that a reference to the seven spirits is implied.

16 Smith, "Holy Spirit's Eternal Procession," 269.

The references to the seven spirits underline three main characteristics of the Holy Spirit vis-à-vis the *missio Dei*. First, it bolsters his divinity and marks him as a worthy member of the Trinity. He is included in the epistolary greeting, marked by the number seven, described as τοῦ θεοῦ (of God), explained in language representative of God's presence, seamlessly connected to the Lamb, and proceeding from the divine throne. Second, it celebrates him as a sending and sent Spirit. He is a co-sender of the divine message along with the Father and Son, but he is also sent. The divine passive ἀπεσταλμένοι (having been sent; 5:6) illustrates the Spirit's missional cooperation with the Godhead as a sent one—not only to the churches but to the whole earth. The contrast between the seven spirits and the three foul spirits in Revelation 16 reinforces this.[17] The latter are sent by the dragon and false prophet (16:13) to prepare the rulers of the world for the battle against God (16:14) and to lead the earth's inhabitants into worshiping the beast (13:8, 12). In contrast, the seven spirits work with God and the Lamb and are sent into all the earth (5:6) to direct worship to God.[18] Both have an earthly missional role, but their allies and purposes are diametrically opposed. The sending of the seven spirits into all the earth also serves an equipping and strengthening role to the churches for faithful witness. Third, the imagery of the Spirit as the Lamb's eyes marks him as one who sees and searches the earth. This searching is missional at its core. As the eyes of the Lamb, the Spirit casts the gaze of the Son on the earth, identifying the heavenly Godhead as one who is intimately and missionally involved on the earth through his Spirit.

## The Spirit

The clearest reference to the Holy Spirit is John's simple appellation τὸ πνεῦμα (the Spirit), which is also the most commonly used descriptor for the Third Person of the Trinity in John's Gospel and Letters. We first encounter this epithet in the letters to the seven churches (Rev 2–3). The formula Ὁ ἔχων οὖς ἀκουσάτω τί τὸ πνεῦμα λέγει ταῖς ἐκκλησίαις ("the one who has ears, let them hear what the Spirit is saying to the churches") appears seven times in the letters, each time at the closing of an exhortation to one of the seven churches (2:7, 11, 17, 29; 3:6, 13, 22). The main speaker in Revelation 2–3 is Jesus, who is vividly introduced to the hearers through John's vision in 1:9–20. Here, his appearance harkens back to Daniel's vision of the heavenly figure in human form (Dan 10:5–6) and the Ancient of Days (7:9). The beginning of each

17 Lee, *Dynamic Reading of the Holy Spirit*, 52.

18 Lee, 86.

letter draws on this imagery, firmly spotlighting Jesus as the speaker. To each church, Jesus utters an οἶδα (I know) phrase, signaling his awareness of deeds, sufferings, and circumstances. After specific corrections, commendations, and encouragements, each letter ends in the formulaic encouragement to hear what the Spirit is saying, coupled with a promised reward to the overcomer. This concluding reference to the Spirit as speaker demonstrates a seamless speaking role between Jesus and the Spirit. The one does not hand over to the other midway; rather, the words of Jesus are affirmed to be the words of the Spirit as each letter concludes. The instructions, encouragements, blessings, and judgment thus proceed from the mouth of the Spirit and the Son, marking the Spirit *both* as speaker and divine agent who commands obedience (implied by the imperative ἀκουσάτω in 2:7, 11, 17, 29; 3:6, 13, 22) and therefore initiates the transformation of God's people.

In 14:13, we encounter τὸ πνεῦμα again. This instance marks the first direct words from the Spirit in Revelation. To understand this reference better, a bird's-eye view of the overarching section is important. While Revelation 6–20 is complex at best, an apt summary of this portion is an ever-increasing unfolding of judgment and decay. Rather than reading it chronologically, readers are encouraged to see the unfolding events in a cyclical manner, each cycle intensifying—almost like waves in the ocean. In Revelation 14, John encounters three angels with three messages. The first angel proclaims an eternal gospel to all people on the earth and signals that God's judgment is imminent (14:6–7). The second angel follows with an Isaiah-like condemnation of Babylon (14:8), essentially condemning the worldly powers that have set themselves up against God. Finally, the third angel announces the judgment of those who will worship the beast and receive its mark (14:9–11). Simplified, judgment is announced, applied to the powers, and then applied to the people. In light of this, John calls God's people to patiently endure (14:12). In verse 13, a divine voice speaks directly, uttering: "Blessed are the dead, those dying in the Lord from now."[19] The encouragement can be narrowly applied to those martyred for Christ but also to those remaining faithful to Christ until death. In verse 13, the Spirit enters into dialogue with the Father with the following words: "Yes . . . for they will rest from their labor, because their works will follow after them." Here, the Spirit says a few significant things. First, he affirms the Father's beatitude; second, he announces a rest for God's people, sharply contrasted to the fate of the beast's worshipers who will have no rest—neither day nor night (v. 11);

---

19 While it is possible for the voice from heaven to be that of the third angel, the contrastive *καί* in verse 13 probably indicates a new speaker.

third, he promises a reward for the faithful, noting that their deeds will count in eternity. Similar to the seamless speaking between Jesus and the Spirit in Revelation 2–3, Revelation 14:13 portrays the seamless speaking between the Father and Spirit in a much-needed encouragement to the faithful who are called to endure. In light of God's pending judgment and the condemnation of Babylon and her followers, John's call for endurance is bolstered by the voice of God from the heavens and the comforting message from the Holy Spirit. The Spirit's dialogue with the Father here demonstrates eschatological insight and care for God's people.

The most puzzling reference to τὸ πνεῦμα in Revelation is found in 19:10. After reprimanding John for falling at his feet and worshiping him, an angel remarks: ἡ γὰρ μαρτυρία Ἰησοῦ ἐστιν τὸ πνεῦμα τῆς προφητείας ("for the testimony of Jesus is the Spirit of prophecy"). Much ink has been spilled on deciphering what the angel is saying to John here. A few things need to be noted. First, γάρ (for) introduces an explanatory clause following the command to worship God (τῷ θεῷ προσκύνησον). What follows is thus the *reason why* John should not worship the angel. Further, the angel earlier calls himself a σύνδουλος (co-servant) of John, his brothers, and those holding to the testimony of Jesus (τὴν μαρτυρίαν Ἰησοῦ). Essentially, the angel is defining his role vis-à-vis this testimony—he is but equal to those who receive it. The Spirit, on the other side, *is* the one who gives the testimony, which is why John must worship God and not the angel. While it is grammatically difficult to translate, the following captures its essence: "Worship God. For the testimony of Jesus is [from] the Spirit of prophecy—[not from me; I am but its recipient]."[20] Such an utterance does two things: First, it establishes a clear hierarchy that extolls the Trinitarian God to a position that no other heavenly being has the right to share and affirms the Godhead as the source of the prophecy delivered to John (see Rev 1:1). This connects Father, Son, and Spirit in a remarkable way. Second, as seen in Revelation 2–3 and 14:13, the Spirit as a unified co-speaker with the other persons of the Godhead is clearly affirmed.[21] Finally, πνεῦμα τῆς προφητείας (the Spirit of prophecy) implies that the Holy Spirit is not only the mediator of the prophecy John

20 Such a reading regards τῆς προφητείας as a descriptive genitive, qualifying the Spirit as the one who inspires or bestows the gift of prophecy. Another approach, which comes down to the same, is seeing τῆς προφητείας as a subjective genitive, denoting the prophecy of or by the spirit (i.e., Spirit-evoked prophecy). Such a view affirms that the testimony of Jesus is inspired and carried by the Spirit that inspires prophecy (see Flemming, *Foretaste of the Future*, 105). I wish to thank my conversation partner, Ms. Estelle Crafford, for her wise input on this difficult verse.

21 Wilson, "Spirit in Revelation," 88–89; Osborne, *Revelation*, 313.

received but also its author. What John received is divinely inspired, which explains the harsh judgment pronounced on anyone who adds or subtracts from it (22:18–19).

Another reference to the Holy Spirit as τὸ πνεῦμα is found in 22:17. Here we encounter the second direct speech made by the Spirit, who, with the bride, says, ἔρχου ("Come!"). A case can be made for either Jesus or the thirsty unbeliever as the recipient of the invitation. The former signals three times that he intends to return (vv. 7, 12, 20), with an identical invitation (ἔρχου) made to Jesus in verse 20. However, verse 17 also contains an invitation to the thirsty to come and drink. Perhaps in true Johannine fashion, both are implied. If the invitation is directed at Jesus, we find, yet again, a harmonious co-speaking of the persons of the Trinity. Not only does the Spirit respond to Jesus's announcement of his imminent arrival (vv. 7, 12), but Jesus, in turn, responds to the Spirit's longings with an affirmative, "Indeed, I am coming soon" (v. 20). Again, the divine dialogue represents a unified picture. While the invitation for Jesus to return is directed to him, it is not there for him. Rather, such an invitation is a signal of readiness from the bride. The Spirit's co-yearnings for the return of Christ essentially remind the church to be ready for her bridegroom, who will come and reward each according to what they have done (22:12). Alternatively, if the invitation here is directed at the thirsty, who are invited to come and drink of the free waters (see Isa 55; John 4), he leads the church in its God-given desire to see the nations come into the new Jerusalem. The Spirit, therefore, does not only speak *to* the churches as seen in chapters 2–3, but he speaks *with* the church.

John's references to τὸ πνεῦμα illuminate the missional role of the Spirit in three ways. First, he is again affirmed as a speaking Spirit, co-speaking with Jesus, the Father, and the church. His co-speaking with Jesus is affirmed seven times—an apocalyptic representation of the Spirit "speaking at all times, to all the local churches, and all the church members."[22] His speaking also implies authority to correct and command. In his co-speaking with the Father (14:13) and the church (22:17), the Spirit demonstrates eschatological insight and foresight coupled with pastoral care for God's people and those who are yet to repent. In his co-speaking with the bride, he directs the gaze of the bride upward to the returning Christ and outward to the thirsty and lost—the former reminding the church of her missional call to prepare and purify herself for the bridegroom and the latter reminding her of her missional role of inviting the nations into the city of God.

22 Lee, *Dynamic Reading of the Holy Spirit*, 91.

Second, as the source of the prophecy (19:10), the Spirit fulfills not only a speaking but also a sending role. He testifies of Jesus and also mobilizes John and his hearers to mission through this testimony. Third, the affirmations of rest (14:13) and invitations to come (22:17) again qualify the Spirit as one who sees. In addition to searching the whole earth (5:6), he now demonstrates a seeing that transcends time. He sees the ultimate reward for the faithful and yearns with the church for its fulfillment, helping her see beyond the here and now. Additionally, the Spirit acts as "mission mobilizer" here,[23] demonstrating that the church's longing for the *eschaton* should not lead to escapism or tunnel vision. Rather, it is deeply missional as it anticipates the nations coming into the new Jerusalem. Remarkably, in a 1967 study conducted by the late Byang Kato in Igbaja, Nigeria, ninety percent of the respondents identified the news of the *eschaton* as the main catalyst in their response to the gospel.[24] The unified response between the Spirit and the bride thus signifies a joining of God and the faithful in "the final mission outreach in the canon."[25]

## The Living Spirit

In Revelation 11:11, John makes a reference to πνεῦμα ζωῆς (the living Spirit). Following God giving the outer court of the temple to the gentiles to trample (11:2), signifying a limited time of persecution,[26] two witnesses emerge who are appointed by God to witness for the same period, clothed in sackcloth (v. 3), and perform many signs that remind the reader of those performed by Elijah and Moses (vv. 5–6). While the Spirit is only explicitly mentioned in verse 11, the imagery of the two olive trees and two lampstands evokes a vision from Zechariah 4:2–6, where the two olive trees represent the two anointed ones (v. 14), namely Joshua the high priest and Zerubbabel the governor.[27] In the context of the rebuilding of the temple, the word of the Lord to the latter is, "Not by might, nor by power, but by my Spirit" (v. 6 ESV). The intertextual reference to the olive trees thus evokes the agency of the Holy Spirit in the lives and testimony of these two witnesses.

What follows is the killing of the witnesses by the beast after the conclusion of their testimony and all the inhabitants of the earth gloating over their death (vv. 9–10). With a reference back to Ezekiel 37 (see also

---

23 Lee, 90.

24 Foday-Khabenje, *Byang Kato*, ch. 5, n117.

25 Tonstad, *Revelation*, 323.

26 See Osborne, *Revelation*, 184.

27 Osborne, 187.

Gen 2:7), John foretells that the living Spirit from God (πνεῦμα ζωῆς ἐκ τοῦ θεοῦ) will enter them and raise them from the dead. In Ezekiel's vision, the Lord interprets the vision as a promise to bring Israel back to their land and to put his Spirit in them (37:12–14). Here, the Spirit raises the witnesses, empowering them for further proclamation and defeating the work of God's enemies through life-giving power. A flipside of this image is seen in Revelation 13:15, where the second beast gives πνεῦμα to the image of the first beast, which causes the image to speak and kill everyone who does not worship it. While demonstrating a similar reviving power, the πνεῦμα of the beast results in a reviving of evil and the persecution of the saints. In contrast, the πνεῦμα of God is described as "living"—it eventually results in God's enemies looking upward (v. 12) and a group of survivors coming to repentance (v. 13; see 14:7).

The discussion of πνεῦμα ζωῆς amplifies the sending role of the Holy Spirit. The revivification of the two witnesses primarily empowers them in their proclamation, ensuring that their mission, which ultimately leads to repentance (11:13), is not prematurely ended. Just as the early church was empowered by the Holy Spirit to proclaim the gospel (e.g., Acts 2:4, 11; 4:8–12, 29–31; 9:17–20; 10:44–48; 13:1–5), the raising of the two witnesses demonstrates the Spirit's power to continue empowering witnesses for God's mission—even amid Satan's onslaughts. Such life-giving also serves as an invitation to the dead churches (3:1–6), as the Holy Spirit is the agent who can again revive them.[28]

## In the Spirit

Another category of πνευ-related words includes John describing his state of being in the Spirit (ἐν πνεύματι) (1:10; 4:2; 17:3; 21:10).[29] Generally, ἐν πνεύματι is used to denote the means or manner by which life is lived, deeds are performed, and speaking occurs, signaling the agency of the Holy Spirit ("by," "with," or even "in the Spirit").[30] Of note is Mark 1:23 and 5:2 where possessed

28 See Lee, *Dynamic Reading of the Holy Spirit*, 85.

29 Adopting a narrative approach, Lee, 55–60, refers to Revelation 1:10–3:22, 4:2–16:21, 17:3–21:9, and 21:10–22:6 as the "four big visions" of John's Apocalypse and argues that the four instances of *ἐν πνεύματι* serve as literary signposts, granting authority to the coming vision and to John as seer.

30 See Matthew 3:11; 12:28; 22:43; Mark 1:8; 12:36; Luke 2:27; 3:16; 4:1; John 1:33; 4:23–24; Acts 1:5; 11:16; 19:21; Romans 2:29; 8:9; 9:1; 14:17; 15:16; 1 Corinthians 4:21; 6:11; 12:3; 12:9; 12:13; 14:16; 2 Corinthians 3:3; 6:6; Ephesians 2:18, 22; 3:5; 5:18; 6:18; Colossians 1:8; 1 Thessalonians 1:5; 1 Timothy 3:16; 1 Peter 1:12; Jude 20. While ἐν πνεύματι in Romans 8:9 is used in a locative manner, implying a being in the realm of the Spirit, as opposed

men are described as being ἐν πνεύματι ἀκαθάρτῳ (lit. "in an impure spirit"). What can be observed from the above examples is the implication of agency.[31] While it is possible that Revelation 17:3 and 21:10 refer to some out-of-body experience (i.e., carried in John's spirit and not the Holy Spirit),[32] John's spirit alone cannot usher him into the divine realm—the Holy Spirit enables the experience as John is "granted access to God's purposes."[33]

While not explicitly serving to characterize the Spirit, John's use of ἐν πνεύματι is missionally significant for two reasons: First, it amplifies the characterization of a speaking Spirit. The Spirit enables John to see and hear heavenly realities that ought to be written down, which is central to John's mandate (see 1:11). Koester therefore argues that "in the Spirit" and "the spirit speaks" are intertwined.[34] Moreover, what John hears and sees is a vivid unfolding of the story of God, climaxing in divine victory. John and the reader are privy to this information and can choose to align themselves with God's mission or that of the soon-to-be-defeated devil. Second, these references reveal the sending Spirit. Here, we see the Spirit sending John into the heavenly and eternal, which, in turn, empowers John to send a message to the churches in Asia Minor. Such a sending enables God to incarnate an eternal message and invite the church to participate as missional agents.

## Concluding Remarks

Revelation presents the final unveiling of God's purposes with the cosmos, which culminates in the final judgment of Satan (20:7–10), the dead (vv. 12–13, 15), the destruction of death and Hades (v. 14), followed by the creation of a new heaven and new earth (21:1), the descension of the new Jerusalem with God dwelling among his people (21:2–4, 9–27), and the restoration of Eden (22:1–5). The salvific mission of God thus comes full circle in John's Apocalypse, and it is brought about by the Trinitarian God. As the Third Person of the Trinity, the Holy Spirit works alongside the Father and Son,

to the realm of the flesh, the expression denotes the agency of the Spirit in the lives of the faithful (see vv. 5–8). Also, 1 Corinthians 14:16 exceeds the instrumental use. Here, Paul is describing a type of prayer, opposed to praying using understandable words (see vv. 14–15). It is possible that Ephesians 6:18 and Jude 20 function like 1 Corinthians 14:16.

31 De Smidt notes that late Jewish and Christian authors understood this phrase as meaning "in the Spirit's control." De Smidt, "Hermeneutical Perspectives," 29.

32 See Aune, *Revelation 1–5*, 83. Aune limits *ἐν πνεύματι* to a supernatural experience that took place in the spirit (lowercase) as opposed to the body.

33 Smith, "Holy Spirit's Eternal Procession," 260.

34 Koester, *Revelation*, 270.

not only to further the *missio Dei* but also to empower the faithful to take up their roles as co-laborers in God's mission. For John and the reader, such participation is most prominently marked by the act of faithful witness, obedience, and endurance. John is commanded to write down what he sees (1:11), which is summarized as the word of God and testimony of Jesus (1:2). The message is primarily for the church, but the value for the world unfolds as the reader progresses through it. Finally, the receiver's mandate is not only to hear but also to obey (1:3). This is bolstered by the affirmation of God's words as trustworthy (21:5; 22:6) and the role of Jesus as chief witness (1:5; 4:14), who proclaims both in word and deed.[35]

In the above survey of the Holy Spirit, the Third Person of the Trinity emerges as a speaking Spirit. He is identified as co-speaker alongside the Father and Son in various instances, including the epistolary greeting, letters to the churches, and the comforting reminders and yearnings for the *eschaton*. Moreover, he is identified as the author of the prophecy, underlining an unmissable role in the mission of faithful witness and obedience. In order to faithfully participate in God's mission, God's people also need eyes to see what God sees. As seeing Spirit, he lifts the gaze of the bride to see God's eternal comfort and Jesus's promise to return and broadens the gaze of the faithful to the nations. The Spirit thus continues to work in the church toward the fulfillment of the gospel reaching the ends of the earth (Acts 1:8). Finally, the Spirit fulfills a remarkable role as one who sends and is sent. He is identified as co-sender (and coauthor) of the divine message and one who mobilizes the faithful by enabling them to see what John saw. When persecution rises, he revives faithful witnesses and transforms the church into a "pneumatic community—the community of the Spirit," empowered to continue Jesus's mission on this earth.[36] He is also a sent agent in this mission. Not only is he sent to the faithful for equipping and strengthening, but he is sent to the whole earth. Such a portrait of the sending and sent Spirit is critical for a fulsome picture of the *missio Dei*. This combats the oft-committed oversight of sidelining the Spirit in discussions of God's mission by reducing it to the Father sending the Son and the Son sending the apostles.[37]

35 Flemming, *Foretaste of the Future*, 98, 100.

36 Padilla, "Holy Spirit," ch. 8, under "Pentecost and the Church."

37 Foday-Khabenje, *Byang Kato*, ch. 5, n90.

Revelation demonstrates that theology of mission cannot be divorced from pneumatology.[38] Such a view holds particular utility in the African context. First, the missional cooperation between the Father, Son, and Spirit and the divine activities and attributes of the Spirit celebrate him as wholly unique from any other created spiritual being. He is the Spirit of God, perfect, whole, and sufficient for those who participate in the *missio Dei*—no other spirit needs to be venerated or consulted for empowerment. Second, Revelation's picture emphasizes *both* the identity and the works of the Third Person of the Trinity, personalizing him as a crucial agent in the whole mission of God as opposed to the oft-misconstrued picture of the Holy Spirit as a mere miracle worker—a well-entrenched misconception in many African churches.[39] Finally, as a continent that has now become the epicenter of Christianity, Revelation reminds us that the Spirit's role in the *missio Dei* exceeds the birth of the church and the making of converts, but that it is carried forth thus:

> To live by the power of the Holy Spirit according to the values of the kingdom of God inserted into history in the person and work of Jesus Christ, in the hope that he who began a good work in the church will in the end carry it on to completion to the glory and praise of God.[40]

## Bibliography

Aune, David E. *Revelation 1–5*. Word Biblical Commentary 52A. Zondervan, 1997.

Boaheng, Isaac. "The Pneumatological Phenomenon in Acts 2:1–6: Implications for Christian Mission in Africa." *Conspectus* 34, no. 1 (2022): 6–19.

Flemming, Dean. *Foretaste of the Future: Reading Revelation in Light of God's Mission*. IVP Academic, 2022. Perlego.

Foday-Khabenje, Aiah Dorkuh. *Byang Kato: The Life and Legacy of Africa's Pioneer Evangelical Theologian*. Langham, 2000. Perlego.

Green, Gene L., Stephen Pardue, and K. K. Yeo, eds. *The Spirit over the Earth: Pneumatology in the Majority World*. Langham, 2016. Perlego.

---

38 See Boaheng, "Pneumatological Phenomenon in Acts 2:1–6," 7, who makes a similar argument primarily from Acts.

39 This can partly be explained by the fact that Africans are in general more descriptive than philosophical, meaning that there is a natural gravitation toward the gifts rather than theology about the person, since the latter is more philosophical. See Ngewa, "Pneumatology," ch. 5, under "Abstract."

40 Padilla, "Holy Spirit," ch. 8, under "Conclusion."

Hultberg, Alan D. "The Origin and Function of the Image of the Seven Spirits in Revelation." *Journal of the Evangelical Theological Society* 66, no. 4 (2023): 685–96.

Koester, Craig R. *Revelation: A New Translation with Introduction and Commentary*. Anchor Yale Bible 38A. Yale University Press, 2015.

Lee, Hee Youl. *A Dynamic Reading of the Holy Spirit in Revelation*. Wipf & Stock, 2014. Perlego.

Mathewson, David L. "The Holy Spirit in the New Creation of Revelation 21:1–22:5." *Journal of the Evangelical Theological Society* 67, no. 1 (2024): 113–24.

Metzger, Bruce M. *A Textual Commentary on the Greek New Testament*. 2nd ed. United Bible Societies, 1994.

Ngewa, Samuel M. "Pneumatology: Its Implications for the African Context." In Green, Pardue, and Yeo, *Spirit over the Earth*.

Osborne, Grant R. *Revelation Verse by Verse*. Lexham, 2016. Perlego.

Padilla, C. René. "The Holy Spirit: Power for Life and Hope." In Green, Pardue, and Yeo, *Spirit over the Earth*.

de Smidt, Kobus. "Hermeneutical Perspectives on the Spirit in the Book of Revelation." *Journal of Pentecostal Theology* 14 (1999): 27–47.

Smith, Brandon D. "The Holy Spirit's Eternal Procession in the Book of Revelation: Theological Interpretation in Pro-Nicene Perspective." *Journal of Theological Interpretation* 17, no. 2 (2023): 255–70.

Tonstad, Sigve K. *Revelation*. Paideia. Baker Academic, 2019. Perlego.

Wilson, Mark. "The Spirit in Revelation: Explorations in Imagery and Metaphor." *Criswell Theological Review*, n.s., 17, no. 1 (2019): 83–96.

# Chapter 4

# The Glorious Revelation of God's Mission of Love

*Sarah Lunsford*

God created for a purpose, moves his creation toward a purposeful end, and communicates with us in his word for a purpose.[1] When we read Scripture missiologically, we therefore expect that his works through the grand narrative flow from his own nature and return to him, having accomplished their intended goal (see Isa 55:11). If the *missio Dei* is rooted in his nature, and if the grand narrative of Scripture communicates the arc of his planned movement, then what can we learn from Revelation about the *telos* of God's mission?[2]

In biblical theology, we find a plethora of possible themes describing the central unifying purpose of Scripture.[3] Indeed, there are so many different proposed themes that some argue there is no one unifying theme, while others claim that we must find unity in the diversity.[4] In this age, we understand "in a mirror dimly" (1 Cor 13:12), with complex and pixelated fragments of insight in our ongoing enterprise of biblical exploration, as we seek to know and love the God who is currently veiled.[5] We struggle to see him clearly, but when the veil is lifted in the final revelation, when we "know fully, even as [we] have been fully known" (1 Cor 13:12), we will see that the *missio Dei* is as unified and simple as the nature of God himself. As Köstenberger and Goswell describe it, "The unity is explained by the fact that it is the revelation of the one God, presented in one canon, which records the story of what God has done and will do in one metanarrative."[6] Our struggle to find meaning and coherence in the imagery of Revelation reflects our struggle to comprehend the *missio Dei* as revealed in his Scripture as a whole, but what we learn of his mission in Revelation will also illuminate our understanding of the full grand narrative and will guide our response to him.

1 As Wright describes, "The writings that now comprise our Bible are themselves the product of and witness to the ultimate mission of God" (*Mission of God*, 48). Hamilton argues that "if the Bible tells a coherent story, it is valid . . . to ask whether the Bible shows us what God's ultimate purpose is" (*God's Glory in Salvation*, 40).

2 Unless otherwise noted, all Scripture quotations are from the ESV.

3 Hamilton, *God's Glory in Salvation*, 51–52.

4 See Köstenberger and Goswell's summation of a variety of diverse themes throughout Scripture and defense of their ultimate unity. *Biblical Theology*, 687–63.

5 See Clark, *To Know and Love God*, xxiiv–xxxii.

6 Köstenberger and Goswell, *Biblical Theology*, 693.

In this chapter, we will employ a missiological reading of Revelation to clarify the unifying purpose of the mission of God. We will consider a few of the dominant themes proposed in missiology to explain God's mission: holiness, glory, and love. We will find that each theme can be misunderstood and misapplied unless each is correctly defined and understood in relation to the others. A missiological reading of Revelation will help us to find these themes united in the revealed Christ, who perfectly reflects the nature of God's love as both the Lamb who was slain and the Lion who judges, which in turn will guide us in how we might glorify him by reflecting the image of Christ, the faithful witness to God's love.

## Common Missiological Perspectives on the *Telos* of the *Missio Dei*

### God's Holiness as the Purpose and Outcome of His Mission

In *Changing the Face of World Missions*, the authors trace shifting missiological motivations through history. They claim that the dominant missionary motivation for much of church history has been the fear of hell.[7] This missionary motivation has been misused to control and manipulate others. The fear of hell is a human response to God's holy judgment. Indeed, when God is described as "holy, holy, holy" in Hebrew, we are reading a profound declaration of the supreme value of his holiness. His holiness explains his acts of redemption and the final judgment. What it does not explain is why God created.

Additionally, if we propose that God's primary purpose in his relationship with his creation is holiness, then we can end up with a distorted vision of God. The image of a God who is primarily angry with all sin and consumed with judgment can lead us to be legalistic and morally harsh, to reach out to the nations as with rubber gloves and plugged noses.[8] Certainly, God is holy, and holiness is a significant element of God's *telos*, but it may not sufficiently encapsulate the *missio Dei* on its own merit.

### God's Glory as the Purpose and Outcome of His Mission

More recently, emphasis has shifted away from God's holiness and final judgment to a current emphasis on the glory of God as his ultimate purpose.[9]

---

7 Pocock, Van Rheenen, and McConnell, *Changing the Face*, 161–81.

8 Michael Reeves notes that overemphasis on holiness and judgment fails to create Christlike missionaries. "If we fear that God's love for us is reluctant or that his approval rests on our performance, we won't feel any real affection for him, our service will be grudging, and the world will likely see through us." Reeves and Hames, *God Shines Forth*, 19.

9 Hamilton, *God's Glory in Salvation*, see 82n74.

There is an overwhelming abundance of Scriptures claiming that God's acts are done "for his glory" and that "glory" will be the final outcome in the eschaton (see Eph 1:11–12; Isa 40:5; 44:23; 48:9–11; 66:18–20; Pss 79:9; 86:9; 115:1). This is not a new concept, but it has received new attention as a unifying theme of Scripture.[10]

The modern missional goal and drive to serve the glory of God coincides with the tremendous popularity and influence of John Piper, who insists that God's purpose is his own glory. "God's own glory is uppermost in his own affections. In everything he does, his purpose is to preserve and display that glory."[11] Piper further claims that "zeal for the glory of God motivates world missions."[12] At this stage in biblical and missiological scholarship, one rarely comes across any publication that fails to present God's glory as the goal and purpose of God's mission.[13]

Despite its prevalence in recent years, this perspective of God's glory as the driving motivation and purpose for the *missio Dei* is not without challenges. There are those who argue that for God to create and redeem, all to serve his goal of receiving more glory for himself, seems out of character. What kind of God would be so consumed with his own glory that he creates a world to praise him and bring him even more glory? A standard response to this challenge says that since God is the only one worthy of praise, it is only right and good that he should receive all glory, and that in fact, it would be idolatry for God to pursue anything less than his own glory.[14] As fair as that point is in arguing for his worthiness, it may not fully answer the question of his character.

In his book *Delighting in the Trinity*, Michael Reeves portrays the problem with a god whose goal is to receive worship or service from his creation. This kind of god cannot be ruler without subjects, cannot be father

---

10 The Westminster Shorter Catechism Question 7 states, "The decrees of God are, his eternal purpose, according to the counsel of his will, whereby, for his own glory, he hath foreordained whatsoever comes to pass."

11 Piper, *Desiring God*, 43.

12 Piper, *Let the Nations*, 29. Likewise, Zane Pratt claims, "The mission of God has the glory of God as its driving passion and as its ultimate goal, as God reveals the amazing spectrum of his glory in creation, judgment, redemption, and restoration." "Heart of Mission," 49.

13 Bruce Waltke says, "The ultimate theological truth that unifies the whole of Scripture is the irruption of the merciful King's rule to his glory" (*Old Testament Theology*, 61, cf. 144). Michael Bird's *Evangelical Theology*, for example, concludes that "God's purposes are primarily doxological—that is, God is concerned with his glory. And the gospel reveals the various tiers of God's plan to manifest his glory" (269).

14 Piper, *Let the Nations*, 24.

without children, or cannot be a god without worshipers. This god's nature is dependent on his creation and is, therefore, no god at all.[15] In the same way, if we say that God's purpose in creating and redeeming is ultimately for his own glory, are we making him out to be dependent on us to bring him glory? This approach seems to imply that God needs us and that he is lacking in some way. However, God's nature is already glorious. He has no need for us to bring him glory, nor does our glory to God benefit him in any way.[16] So, then, if God is already sufficiently glorious and not in need of additional praise, then we are still left wondering—Why? Why does the glorious God need or want more glory? Is having an audience beyond his Trinitarian nature a necessary element of glory itself?

Similarly, if we say that the missional purpose of God is his own glory, then our understanding of how the church participates in God's mission can be misconstrued. As Telford Work says, the idea that the *telos* of our lives is to glorify God lacks specificity; it is too vague to be helpful.[17] Indeed, some missionaries are consumed with zeal for winning the nations so that they can offer God more of the glory he deserves. This implies that in some way, we are able, by our works, to make him more glorious or to increase his stores of magnificence. It suggests that God's glory is outside of himself, that glory is in the voices of praise, and that the more the worshipers, the greater the glory.[18] This gives missionaries more power than seems appropriate.

### God's Love as the Purpose and Outcome of His Mission

In contrast to those gods who need a creation to serve them and to establish their preeminence, Reeves describes our Trinitarian God as a God of love, whose very nature already gives and receives love within the Godhead. Reeves demonstrates that it is out of the abundance and overflow of God's love that he is motivated to create, to pursue that creation with a redemptive plan that cost him dearly, and to aim for a loving community as his ultimate purpose.[19] This perspective of "love" as the ultimate *telos* for God's mission seems a bit more consistent with what we know of God's nature and character.

15 Reeves, *Delighting in the Trinity*, 39–47.

16 Reeves, 47–52.

17 Work, *Jesus*, 170.

18 Certainly, this is a bit of a caricature, but it serves to highlight ways that we can be misguided if we pursue God's glory as the sole end goal.

19 Reeves, *Delighting in the Trinity*, 41–43.

John Stott teaches that mission arises from God's loving nature.[20] He points out that the Johannine Commission (John 20:20; also 17:18) sends us out in the same suffering servant manner that Christ was sent, and that this kind of humble and generous self-sacrifice is a clear testament to God's loving mission. This perspective on God's mission is self-justifying and has explanatory power because love loves for love's sake.[21] As opposed to the creation-reliant implications of a *telos* of glory, Stott explains that just as God does not love with expectation of return, so also missional engagement, done out of love, does not expect or demand results but radiates God's generous invitation for the world to join his community of love.[22]

For all the coherence and clarity that a *telos* of love in the *missio Dei* provides, our interpretation faces challenges. Some missionaries whose main focus is love can be unfaithful to biblical teaching on God's holiness, as they generously pour out their lives in social work and gracious empathy, eschewing aspects of the gospel that include judgment or condemnation.[23] Similarly, a coherent and consistent missiological position on the ultimate purpose of God's mission cannot justify neglecting the weighty biblical representation of his motivations for his own glory, especially if we agree that the Bible is written in "witness to the ultimate mission of God."[24]

Thus far, we have examined holiness, glory, and love separately as alternative options to define God's primary missiological purpose. However, most scholars recognize that while holiness, glory, and love are all key aspects in the *telos* of God's mission, they need to be understood in relation

20 "God is love, always reaching out after others in self-giving service." Stott, *Christian Mission*, 21.

21 As both Augustine and Aquinas agree, love is the ultimate motivation behind all actions (Aquinas, *Summa Theologica* 2.28.6; and Augustine, *Civ.* 14.7, 9). Wright suggests that the great commandment to love God and neighbor is a better descriptor of the mission of the church than the Great Commission is. He argues that the grand narrative is just as much a story of biblical ethics as anything else, in that creation is meant to reflect God's loving nature. "Here, then, we have a very clear imperative—to love God with the totality of our being and to love our neighbor as ourselves. This could easily be described with even more textual justification, as 'the great commission,' for it governs the whole of life whatever our specific calling. This fundamental twin commandment certainly precedes, underlies and governs the so-called Great Commission itself, for we cannot make disciples of the nations without love for God and love for them." *Mission of God*, 60.

22 "If good works are visible loving, then they are 'expecting nothing in return' (Luke 6:35)." Stott, *Christian Mission*, 27.

23 Granted, this kind of missional application assumes a faulty definition of "love." In fact, the relationship between proclamation and service in our mission efforts is the topic of Stott's *Christian Mission*, and his full explanation of how a proper understanding of love clarifies the balance is well worth reading.

24 Wright, *Mission of God*, 48.

to one another.[25] The fact that these three themes are dominant throughout Scripture cannot be denied, but the precise relationship between God's missional motivation and purpose regarding holiness, glory, and love needs further exploration. To that end, we will turn to Revelation for clarity on God's unifying purpose throughout the grand narrative.

## Exploring the Revelation of Jesus Christ

### In Search of the Unifying Theme

James Hamilton argues that the unifying theme of Revelation, and of biblical theology as a whole,[26] is "God glorifying himself by saving his people through the judgment of his and their enemies."[27] Hamilton clarifies that salvation reveals God's love and that judgment reveals God's holiness, but neither of them are ends in themselves. Rather, God's love and holiness are a "means to the end of displaying his own glory."[28]

Hamilton is not the only scholar to position God's love and holiness in service to his ultimate goal of glory,[29] but the idea that God acts in love and preserves his holiness all to magnify his glory does not sit right with everyone. Schreiner agrees that the glory of God in Christ is the central theme of Paul's writings,[30] but in his commentary on Revelation, he positions glory in service to holiness. He notes that the angel cries out in Revelation 14:7, "Fear God and give him glory, because the hour of his judgment has come." Schreiner points to its parallel with Jeremiah 13:16 and argues that we are to glorify God in order to avoid judgment.[31]

Richard Hays argues that, despite the centrality of love as a New Testament theme, since love is not a prominently displayed theme in Revelation,[32] love

---

25 For example, Bird believes that "God's purpose is to glorify himself by the effusion of his holy love operating through the Son and the Spirit in order that we should partake of God's life, share in God's glory, and participate in God's reign over all things." *Evangelical Theology*, 269.

26 Hamilton, *God's Glory in Salvation*, 40.

27 Hamilton, 718. He sees the Revelation in three parts: Jesus and the letters (1:9–3:22), with emphasis on the glory of the risen Christ (1:9–20); the throne and the judgments (4:1–16:21); and the harlot, the king, and the bride (17:1–22:9). He proposes a chiastic structure to the Revelation, centered on God and Christ taking the kingdom in 11:15–19.

28 Hamilton, *God's Glory in Salvation*, 54.

29 Cf. Bird, *Evangelical Theology*, 269–74.

30 Schreiner, *Paul*, 15–35.

31 Schreiner, *Revelation*, 679.

32 However, Hays does believe that love is a focal theme in Paul's writings (Rom 13:8; 1 Cor 12:31–13:13) and John's writings (John 13:34–35; 1 John 4:7–8). *Moral Vision*, 200–203.

cannot be the unifying theme of all Scripture.[33] However, Andreas Köstenberger and Gregory Goswell insist that love is the unifying theme of both Revelation and the full grand narrative, saying that despite the heavy emphasis on judgment throughout Revelation, the book opens and closes with the dominant theme of love. We read in 1:5b–6 that the reason Christ is worthy of glory is because of his love and sacrifice—"To him who loves us and has freed us from our sins by his blood and made us a kingdom, priests to his God and Father, to him be glory and dominion forever and ever. Amen." Revelation then concludes with the marriage supper of the Lamb (19:6–7). "Thus, the proper climax of the Bible's theology is . . . the consummation of the love relationship between God and his people in and through Christ, the Bridegroom, whose love for his people found tangible expression in his sacrificial, vicarious death on the cross."[34] On the basis of this argument for love as the unifying theme and *telos*, we will explore the beginning and the end of Revelation, focusing primarily on 1:1–8 and interacting with the end in Revelation 21.

**The Revelation**

Revelation opens with the word *apokalypsis* (1:1). The word is translated "revelation," but its meaning is "to make visible," or more specifically, "to remove the veil." This harkens back to the temple veil that separated God from man. Jumping from the beginning of Revelation to its end, we see the final "unveiling" in Revelation 21. The new Jerusalem takes on the full type of the temple.[35] The veil that has separated God from man will finally be removed, and God will directly tabernacle with his holy people.[36] The word *apokalypsis* is related to *anakalypsis*, often referring to the lifting of a bridal wedding

---

33 Nor is it dominant in Mark, Acts, or Hebrews, according to Hays (200–203). Cf. Köstenberger and Goswell's response in *Biblical Theology*, 735–39. Köstenberger and Goswell counter that one must read the Revelation in light of the full Johannine corpus. John the Revelator also wrote that "God is love" (1 John 4:16), that "God so loved the world that he gave his only Son" (John 3:16), that "greater love has no one than this, that someone lay down his life for his friends" (John 15:13), that "we love because he first loved us" (1 John 4:19), and that our new commandment is to love one another as he loved us (John 13:23–35; 1 John 2:7–8). Therefore, Köstenberger and Goswell insist that love is indeed the dominant theme of Revelation as the ultimate expression of the unifying theme of Scripture.

34 Köstenberger and Goswell, 686.

35 Beale says that in Revelation 21 the concepts of temple and city are conjoined into the central idea of God's presence with his people (Beale, *Revelation*, 1070).

36 According to Bauckham, "God's creation reaches its eschatological fulfilment when it becomes the scene of God's immediate presence" (*Theology of the Book*, 140). See also Ngundu, "Revelation," 1604. In fact, Ngundu argues that because the unveiling ("unmasking") is such a powerful move, Revelation's theme is more about power rather than love (1570).

veil,[37] another symbolic unveiling at the end of Revelation (19:6–7; 21:2) that likewise portends the coming union between God and his people. The end of the whole grand narrative of Scripture is perfect *koinonia* fellowship between God and his people.[38] The unveiling is the *telos* of the *missio Dei*, as God's people join the loving communion of the Trinity.[39]

**The Revelation of Jesus Christ**

There is some ambiguity in the genitive phrase "of Jesus Christ" (1:1). Is the phrase to be translated subjectively or objectively? Is Jesus the one revealing or the one being revealed? While many scholars argue for the more direct interpretation that Jesus is passing along a revelation from God to John,[40] there is a case to be made for Christ himself as the one being revealed throughout the highly Christocentric book of Revelation.[41] Many agree that Jesus Christ is both the one who reveals and the one who is unveiled.[42]

As we see in Revelation 21, the glory of the Lord fills the city. In its fullest biblical sense, "glory" is the manifestation of God's inherent nature, God's self-revelation, which cannot be understood correctly apart from Christ. Despite its widespread adoption as the *telos* of God's mission, the subject of "glory" itself has received paltry attention.[43] Perhaps some of our confusion in finding unity between the themes of holiness, glory, and love lies in the fact that "glory" has not been clearly defined. We tend to think "glory" refers to "honor," but the terms are used separately throughout most of Revelation (4:9, 11; 5:12, 13; 7:12; 19:1, 17; 21:24, 26). The Greek term *doxa* did originally have that emphasis, but once it was used to translate the Hebrew term *kavod*, its meaning was greatly expanded in its New Testament usage.

---

37 Huber, "Revealing Christ in Revelation," 98.

38 Santiago, *Fellowship of the Throne*, 14, 87, 90. See also Ekem, "Revelation 21:1–4," 59; and Robinson, *Temple of Presence*, 124.

39 See Santiago, *Fellowship of the Throne*, 14. Note especially footnote 89 for his argument based on the biblical canon that the final koinonia fellowship ending Revelation is also the telos of the grand narrative. See Kärkkäinen, *Introduction to Ecclesiology*, 22, where he states that it's almost universally agreed across denominations that koinonia anchors our present fellowship in the life of the Trinity and thus with each other (294).

40 Beale, *Revelation*, 183. Hamilton agrees that "apocalypse" in 1:1 means to "unveil," but he focuses on how it will unveil the future rather than unveiling the veiled God. *Revelation*, under "Revelation of God's Justice and Mercy."

41 Huber, "Revealing Christ in Revelation," 98.

42 Santiago, *Fellowship of the Throne*, 94. See also Khatry, "Revelation," 1772.

43 Cole, *Glorification*, 14.

Robinson explains that glory is a theophanic term that implies the physical substance of God himself.[44] Reeves and Hames argue that "Jesus is not only glorious in a descriptive way; he is God's Glory in a definitive way . . . Jesus is the Glory of God: the very outshining radiance of his being."[45] Therefore, when the veil between God and man is fully removed, the glory we will see is God in Christ, who fully manifests the loving nature of God. Indeed, Jesus is the glory to be unveiled, the object of revelation.

**The Revelation of What Must Soon Take Place**

Jesus is also the one showing the revelation of what "must soon take place" (1:1). What events need to happen for the veil to be removed so that the glory of God in physical substance can fully dwell in loving communion with his people? The temple veil represents the necessary separation between a holy God and a sinful people, so it is the purifying judgment that will render God's people holy enough to dwell in communion with God's presence. This is why so much of Revelation is about the coming judgment—it is the path to the final unveiling.

As with our understanding of "glory," the concept of holiness needs to be understood theologically. The heart of the law, as Jesus taught, is the great commandment—to love the Lord and others as oneself (Matt 22:36–40); thus, all sin is a perversion of love, improperly aligned with the God who *is* love. Reeves explains that Adam and Eve "were created *as lovers* in the image of God, and they could not undo that. Instead, their love *turned*. . . . Created to love God, we turn to love ourselves and anything but God."[46]

Just as all sin is a twisted love, failing to be properly oriented toward God, all sin "fall[s] short of the glory of God" (Rom 3:23) by failing to fully image that perfect love. The radiance of God's glorious nature burns away all that falls short. Holiness is a necessary aspect of God's love.[47] Perfect love cannot dismiss or tolerate anything that is unloving. No one who truly loves can ignore or dismiss a cruelty or injustice committed against their beloved. Perfect love *must* judge. Amazingly, though, we see that the God who has so faithfully loved his creation, who has endured unimaginable abuses and betrayals from a fallen people and witnessed horrors committed against

44 Robinson, *Temple of Presence*, 133–34.

45 Reeves and Hames, *God Shines Forth*, 22.

46 Reeves, *Delighting in the Trinity*, 65 (emphasis original).

47 For a description of Aquinas and Augustine on God's holiness in relation to his love, see Lunsford, *Missiological Triage*, 50–61.

his beloved creation, is also so perfect in love and so committed to a *telos* of loving union that he takes upon himself all punishment for the world's unloving (idolatrous) behaviors! Furthermore, out of God's perfect love, he veils his holiness, showing abundant mercy as he patiently gives us time to repent and turn to him (cf. 2 Pet 3:9).

In Revelation 5, the final judgment awaits one who is worthy to open the scroll, and Christ alone, the Lamb of God, is presented as worthy to judge all sin. As the holy Lamb who so perfectly reflected the very image of God's love, without any twisting or perversion, by humbling himself even to death to redeem his rebellious people, Christ alone radiates the full power and fiery radiance of God's nature, including his holy judgment. He does not condemn out of revenge or impatience or pride but from a place of humble entreaty and patient invitation. When the final judgment comes after millennia of astounding patience, mercy, and abundant invitation, the overwhelming fairness of that judgment—when the one who judges is the primary "victim" and simultaneously the one who willingly received the worst possible penalties in his own body, all to offer reconciliation—will literally silence all retorts and leave heaven in awe (8:1; see also Rom 3:19). We will be dumbfounded to realize that the most fearful judgment is also the most perfect demonstration of love.

### Alpha and Omega

At the crucifixion of the Lamb, we saw that the temple veil was ripped from top to bottom (Matt 27:51). At the final judgment of the Lion, we will see the veil completely removed. In this way, not only is Jesus Christ the one revealed, but he is also the one who reveals. Jesus removes the veil. He is indeed the Alpha and Omega, the beginning and the end, the one who is and was and is to come (1:8; 22:13). He is the glory revealed and the one who lifts the veil so that God's people can enter the presence of God and join the communion of the Trinity. The *telos* of Revelation and of the *missio Dei* is loving fellowship, made possible by the loving sacrifice of Christ, the Lamb who makes us holy so that we can finally see the full manifestation (glory) of God's presence.

### The Revelation Shown to His Servants

God gave the revelation to Jesus to show to his servants. Jesus sent his angel, who gave it to John, who shared it with the churches, with the repeated injunction to read the revelation aloud and share it abroad (1:1–3). This is reminiscent of God's missiological sending—the Father sends the Son, the Son sends the Spirit, and the Spirit sends the church. If we say that the beginning and end of Revelation is Jesus, who is the glory of God in that he manifests God's loving nature and holy mission toward the *telos* of full *koinonia* fellowship between God and his people, then what is the primary message for "his servants"? How does the *telos* of the *missio Dei* inform the mission of the church?

First, we can note that the revelation of Jesus Christ was shown to his *beloved* disciple, John, who in turn shares it with the churches, the future *beloved* bride (19:7). Second, we can note that Jesus has made his beloved to be his priests (1:6). When Jesus was crucified, the temple veil was torn, and when he ascended, he sent us his Spirit to dwell within us, a down payment on the full *koinonia* fellowship we will have with God when the veil is fully removed. John received the vision of Revelation while he was "in the Spirit," and each of the letters to the seven churches ends with the same words—"He who has an ear, let him hear what the Spirit says to the churches" (2:7, 11, 17, 29; 3:6, 13, 22). In the consummation, the entire city will be the temple, but in this age, our bodies are the temple of the Spirit. God is still veiled to those who are lost (2 Cor 4:3–6), but we have fellowship with God through the indwelling Spirit and reveal him to the world as ambassadors of reconciliation (2 Cor 5:20). We are empowered through the Spirit to reflect the glory of God, to properly fulfill the great commandment, and to testify through word and deed to reconciliation with God.

Many scholars have recognized that glory is the manifestation of God and is thus related to us in our nature as image-bearers. While God is veiled in this age, we his image-bearers glorify him by reflecting his holy love.[48] Constantine Campbell teaches that "glory is understood as an element of the visible manifestation of believers' union with Christ. When revelation occurs, so too will glorification."[49] Donald Berry states that "humans, as image-bearers, were created to see God's glory and to share in his glory. And through righteous lives that put the worth and truth of God on display (cf. Rom 1:25), humans were to show forth God's glory in the earth."[50] Graham Cole writes,

> In the light of the great rupture delineated in Genesis 3, God has a plan to reclaim and restore his divine image bearers to himself. Divine love

48 See Peñamora, "Asia and God's Cruciform," 105–27.

49 Campbell, *Hope of Glory*, 280.

50 Berry, *Glory in Romans*, 193.

> motivates the plan. Divine glory is the ultimate goal of the plan. To be restored to the divine image is to become a glorious being.[51]

The authors of *The Changing Face of World Missions* likewise write, "Christians are called to taste the glory of God—to be with him, to reflect his glory, and to perceive life beyond these human bounds—is the core of Christian motivation."[52]

**Behold Jesus Christ, the Faithful Witness**

The word "behold" (ἰδού) is repeated twenty-six times throughout Revelation. Jesus Christ is at the heart of all that is revealed—the beginning, the end, and the means of the unveiling of God's presence, resulting in full *koinonia.* The book of Revelation demands that we *behold* him in his full glory, as he perfectly shows us the face of God.

In these first verses of the revelation of Jesus Christ, we see his key descriptor as "faithful witness" (1:5). John originally referred to Jesus in this way in John 1:1–18, describing the testimony of Jesus as the Word made flesh, culminating in the declaration that "no one has ever seen God. The one and only Son, who is himself God and is at the Father's side—he has revealed him" (v. 18). John did not say that the Son *will* reveal God but that he already has. The incarnate Christ revealed (glorified) the God who is veiled by living in perfect alignment with the loving nature of God and in humble submission to his loving mission. Reeves and Hames explain that "the glory of God that will fill the earth at the end is the same glory we see in the death of Jesus. Specifically, the self-giving glory of the cross is the key to understanding the glory that is to come."[53] In fact, as the ultimate demonstration of God's love, it was the suffering of Christ that best manifests God's nature, the essence of his glorification (John 12:23).[54]

In Revelation, we see the image of a radiant Christ in his fully glorified condition (1:12–18). He is worthy and glorified because he is the "faithful witness" (1:5). As the Lamb who was slain, who so perfectly manifests the love of God (Rev 1:5–6; cf. John 15:13), he is worthy to be the Lion of the tribe of Judah (5:5) and to serve as holy judge (19:11–16). In this age where God's face is veiled, Jesus is the faithful witness because in his life, death, and resurrection, he reveals God's loving mission.

---

51 Cole, *Glorification*, 15.

52 Pocock, Van Rheenen, and McConnell, *Changing the Face*, 173.

53 Reeves and Hames, *God Shines Forth*, 113.

54 Harrison, "Glory," 341–42.

How does a book that focuses our attention on Jesus contain a message for his servants? As his beloved servants made priests, we are called to glorify him, to reveal his love to the world as both a warning of eternal separation from God and an invitation to loving union with him, to follow his example as faithful witnesses to the nature and mission of the God who *is* love. As image bearers, we reflect that which we gaze upon. How can we reflect the image of God unless we focus our eyes on him? How can we glorify him unless we anchor the full weight of our love in his nature, as revealed in Christ? Fix your eyes on Jesus, the author and finisher of our faith (Heb 12:2)! Behold the Lamb who was slain, the faithful witness to the love of God!

Our missiological reading of Revelation, therefore, leads us to glorify God by reflecting the image of Christ. Like him, we are called to be faithful witnesses. We do this, first, by holding fast to our "first love" (2:1–4). Love for him guides us in how to participate in his mission and fuels us with motivation. Reeves and Hames say it well,

> God's glory is not only the fuel of mission in the sense of being its grand objective. God's glory—his own naturally overspilling life, showcased in his Son—is mission's rationale and its motor. . . . Seeing in Jesus what our God is really like causes us to shine like him. We come to share his great heart's desire that his love, goodness, and righteousness would bless all the world.[55]

Out of a pure love for God and for others, we glorify him when we face suffering and persecution in the same humble and self-sacrificing manner as Christ did (cf. 2:8–11; 3:7–13). We live lives that are molded and shaped by holy love for one another, and we faithfully defend the purity of his gospel (cf. 2:12–24). True and faithful love that reflects the glory of Christ will be passionate in pursuit of God and his loving mission to reveal himself to the world (cf. 3:1–6, 14–22).

This insight brings coherence to the themes of suffering throughout Revelation (10:1–11:14), the glory of the martyred saints (7:9, 14; 12:11–12), and the emphasis on enduring as faithful witnesses (14:4–5). Köstenberger and Goswell point to the imagery of the lampstand to picture the church (1:12, 20; cf. 2:1, 5) and the witnesses (11:4) in that it shows God's people as lights in a dark world who will experience Satan's wrath (11:7–10) but also bring unbelievers to repentance by their enduring witness (11:11–13).[56]

---

55 Reeves and Hames, *God Shines Forth*, 29.

56 Köstenberger and Goswell, *Biblical Theology*, 680.

This perspective of glorifying God by reflecting his nature as his image-bearers can give new insight into what it means to say that "they will bring into [the city] the glory and the honor of the nations" (21:26). If the glory of all creation is its ability to reveal God's nature, then the glory of the nations is not something they possess apart from God. This suggests that each nation is able to reflect God's nature in a unique manner. Perhaps each unique context provides a specific opportunity to reveal God's love. We see this community of image bearers magnifying God's glory through their diverse situations and testimonies even in the way that God reveals his word to us. Just as he revealed his mission through sixty-six books and forty authors over a period of 1,500 years, and just as he revealed the life and death of Jesus through four different gospel testimonies, so also he reveals himself through a multitude of people, churches, and nations.

Only Christ is a perfect image of God; we, his people, glorify him best when we do so in community with one another, an image of the final consummation. Therefore, if we see "glory" as the revelation of God's nature, and if we hold to a *telos* of love in that final revelation of the full *missio Dei*, then we will be moved toward unity, community, shalom, hospitality, and priesthood in the kingdom of God. Rather than approaching the nations with an ethnocentric interpretation of holiness in our own cultural image, we glorify him when we image his holy love revealed in Christ by loving one another, showing honor and respect for the unique reflection of his glory that each nation bears.

Understanding glory as the radiance of God's loving nature also explains what it means that we will be glorified when we are finally united with him in the marriage supper of the Lamb (19:7–8). He will be unveiled, and the city will be lighted by his own glory (22:5). The essence of his glory is his sacrificial, faithful love; we glorify him when we image his love, the perfection of holiness; and we will be most fully glorified when we are united with him in love.[57]

## Conclusion

God's glory is not outside of his nature but a revelation of his nature. He shares that glory with us by creating us in his own image through the power of the indwelling Spirit, our deposit on the future fellowship in the final revelation,

57 "Yes, the culmination of history is the glory of God. Not glory taken but glory given. The whole creation suffused with his light, his creatures filled and made happy in his goodness, his bride drenched eternally in his love." Reeves and Hames, *God Shines Forth*, 122.

and by transforming us into the image of Christ, who alone perfectly radiates the love of God and its corresponding holiness. "And we all, with unveiled face, beholding the glory of the Lord, are being transformed into the same image from one degree of glory to another. For this comes from the Lord who is the Spirit" (2 Cor 3:18). The radiance of God's loving nature shines on us, and when we turn our hearts toward him, we reflect that light into a dark world.

Thus, we see that God's passion for his glory *is* his passion for revelation. In his love, he eagerly anticipates the day when he will be unveiled, when he will be known by his people, even as he fully knows us (1 Cor 13:12), when we will finally "know the love of Christ that surpasses knowledge" in all its "breadth and length and height and depth" (Eph 3:18–19). God's passion for his glory is the Bridegroom's passionate anticipation for his marriage feast, when he will no longer be veiled but will be truly known, united with the creation he has so faithfully loved.

## Bibliography

Aquinas, Thomas. *A Summa of the Summa*. Edited by Peter Kreeft. Ignatius, 1990.

Augustine. *City of God*. Translated by Henry Bettenson. Penguin, 2004.

Bauckham, Richard J. *The Theology of the Book of Revelation*. Cambridge University Press, 1993.

Beale, G. K. *The Book of Revelation: A Commentary on the Greek Text*. New International Greek Testament Commentary. Eerdmans, 1999.

Berry, Donald. *Glory in Romans and the Unified Purpose of God in Redemptive History*. Wipf & Stock, 2016.

Bird, Michael. *Evangelical Theology: A Biblical and Systematic Introduction*. 2nd ed. Zondervan, 2020.

Campbell, Constantine R. *Paul and the Hope of Glory: An Exegetical and Theological Study*. HarperCollins, 2020.

Clark, David K. *To Know and Love God: Method for Theology*. Crossway, 2023.

Cole, Graham A. *Glorification: An Introduction*. Crossway, 2022.

Ekem, John D. K. "Revelation 21:1–4 from an African Perspective." In Green, Pardue, and Yeo, *All Things New*.

Green, Gene L., Stephen T. Pardue, and K. K. Yeo, eds. *All Things New: Eschatology in the Majority World*. Langham, 2019.

Hamilton, James M. *God's Glory in Salvation Through Judgment: A Biblical Theology*. Crossway, 2010.

Hamilton, James M. *Revelation: The Spirit Speaks to the Churches*. Preaching the Word. Crossway, 2012.

Harrison, E. F. "Glory." In *Evangelical Dictionary of Theology*, edited by Daniel J. Treier and Walter A. Elwell. 3rd ed. Baker Academic, 2017.

Hays, Richard B. *The Moral Vision of the New Testament: A Contemporary Introduction to New Testament Ethics*. HarperOne, 1996.

Huber, Lynn R. "Revealing Christ in Revelation." In *Narrative Mode and Theological Claim in Johannine Literature: Essays in Honor of Gail R. O'Day*, edited by Lynn R. Huber, Susan Hylen, and William M. Wright. SBL Press, 2021.

Kärkkäinen, Veli-Matti. *An Introduction to Ecclesiology: Historical, Global, and Interreligious Perspectives*. IVP Academic, 2021.

Khatry, Ramesh. "Revelation." In *South Asia Bible Commentary: A One-Volume Commentary on the Whole Bible*, edited by Brian C. Wintle. Zondervan, 2015.

Köstenberger, Andreas, and Gregory Goswell. *Biblical Theology: A Canonical, Thematic, and Ethical Approach*. Crossway, 2023.

Lunsford, Sarah. *Missiological Triage: A Framework for Integrating Theology and Social Sciences in Missiological Methods*. Pickwick, 2023.

Ngundu, Onesimus. "Revelation." In *Africa Bible Commentary*, edited by Tokunboh Adeyemo. WordAlive, 2006.

Peñamora, Aldrin. "Asia and God's Cruciform Eschatological Reign." In Green, Pardue, Yeo, *All Things New*.

Piper, John. *Desiring God: Meditations of a Christian Hedonist*. Multnomah, 2003.

Piper, John. *Let the Nations Be Glad!* Baker Academic, 2010.

Pocock, Michael, Gailyn Van Rheenen, and Douglas McConnell. *The Changing Face of World Missions*. Baker Academic, 2005.

Pratt, Zane. "The Heart of the Mission: Redemption." In *Theology and Practice of Mission: God, the Church, and the Nations*, edited by Bruce Ashford. B&H, 2011.

Reeves, Michael. *Delighting in the Trinity: An Introduction to the Christian Faith*. IVP Academic, 2012.

Reeves, Michael, and Daniel Hames. *God Shines Forth: How the Nature of God Shapes and Drives the Mission of the Church*. Crossway, 2022.

Robinson, Andrea L. *Temple of Presence: The Christological Fulfillment of Ezekiel 40–48 in Revelation 21:1–22:5*. Wipf & Stock, 2019.

Santiago, Fabián. *The Fellowship of the Throne in John's Apocalypse: A Theo-Political Inquiry into Authority and Society and Their Christological Bond*. Langham, 2020.

Schreiner, Thomas R. *Paul, Apostle of God's Glory in Christ*. IVP Academic, 2001.

Schreiner, Thomas R. *New Testament Theology: Magnifying God in Christ*. Baker Academic, 2008.

Schreiner, Thomas R. *Revelation*. Baker Exegetical Commentary on the New Testament. Baker Academic, 2023.

Stott, John R. W. *Christian Mission in the Modern World: What the Church Should Be Doing Now!* IVP, 1975.

Waltke, Bruce K., with Charles Yu. *An Old Testament Theology: An Exegetical, Canonical, and Thematic Approach*. Zondervan Academic, 2007.

Work, Telford. *Jesus—the End and the Beginning: Tracing the Christ-Shaped Nature of Everything*. Baker Academic, 2019.

Wright, Christopher J. H. *The Mission of God: Unlocking the Bible's Grand Narrative*. IVP Academic, 2006.

# Chapter 5

# "God's Dwelling Is with Humanity"

## The Eschatological Reality and Hope of Being God's People in God's Presence

*Alistair I. Wilson*

At the heart of biblical theology lies God's covenant promise to enter into a relationship of loyalty and presence with his people.[1] They will be with him as his people, and he will be with them as their God. As Michael Morales states, "The divine desire to dwell with humanity, the goal of both creation and redemption, is the essence of covenant theology—its promissory root, its redemptive-historical vine and its eschatological fruit realized in the new heavens and earth."[2] This form of words (with some variations in the precise wording) is often described as the "covenant formula."[3]

In this chapter, I will offer a missiological (or missional) reading of Revelation that highlights the way in which John's apocalyptic work brings this central biblical promise into fresh light as it becomes evident that God's people are, in fact, God's peoples.

My thesis is that Revelation places the experience of being the people of God in God's presence at the heart of eschatological hope and, indeed, of the comfort available to believers in every age as they experience a sense of vulnerability and displacement.

I will begin by providing a definition of eschatology and explaining how I understand the missiological/missional approach I will take. I will then identify key texts within Revelation and the most significant antecedents in the Old Testament Scriptures.

### Defining Eschatology

According to Roland Chia, "Traditionally the word eschatology refers to the study or the doctrine of the last things. Eschatology deals with questions concerning the consummation of history and the completion of

---

1 Stewart, *Revelation*, 236.

2 Morales, *Who Shall Ascend the Mountain*, 103.

3 Morales, drawing on the work of Rolf Rendtorff, states, "The covenant formula varies throughout Scripture according to contextual emphasis, and is delineated by Rendtorff as follows: Formula A: I will be your God; Formula B: You shall be my people; Formula C: I will be your God and you shall be my people." Morales, *Who Shall Ascend the Mountain*, 103, citing Rendtorff, *Covenant Formula*, 13.

God's work in the world."[4] This definition is quite appropriate, so long as it is recognized, first, that "the last things" is not itself a biblical expression and, second, that "the last days" (or similar expressions) is a phrase used in Scripture by authors of New Testament documents to refer to the events that have overtaken them in their own day on account of the life, death, resurrection, and ascension of Jesus of Nazareth.[5] According to Beale, "Without exception [the phrase "latter days," or similar expressions] is used to describe the end times as beginning in the events associated with the life, death and resurrection of Jesus Christ."[6]

The Revelation of John is sometimes read (at a popular level, at least) as speaking of realities and events related to a time remote from the author and also from both ancient and modern readers. In this chapter, I follow many New Testament scholars in regarding Revelation as a document intended to make sense to first-century readers and to provide them with comfort and encouragement.[7]

## A Missiological Reading of Revelation

First, it is important to state that I understand the terms *missiological* and *missional* to be synonymous. I will use them interchangeably, recognizing that the former term has been chosen for the titles of this series of books but that the latter term is more commonly used in recent academic publications. I do not intend to draw any distinction in meaning between these two terms.

Second, I do not restrict the sense of missiological and missional to an etymological definition related to "sending." While there are "sending" texts that are relevant to mission, the modern family of terms is used both in popular Christian conversation and academic discourse with a much wider

4 Chia and Katongole, "Eschatology," 277.

5 See, for example, Acts 2:16–17; 1 Corinthians 10:11; Hebrews 1:2.

6 Beale, "Eschatology," 330. Similarly, Wells, "Mission in the Light of Covenantal Eschatology," 105–6.

7 So deSilva: "Many popular interpreters of Revelation try to make sense of its visions by looking to the future, decoding its images in terms of contemporary politics and forecasting how our history will unfold. In so doing they ignore the basic principle of exegesis that a text is written to make sense to its original audience." *Introduction to the New Testament*, 786. Similarly, Koester writes, "Revelation is a book for its own time, and that it was written to communicate with Christian congregations in first-century Asia Minor (modern-day Turkey). If futuristic interpreters assume that Revelation's message will become clearer as the final days approach, most scholars take the opposite view. Assuming that Revelation's message would have been clearest to those who lived in John's own time, they search for clues to understanding the book not by combing recent headlines or news broadcasts but by studying the language and literature of the ancient world." *Revelation and the End*, 27.

range of connotations. There are a few verses in Revelation that include the verb ἀποστέλλω and related words (see 1:1; 2:2; 18:20; 21:14; 22:6) and the verb πέμπω (see 22:16),[8] but none of these are particularly significant for an understanding of mission as the term is usually understood. Some scholars prefer to use the term *mission* in a narrower sense than others,[9] but even those who argue for a narrower sense recognize that there is a valid broader sense. Any attempt to argue that one sense rather than another is the correct sense seems to be an exercise in futility.

Third, and as the corollary of my previous point, I understand the terms *missiological* and *missional* to be indicators that I am asking questions of the biblical text that are raised by academic discussions within the field of missiology and, by extension, the field of World Christianity. Heeding the concern of Michael Stroope,[10] I do not wish to claim that John has a theology of mission or a missional intention. Such language is a modern construct, and we have no reason to think that John would have thought of his work in those terms. This is not to say, of course, that John did not intend to make disciples or to proclaim the gospel. I see no reason to doubt that he did! It is simply to say that I do not believe that it is possible to restrict a missiological reading only to texts that make explicit reference to sending or some other term. A missiological reading, in my view, should be open to engage with the issues that missiologists discuss.

Fourth, I will focus on God's express purposes (as revealed in Scripture) as the foundation of a missiological reading (the so-called mission of God). There is, therefore, a close connection between a missional reading of Scripture and a reading of Scripture that draws out the "narrative arc" or "drama" of Scripture.[11] In particular, I will emphasize God's purposes to reconcile a people to himself from all nations.

**Recent Discussion of a Missiological/Missional Reading of Revelation**

I am aware of only one book that is explicitly described as a missional reading of Revelation: Dean Flemming's *Foretaste of the Future: Reading Revelation in Light of God's Mission*. Flemming contrasts his work with some examples

8 All scripture references are taken from CSB, unless otherwise noted.

9 For example, compare the approach of DeYoung and Gilbert's *What Is the Mission of the Church?* with that of Wright, *Great Story and the Great Commission*.

10 "Even more confusing is to convey the notion that actors in the early church or those who wrote the New Testament documents had a 'missiology.'" Stroope, *Transcending Mission*, 85.

11 See, for example, Wright, "Reading the New Testament Missionally," 181; Bartholomew and Goheen, *Drama of Scripture*, xvii.

of popular approaches to Revelation, saying, "I propose that a *missional* reading of Revelation will lead us to read [Revelation] in a more faithful and responsible way."[12] Flemming also highlights how a missional reading of Scripture pays particular attention to a wide range of voices from the global church. He states,

> As I explore a missional reading of Revelation in this book, I will seek to include perspectives from people representing various cultures and contexts. Such an approach, in fact, rings true to Revelation itself, where those from every tribe, language, and nation make up the people of God (Rev 7:9).[13]

Closely associated with a missional reading of Scripture is a commitment to hear voices from diverse parts of the global church. There have been relatively few academic studies of Revelation written by Majority World scholars. Most of the major exegetical commentaries have been written by English-speaking authors originating from Europe and North America. One exception to this pattern is Amos Yong's recent commentary on Revelation in the Belief series. Yong describes himself as an "Asian American," but more specifically as "a first-generation immigrant from Malaysia,"[14] and he pays particular attention to how his context affects his reading of Revelation.

Another contribution to the interpretation of Revelation from beyond the English-speaking, North Atlantic community of scholars, although a briefer work than most single-volume commentaries, is the work of Juan Stam on the "Apocalipsis" in the *Comentario Bíblico Contemporáneo*, a one-volume Spanish commentary on the whole Bible from Latin America. Several books on mission include some discussion of Revelation, and we will refer to some of these at appropriate points in this chapter.

**Key Text: Revelation 21:3–4**

The most significant text for our purposes is Revelation 21:3–4, which Lanier describes as "perhaps the most glorious words of Revelation."[15] In these verses, John hears a "loud voice from the throne" declaring,

---

12 Flemming, *Foretaste of the Future*, 5 (emphasis original).

13 Flemming, 5.

14 Yong, *Revelation*, 2. More specifically, Yong describes his experience in the following terms: "Mine is a Malaysian Chinese experience currently in Southern California but with prior sojourn in the Pacific Northwest, the Northeast, the Upper Midwest, and the Eastern seaboard" (2–3).

15 Lanier, "Covenant in the Johannine Epistles and Revelation," 284.

> Look, God's dwelling is with humanity, and he will live with them. They will be his peoples, and God himself will be with them and will be their God. He will wipe away every tear from their eyes. Death will be no more; grief, crying, and pain will be no more, because the previous things have passed away. (Rev 21:3–4)

The Greek text of these words reads,

> ἰδοὺ ἡ σκηνὴ τοῦ θεοῦ μετὰ τῶν ἀνθρώπων, καὶ σκηνώσει μετ' αὐτῶν, καὶ αὐτοὶ λαοὶ αὐτοῦ ἔσονται, καὶ αὐτὸς ὁ θεὸς μετ' αὐτῶν ἔσται [αὐτῶν θεός], καὶ ἐξαλείψει πᾶν δάκρυον ἐκ τῶν ὀφθαλμῶν αὐτῶν, καὶ ὁ θάνατος οὐκ ἔσται ἔτι οὔτε πένθος οὔτε κραυγὴ οὔτε πόνος οὐκ ἔσται ἔτι, [ὅτι] τὰ πρῶτα ἀπῆλθαν. (Rev 21:3–4 NA$^{28}$)

The central declaration is *καὶ αὐτοὶ λαοὶ αὐτοῦ ἔσονται*. The plural forms in this statement are noteworthy and should be translated, "[and] they will be his peoples."[16] We will pay particular attention to this text, read in light of the rest of Revelation and the whole canon of Scripture.

As we consider the whole of Revelation, we discover numerous other references to *λαός* in either singular or plural forms (5:8–10; 7:9; cf. 10:11; 11:9; 13:7; 14:6; 17:15; 18:4).

In Revelation 21:3, the powerful voice from the throne declares (referring to God in the third person), "They will be his peoples, and God himself will be with them and will be their God." This declaration, like much of the language of Revelation, is drawn from the Old Testament. It is covenantal language, expressing God's commitment to his people in solemn terms. In the following section, we will observe various places in the Old Testament where similar language is used. We will see that the eschatological hope set out in Revelation 21:3 is not, in fact, restricted to a future experience but has been realized to a greater or lesser extent through the whole history of God's covenant relationship with his people.

This truth has missional significance. As Christopher Wright says with reference to Revelation 21:3–4, "The mission of God's people is not only driven forward by the command of Christ, it is also drawn forward by the promise of God."[17]

**God's Promise to Be God to His People in the Old Testament**

My first claim in this chapter, then, is that the eschatological hope expressed in Revelation 21:3 is central to the whole narrative of Scripture. Several Old

16 So Bauckham, *Theology of the Book*, 137.

17 Wright, *Mission of God's People*, 44.

Testament texts are relevant. I will briefly mention some early references to Yahweh's promise of relationship with his people and then devote more sustained attention to Leviticus 26.

The first reference to Yahweh's promise to be God to his people is found in Genesis 17:7–8 in the context of God's covenant with Abraham. Yahweh promises that the covenant he makes with Abraham is a "permanent covenant to be your God and the God of your offspring after you" (17:7) and again with reference to Abraham's offspring, "I will be their God" (17:8).

This reference does not have the balanced form of the covenant formula, which is found in multiple locations in Scripture, but the key affirmation is clear enough: "I will be their God" is a promise to Abraham and his future offspring that is built into the heart of God's covenant commitment to Abraham. This covenant has a distinctly universal aspect to it alongside the promise of blessing to Abraham's own family, as is seen in the Lord's earlier statement to Abram (Gen 12:2–3). God's purposes for Abraham are bound up with his purposes for "all the families/tribes of the earth." James Keown recognizes this emphasis, commenting,

> The promise of the land is both introduced and concluded by the important statement that God's relationship with Abraham will be perpetuated among his descendants. Abraham's special links with Israel are the main focus of Genesis, but this is not an exclusive relationship and Abraham's descendants are found in other nations too.[18]

We cannot understand this declaration apart from the covenants of God.

A similar commitment by Yahweh to be God to his people is found in Exodus 29:45: "I will dwell among the Israelites and be their God." Once again, we do not have the familiar balanced "relational formula" here, but the language of Revelation 21:3 picks up the commitment of God to both dwell with his people and be their God.

Leviticus 26 deals with the consecration of the priests who will administer the sacrificial system. In 26:11–12, 45, we see the three elements of God's commitment found in Revelation 21:3: God will be present with his people ("I will place my residence among you"); the people will be "my people" and Yahweh will be "their God." As Daniel Santos explains, "The whole liturgical and ceremonial structure of the priesthood was the means to achieve the presence of God with the people."[19]

18 McKeown, *Genesis*, 101.

19 Santos, "Éxodo," 137 (author's translation).

This text provides the full expression of what has been seen in part in Genesis 17:7–8 and Exodus 29:45. The balanced form of this text ("I will place my residence among you, and I will not reject you. I will walk among you and be your God, and you will be my people.") appears to lie behind Revelation 21:3.

The people (singular) in question in these texts is the people of Israel whom Yahweh "brought out of the land of Egypt in the sight of the nations" (Lev 26:45). This is a striking reference because it places these promises in the context of Yahweh's covenant faithfulness expressed in the Exodus while standing in contrast with what we will see in Revelation.

The words of promise in Leviticus 26 are expressed in the context of covenant conditions ("If you follow my statutes and faithfully observe my commands," v. 3; "But if you do not obey me and observe all these commands," v. 14). As the narrative of Scripture progresses, we see that Israel does not fulfill its obligations. The promise of God appears to stand in jeopardy. "The Lord's goal to become the only God of the people is actualized only with the transformation of their hearts."[20] We shall see in the prophetic writings how Yahweh will accomplish this transformation by the new covenant.

As we move on to consider selected texts from the Prophets, the covenant formula remains significant. There are numerous references we might consider in the prophecy of Jeremiah (Jer 7:23; 11:4–5; 24:7; 30:22; 31:1), which demonstrate that the relational formula, expressed most concisely as "You will be my people, and I will be your God," is repeated in one form or another numerous times in the Torah and the Prophets. The wording varies to some extent from one text to another (sometimes the clauses are reversed; sometimes first- and second-person pronouns are employed; sometimes first- and third-person pronouns are used), but the fundamental formula is a recurrent motif throughout Scripture.

One further reference in Jeremiah and one in Ezekiel deserve particular attention because these passages speak not only of God's covenant commitment to his people but of the new covenant.

The first passage is perhaps the most familiar:

> "Look, the days are coming"—this is the LORD's declaration—"when I will make a new covenant with the house of Israel and with the house of Judah. This one will not be like the covenant I made with their ancestors on the day I took them by the hand to lead them out

20 Kiuchi, *Leviticus*, 487.

> of the land of Egypt—my covenant that they broke even though I am their master"—the LORD's declaration. "Instead, this is the covenant I will make with the house of Israel after those days"—the LORD's declaration. "I will put my teaching within them and write it on their hearts. I will be their God, and they will be my people. No longer will one teach his neighbor or his brother, saying, 'Know the LORD,' for they will all know me, from the least to the greatest of them"—this is the LORD's declaration. "For I will forgive their iniquity and never again remember their sin." (Jer 31:31–34)

John Goldingay highlights the relational heart of the new covenant promise:

> Then, *I will be God for them and they will be a people for me.* In one sense, there will be nothing new there; Yahweh is picking up the language of Sinai and the basis on which the relationship already worked (7:23; 11:4; cf. 30:22; 31:1). But the relationship will now function properly. The new pledge will not be "fragile."[21]

We see a similar pattern in Ezekiel as in Jeremiah. There are numerous references to the relational promise (e.g., Ezek 11:20; 14:11; 37:23, 27). There is also a recurrence of the formula in the context of a passage similar to that of Jeremiah 31:31–34. There is no explicit mention of the "new covenant" in Ezekiel 36:24–30, but there are several similarities, notably the reference to the activity of God with respect to the "heart" of the people. The other common feature is the covenant formula: "You will be my people, and I will be your God" (Ezek 36:28).

Just a little later in Ezekiel, there is another passage that presents a remarkable picture of future hope (Ezek 37:21–24). These passages, which point to a future united people in relationship with God, become particularly significant in canonical perspective when read in light of Jesus's reference to the new covenant. One final example of the relational formula is found in Zechariah 8:8: "I will bring them back to live in Jerusalem. They will be my people, and I will be their faithful and righteous God." This survey of texts demonstrates that the words John recounts in the voice from the throne resonate throughout the Hebrew Scriptures.

21 Goldingay, *Jeremiah*, 654.

## God's Presence with His People in the New Testament

Numerous texts in the New Testament reiterate the Lord's promise to be present with his people. We will focus our attention on the language of Revelation 21:3: "Look, God's dwelling is with humanity, and he will live with them. They will be his peoples, and God himself will be with them and will be their God." As we will see, this declaration refers not only to a future reality but to a reality that God's people have already come to experience in their relationship to Jesus Christ. The verse has two elements: first, the statement about God dwelling with his people; and second, the relational formula that, as we have seen, reasserts the recurring theme of many Old Testament texts. Both elements reinforce each other.

### God's Dwelling Is with Humanity

The first portion of Revelation 21:3 reads, "Look, God's dwelling is with humanity, and he will live with them." The noun phrase "the dwelling of God" (ἡ σκηνὴ τοῦ θεοῦ) and the related verb "he will dwell" (σκηνώσει) recall a highly significant theme within biblical theology, namely God's presence with his people in the "tabernacle" or "temple." Gregory Beale's work on this theme highlights its significance for mission.[22] The use of the verb σκηνόω is striking because it is a distinctive feature of the New Testament Johannine literature, namely John 1:14. In fact, the verb σκηνόω (to dwell) occurs in the New Testament only in John 1:14 and in four verses in Revelation (7:15; 12:12; 13:6; 21:3).[23] Although the question of common authorship of the Gospel according to John and the Revelation of John is debated (particularly if common authorship is ascribed to John, the Beloved Disciple),[24] there is no doubt that there are numerous strong linguistic affinities between the two documents. The verb is not used commonly in biblical literature. In the LXX, it is found only in Genesis 13:12, where we are told, "Lot lived in the cities

22 "How does the vision of the worldwide temple in Revelation 21–22 relate to Christians and their role in fulfilling the mission of the church? We, as God's people, have already begun to be God's end-time temple where his presence is manifested to the world, and we are to extend the boundaries of the new garden-temple until Christ returns, when, finally, they will be expanded worldwide." Beale, *Temple and the Church's Mission*, 395.

23 Danker, et al., *Greek-English Lexicon*, 929.

24 See the discussion in deSilva, *Introduction to the New Testament*, 341–44. Leithart strongly affirms the connection on the basis of common authorship: "The introduction of the tabernacle motif is significant at several levels (21:3). Structurally, it connects to the opening chapter of John's Gospel, the only place outside of Revelation where σκηνόω is used. John's Gospel begins with the incarnational Word tabernacled in flesh and his vision ends with God tabernacled among men, a neat inclusio around his two-volume work." *Revelation*, 350.

on the plain and set up his tent [ἐσκήνωσεν] near Sodom." It so happens that this Greek verb meaning "take up residence"[25] bears a similarity in terms of assonance with the Hebrew term, which also means "to dwell" (although there does not appear to be any etymological relationship between the terms). As C. K. Barrett explains,

> It recalls, in sound and in meaning, the Hebrew שכן which means "to dwell"; the verb is used of the dwelling of God with Israel (e.g. Exod. 25:8; 29:46; Zech. 2:13), and a derived noun שכינה (*shechinah*) was used (though not in the Old Testament) as a periphrasis for the name of God himself. Further, the bright cloud settled down (שכן) upon the Tabernacle (Exod. 24:16; 40:35), and since this cloud was the visible manifestation of the presence of God (cf. ὀφθήσομαι, Exod. 25:7 LXX) the abiding presence of God suggested his glory (כבוד, δόξα; see below).[26]

Throughout the Old Testament, Yahweh made himself accessible to his people in a place: the tabernacle, initially, and then in the temple in Jerusalem. But with the incarnation, everything changed. John writes, "The Word became flesh and dwelt [ἐσκήνωσεν] among us" (John 1:14). The word John uses in the Gospel echoes the term for the tabernacle in the Old Testament. Jesus becomes the place where God's presence dwells and is accessible to human beings.

When, therefore, John in Revelation states that "the dwelling of God" (ἡ σκηνὴ τοῦ θεοῦ) is with humans and "he will dwell" (σκηνώσει) with them, the repeated use of the related terms creates a significant canonical association. While we cannot say with certainty whether the first recipients of the Apocalypse would have had access to the Gospel according to John, any reader (including any modern reader) who has access to both texts can see how they interpret each other.[27] The Greek translated "God's dwelling is with humanity" does not, in fact, include a verb. It is a verbless clause (ἡ σκηνὴ τοῦ θεοῦ μετὰ τῶν ἀνθρώπων) so that the verb must be supplied. In principle, the supplied verb might indicate either a past or future state. Most translations supply the present form of the verb "to be," and this seems quite appropriate.

25 Danker, et al., *Greek-English Lexicon*, 929.

26 Barrett, *Gospel According to St. John*, 165.

27 Thomas and Macchia write, "Discerning Johannine hearers would be aware that, in the life and ministry of Jesus, the presence of God among them was made even more immediate (John 1:14)." *Revelation*, 366.

Although there is certainly a future aspect to God's dwelling with his people (the future verb form is explicit), readers (in John's day or our own) who see the connection to the Word who became flesh and "dwelled among us" can be assured that the Word, who came to dwell with his people at a specific moment in history and who will dwell with them in the new heavens and the new earth, has not abandoned them in the interim. The eschatological hope of God dwelling with his people is neither entirely a future prospect nor entirely realized. Rather, it is "inaugurated." It is a present reality, experienced in part, but also a full reality that is anticipated eagerly.

The reason that there can be hope of a people ultimately dwelling with God is that the Word dwelled among a people that rejected him. He was rejected and crucified but then raised to life so that he became "one like a slaughtered lamb standing in the midst of the throne" (Rev 5:6). That Lamb is the one who accomplishes all that the covenant formula promises.

**"They Will Be His Peoples"**

As mentioned earlier, the second sentence in Revelation 21:3 reads, "They will be his peoples, and God himself will be with them and will be their God" (*καὶ αὐτοὶ λαοὶ αὐτοῦ ἔσονται, καὶ αὐτὸς ὁ θεὸς μετ' αὐτῶν ἔσται [αὐτῶν θεός]*). This wording clearly picks up the refrain of the covenant formula of the Old Testament texts we have surveyed. In the context of Revelation, however, we read the reference to the people of God in light of the great multitude gathered from "every people" (Rev 7:9). This new perspective on the people of God as "peoples" rather than the single ethnic people of Israel is emphasized by the plural term.[28] Bryan comments,

> Now, however, the marriage covenant is not with Israel alone but with the "peoples" of the world: "Look, God's dwelling is with human beings, and he will live with them. They will be his *peoples*, and God himself will be with them and will be their God" (Rev. 21:3 AT).[29]

The blending of place and people in Revelation 21 (the new Jerusalem is the bride) points to God's intention that his relationship with his people is no longer tied to a particular place, a particular ethnicity. John expresses

---

28 Bauckham comments, "The text given [the plural form] is the most probably original form of the text. The major variant readings . . . are explicable as attempts to conform the text to the standard Old Testament covenant declarations: 'They shall be my people and I will be their God' (e.g., Ezek 37:23; Zech 8:8)." *Climax of Prophecy*, 310. So also, Koester, *Revelation*, 798.

29 Bryan, *Cultural Identity and the Purposes of God*, 245. See also, Flemming, *Foretaste of the Future*, 189–90; Ekem, "Revelation 21:1–4 from an African Perspective," 632.

this by a tiny change in one word, which is reflected accurately in the CSB translation. There is not a fundamental difference in meaning, but the plural in Revelation 21:3 points to a reality that is reflected in other texts in Revelation: God's people are to be gathered "from every nation, tribe, people and language" (Rev 7:9). Peter Leithart effectively draws out some of the implications of this language,

> The city is a bride and this city-bride is also a "them," the "peoples" that God claims as his own (v. 3).
>
> Some texts of verse 3 have the singular λαός, while others contain the plural λαοί. The textual evidence favors the latter . . . , and the ecclesiological implications are significant. To be sure, the church is one—one body, one temple, one family of the sons of Abram. But it is equally a company of nations, all of which retain their own prior histories, cultures, languages, spiritual instincts, and orientations. The church does not transform the rich diversity of humanity into a boring uniformity; it brings each historical community to its completion in Christ. Chinese churches will be different from Indian and Nigerian churches, but each church will represent the fulfillment of the peoples. In Christ, incorporated into his body by his Spirit, Chinese, Indian, Nigerian, and all other cultures will reach their richest fulfillment. Kings' treasures reach their ultimate purpose when they are brought into the heavenly city.[30]

Yong also recognizes the crucial significance of the wording in 21:3:

> A loud voice from the throne (21:3a), similar to that heard from right before the last hallelujah (19:5–6), confirms that the chasm between heaven and earth is now overcome: "See, the home of God is among mortals. He will dwell with them as their God; they will be his peoples, and God himself will be with them" (21:3). Notice that the covenantal language of the Old Testament linking a transcendent God (in much of the Hebrew Bible canon) with the terrestrial people (singular) of Israel is here not only enlarged to include the gentiles, the peoples (plural) of the world, but also to indicate the immanent presence of the divine in an integrated new heaven and earth. Hence, the creator and lord of the world now enters into intimate relationship with people from every nation, tribe, and language (see 5:9; 7:9).[31]

30 Leithart, *Revelation*, 2:345–46.

31 Yong, *Revelation*, 243.

God has made us as embodied people. Where we live is important. But it is not ultimate. We can be at home where God's people are because there God has promised to be.

## Conclusion

Revelation offers readers an eschatological vision. While some readers become obsessed and perplexed by the interpretation of challenging symbols, certain aspects of the message are clear and provide significant pastoral comfort.[32] I have offered a missiological reading of eschatology in Revelation focusing on one of the clearest, most comforting, and most expansive texts in the Apocalypse. In Revelation 21:3–4, we see how God will bring his covenant purposes to perfect fulfillment in the closest relationship with his people while expanding the boundaries to include the peoples.

The Bible tells the story of how the Creator God solemnly promises to commit to a people he will rescue so that they will be his people, and he will be their God. This is made possible because of all that Jesus, the "one like a slaughtered lamb standing in the midst of the throne" (Rev 5:6), accomplished.

Revelation makes it clear that "God's people" will also be "God's peoples," gathered from all nations. This reality has already been inaugurated as disciples of Jesus experience the presence of God by his Spirit and as they make halting attempts to demonstrate unity and love for one another. While they await the full realization of God's covenant promise of his unending and unhindered presence, wherever God's people find themselves, they can know that God is with his people now according to his promise. And however disoriented and rootless God's people may find ourselves in this present experience, we can hold on to God's promise that he will bring us in the end to a place where we truly belong.

32 See particularly, the excellent presentation of the message of Revelation in Bauckham, *Theology of the Book*.

## Bibliography

Barrett, C. K. *Gospel According to St. John: An Introduction with Commentary and Notes on the Greek Text*. 2nd ed. SPCK, 1978.

Bartholomew, Craig G., and Michael W. Goheen. *The Drama of Scripture: Finding Our Place in the Biblical Story*. 3rd ed. Baker Academic, 2024.

Bauckham, Richard J. *The Climax of Prophecy: Studies on the Book of Revelation*. T&T Clark, 1993.

Bauckham, Richard J. *The Theology of the Book of Revelation*. Cambridge University Press, 1993.

Beale, G. K. "Eschatology." In *Dictionary of the Later New Testament and Its Developments*, edited by Ralph P. Martin and Peter H. Davids. IVP Academic, 1997.

Beale, G. K. *The Temple and the Church's Mission: A Biblical Theology of the Dwelling Place of God*. New Studies in Biblical Theology 17. IVP Academic, 2004.

Bryan, Steven M. *Cultural Identity and the Purposes of God: A Biblical Theology of Ethnicity, Nationality, and Race*. Crossway, 2022.

Chia, Roland, and Emmanuel Katongole. "Eschatology." In *Global Dictionary of Theology: A Resource for the Worldwide Church*, edited by William A. Dyrness and Veli-Matti Kärkkäinen. IVP Academic, 2008.

deSilva, David A. *An Introduction to the New Testament: Contexts, Methods and Ministry Formation*. 2nd ed. IVP Academic, 2018.

DeYoung, Kevin, and Greg Gilbert. *What Is the Mission of the Church? Making Sense of Social Justice, Shalom, and the Great Commission*. Crossway, 2011.

Ekem, John D. K. "Revelation 21:1–4 from an African Perspective." In *Majority World Theology: Christian Doctrine in Global Context*, edited by Gene L. Green, Stephen T. Pardue, and K. K. Yeo. IVP Academic, 2020.

Flemming, Dean. *Foretaste of the Future: Reading Revelation in Light of God's Mission*. IVP Academic, 2022.

Goheen, Michael W., ed. *Reading the Bible Missionally*. Gospel and Our Culture Series. Eerdmans, 2016.

Goldingay, John. *The Book of Jeremiah*. New International Commentary on the Old Testament. Eerdmans, 2021.

Kiuchi, Nobuyoshi. *Leviticus*. Apollos Old Testament Commentary 3. Apollos, 2007.

Koester, Craig R. *Revelation: A New Translation with Introduction and Commentary*. Anchor Yale Bible 38A. Yale University Press, 2014.

Koester, Craig R. *Revelation and the End of All Things*. 2nd ed. Eerdmans, 2018.

Lanier, Gregory R. "Covenant in the Johannine Epistles and Revelation." In *Covenant Theology: Biblical, Theological, and Historical Perspectives*, edited by Guy Prentiss Waters, J. Nicholas Reid, and John R. Muether. Crossway, 2020.

Leithart, Peter J. *Revelation 12–22*. International Theological Commentary. Bloomsbury T&T Clark, 2018.

Mathewson, David L. *Revelation: A Handbook on the Greek Text*. Baylor Handbook on the Greek New Testament. Baylor University Press, 2016.

McKeown, James. *Genesis*. Two Horizons Old Testament Commentary. Eerdmans, 2008.

Morales, L. Michael. *Who Shall Ascend the Mountain of the Lord? A Biblical Theology of the Book of Leviticus*. New Studies in Biblical Theology 37. IVP Academic, 2015.

Padilla, C. René, Milton Acosta Benítez, and Rosalee Velloso Ewell. *Comentario Bíblico Contemporáneo*. Editorial Lampara, 2019.

Rendtorff, Rolf. *The Covenant Formula: An Exegetical and Theological Investigation*. Translated by Margaret Kohl. T&T Clark, 1998.

Santiago, Fabián. *The Fellowship of the Throne in John's Apocalypse*. Langham, 2020.

Santos, Daniel. "Éxodo." In *Comentario Bíblico Contemporáneo: Estudio de Toda La Biblia Desde América Latina*, edited by C. René Padilla, Milton Acosta Benítez, and Rosalee Velloso Ewell. Editorial Lampara, 2019.

Stam, Juan. "Apocalipsis." In *Comentario Bíblico Contemporáneo*, edited by C. René Padilla, Milton Acosta Benítez, and Rosalee Velloso Ewell. Editorial Lampara, 2019.

Stewart, Alexander E. *Revelation*. Exegetical Guide to the Greek New Testament. B&H Academic, 2024.

Stroope, Michael W. *Transcending Mission: The Eclipse of a Modern Tradition*. IVP Academic, 2017.

Thomas, John Christopher, and Frank D. Macchia. *Revelation*. Two Horizons New Testament Commentary. Eerdmans, 2016.

Wells, Paul. "Mission in the Light of Covenantal Eschatology." In *A Covenantal Vision for Global Mission*, edited by Paul Wells, Peter A. Lillback, and Henk Stoker. P&R, 2020.

Wright, Christopher J. H. *The Great Story and the Great Commission*. Baker Academic, 2023.

Wright, Christopher J. H. *The Mission of God: Unlocking the Bible's Grand Narrative*. IVP Academic, 2006.

Wright, Christopher J. H. *The Mission of God's People: A Biblical Theology of the Church's Mission*. Biblical Theology for Life. Zondervan, 2010.

Wright, N. T. "Reading the New Testament Missionally." In Goheen, *Reading the Bible Missionally*.

Yong, Amos. *Revelation*. Belief: A Theological Commentary on the Bible. Westminster John Knox, 2021.

Part 2

# The Missionary Message of Revelation

# Chapter 6

# Judgment and Salvation

## The Message of Mission in Revelation

*John D. Harvey*

Revelation can be confusing, not only with regard to its symbolism but also with regard to its authorship, date, audience, genre, and structure. This chapter identifies the apostle John as the author and suggests a late date of around AD 95.[1] Members of the audience have experienced sporadic persecution in the past (cf. 2:3, 9, 13; 3:8) and will experience intensified persecution in the future (cf. 6:9–11; 11:3–6).[2]

The question of genre is complex, since John identifies the work as both an "apocalypse" (1:1) and a "prophecy" (1:3). Further, the book has an epistolary introduction (1:1–8) and an epistolary conclusion (22:6–21). Is the book a letter, a prophecy, or an apocalypse? In fact, it combines all three genres. The form is a circular letter. The message is one of prophetic revelation. The imagery is apocalyptic symbolism. Beale suggests that the book is "a prophecy cast in an apocalyptic mold and written down in letter form."[3]

The epistolary introduction (1:1–8) consists of a superscription (1:1–3), a salutation (1:4–5a), and an expanded benediction (1:5b–8). The epistolary conclusion (22:6–21) consists of a summary (22:6–11), a promise (22:12–15), an invitation (22:16–20), and a benediction (22:21). Numerous proposals for the structure of the body of the book exist, but there are two repeated verbal keys to understanding that structure. The first is "to show . . . the things which must take place," which occurs three times at significant points in the book (1:1; 4:1; 22:6). The second is "in the Spirit," which occurs four times (1:10; 4:2; 17:3; 21:10).[4] Each of the four occurrences of the latter phrase marks the beginning of an extended vision that John sees while he is under the Spirit's control. The following table sets out the resulting structure.

---

1 Mounce has a balanced discussion of authorship and leans toward John, the apostle (*Revelation*, 8–15). Beale has an extended discussion of the date and leans toward a late date (*Revelation*, 4–27).

2 All Scripture quotations are from the NASB unless otherwise indicated.

3 Beale, *Revelation*, 39. Onesimus Ngundu takes a different approach and views the book as a seven-act drama with seven scenes in each act ("Revelation," 1570).

4 Tenney suggested that the four occurrences of the phrase "in the Spirit" are key to understanding the book's structure (*Interpreting Revelation*, 32–33). This chapter embraces that suggestion.

**Table 6.1. The Structure of Revelation**

| | |
|---|---|
| 1:1-8 | Epistolary Introduction |
| 1:9-3:22 | Vision 1: The Churches in Asia |
| 4:1-16:21 | Vision 2: The Seals, Trumpets, and Bowls |
| 17:1-20:15 | Vision 3: The Coming of Christ |
| 21:1-22:5 | Vision 4: The New Heaven and New Earth |
| 22:6-21 | Epistolary Conclusion |

Twin themes run throughout the book. Those themes—judgment and salvation—appear in all four of the visions as well as in the epistolary conclusion. Together, they form the message of mission in Revelation. This chapter will trace these themes as John develops them to warn those individuals who practice unrighteousness and to encourage those individuals who practice righteousness (22:10–15).

## Judgment and Salvation in the Vision of the Churches in Asia (Rev 1:9-3:22)

The first vision focuses on congregations for which John was responsible. Like the author, their members were persevering in the face of tribulation because of their testimony for Jesus (1:9). The section begins with John's commission to write (1:9–20) and includes prophetic messages to seven churches on a circular postal route in the Roman province of Asia.[5] Each message consists of an opening address, a prophetic assessment of the church, and a closing exhortation. Although the Greek words for judgment (*krima/krinō/krisis*) and salvation (*sōtēria/sōzō*) do not appear in the vision, both concepts are clearly present in the warnings and promises of the messages.[6]

5 Although "letters" is the common designation for the messages, it is better to think of them as prophetic oracles, similar to those spoken by the Old Testament prophets. The phrase "thus says [*tade legei*] . . ." appears at the beginning of each message in the Greek text. It parallels the way the LXX translates the prophetic declaration "Thus says the Lord . . ." (*tade legei ho kurios*). In the seven messages of Revelation 2–3, a description of the glorified Son of Man from the vision in 1:9–20 replaces "the Lord."

6 "Judgment" words (*krima/krinō/krisis*) occur sixteen times in the book; "salvation" words (*sōtēria/sōzō*) occur four times. The two themes, however, extend beyond those specific words.

**Table 6.2. Warnings and Promises to the Seven Churches**

| Church | Warning | Promise |
|---|---|---|
| Ephesus (2:1-7) | *Repent* or face removal of the lampstand (2:5) | *Overcome* and eat of the tree of life in the paradise of God (2:7) |
| Smyrna (2:8-11) | [hurt by the second death] | *Overcome* and avoid the pain of the second death (2:11) |
| Pergamum (2:12-17) | *Repent* or face war with Jesus (2:16) | *Overcome* and receive hidden manna, a white stone, and a new name (2:17) |
| Thyatira (2:18-29) | *Repent* or face great tribulation and death by pestilence (2:22) | *Overcome* and receive authority to rule over the nations (2:26-28) |
| Sardis (3:1-6) | *Repent* or face sudden destruction (3:3) | *Overcome* and receive white garments and a place in the book of life (3:5) |
| Philadelphia (3:7-13) | [bow at the feet of the faithful] | *Overcome* and become a pillar in the temple of the new Jerusalem (3:12) |
| Laodicea (3:14-22) | *Repent* or face reproof and discipline (3:19) | *Overcome* and sit on the throne with Jesus and the Father (3:21) |

Calls to repent (*metanoeō*) introduce five of the seven warnings and highlight the importance of that element of the message of mission.[7] Four consequences of failing to repent are explicitly stated (2:5, 16, 22; 3:19). One is implied (3:3) by the "thief" metaphor used elsewhere in the New Testament, which signifies destruction (cf. 2 Pet 3:10; cf. 1 Thess 5:2–3; Matt 24:42–44). Two are not stated as warnings but are clear from the context—being hurt by the second death (2:11) and bowing at the feet of the faithful (3:9).

A variation of "the one who is overcoming" (*ho nikōn*) introduces each of the seven promises.[8] Overcoming involves perseverance (*hypomonē*; 2:2, 3, 19; 3:10) and holding fast (*krateō*; 2:13, 25; 3:11), and it leads to rewards that accompany Christ's coming or are part of existence in the new heaven and earth. Those rewards include eating from the tree of life (2:7; cf. 22:2), not being hurt by the second death (2:11; cf. 20:14), receiving a new name (2:17;

7 The verb *metanoeō* (to repent) occurs twelve times in the book. Eight of the occurrences are in the first vision, while four are in the second vision. The noun *metanoia* (repentance) does not occur in the book.

8 The verb *nikaō* (to overcome) occurs sixteen times in the book. Eight of the occurrences are in the first vision, six are in the second vision, one is in the third vision (17:14), and one is in the fourth vision (21:7). The noun *nikē* (victory) does not occur at all in the book.

cf. 22:4), ruling over the nations (2:26; cf. 20:4), having names written in the book of life (3:5; cf. 21:27), becoming citizens of the new Jerusalem (3:12; cf. 21:24–26), and sitting with Jesus on his throne (3:21; cf. 22:5).

The vision of the churches in Asia makes it clear that Jesus's followers and those with whom they share the message of mission must understand the consequences of their responses to that message. On one hand, willful failure to repent leads to death and destruction. On the other hand, faithful willingness to persevere leads to life and blessing.

## Judgment and Salvation in the Vision of the Seals, Trumpets, and Bowls (Rev 4:1–16:21)

The second vision begins with both verbal keys that inform the understanding of the book's structure: "I will show what must take place after these things" (4:1), and "immediately I was in the Spirit" (4:2). It is the longest of the four visions and includes many characteristics that allow John to refer to the book as an "apocalypse."[9] Throughout the vision the twin themes of judgment and salvation interlock.

The seven seals, seven trumpets, and seven bowls that are part of the second vision are familiar to most readers. References to divine wrath connect the three series (6:16–17; 11:17–18; 16:1). It is clear that the events describe the judgment that precedes the second coming of Christ. It is also worth noting that Jesus's Olivet Discourse describes three sets of events that culminate in his return: the beginning of birth pangs, the time of great tribulation, and the coming of the Son of Man. It is possible—although by no means certain—that the seals, trumpets, and bowls correlate to those three sets of events.[10]

---

9 Collins defines an apocalypse as "a genre of revelatory literature with a narrative framework, in which a revelation is mediated by an otherworldly being to a human recipient, disclosing a transcendent reality which is both temporal, insofar as it envisages eschatological salvation, and spatial insofar as it involves another, supernatural world." "Toward the Morphology of a Genre," 9.

10 Johnson notes, "This parallel to major parts of Revelation is too striking to be ignored." "Revelation," 472.

**Table 6.3. Jesus's Olivet Discourse and Revelation 6–16**

| | Matthew | Mark | Luke | Revelation |
|---|---|---|---|---|
| Beginning of Birth Pangs | 24:4-14 | 13:5-13 | 21:8-19 | 6:1-8:5 |
| Great Tribulation | 24:15-28 | 13:14-23 | 21:20-24 | 8:6-11:19 |
| Coming of the Son of Man | 24:29-31 | 13:24-29 | 21:25-28 | 16:1-21 |

Opening the seals results in conflict (6:1–2), war (6:3–4), famine (6:5–6), death (6:5–6), and cosmic distress (6:12–17).[11] Sounding the trumpets results in the destruction of one-third of the earth's surface and vegetation (8:7), the destruction of one-third of sea life and commerce (8:8–9), the embittering of one-third of the fresh waters (8:10–11), the darkening of one-third of the sun, moon, and stars (8:12), and the killing of one-third of humankind (9:13–19). Pouring out the bowls of wrath results in malignant sores afflicting humankind (16:2), the sea turning to blood (16:3), the rivers turning to blood (16:4–7), the sun scorching humankind with heat (16:8–9), and deep darkness covering the earth (16:10–11).[12] Despite the severity of the judgments, those who experience them refuse to repent of their works or give God glory; instead, they blaspheme him (9:20–21; 16:9, 11).

The other section of the second vision that emphasizes judgment describes the activities of four angelic messengers (14:6–20). The first angel preaches "an eternal gospel" that calls on every nation, tribe, tongue, and people to fear God, give him glory, and worship him as creator and judge (14:6–7). The second angel announces God's judgment on Babylon the Great (14:8). The third angel announces doom for anyone who worships the beast from the sea (14:9–12; cf. 13:1–10). The fourth angel announces the reaping of the earth and the treading of the winepress of God's wrath (14:11–20). Together, the seals, trumpets, bowls, and angelic announcements make it clear that human repentance and divine judgment are essential components of the gospel that Jesus expects his disciples to preach to everyone living on the earth.

11 The fifth seal also refers to judgment, when the souls of the martyrs ask God how long he will delay it (Rev 6:9–11).

12 Numerous scholars have discussed the similarities between the seals, trumpets, and bowls in Revelation and the plagues in Exodus. Ramesh Khatry concludes that it is not possible to know for certain whether the seals, trumpets, and bowls are cyclical, consecutive, or progressive, although it is clear that "each makes the judgment more intense with the last one leading to the climax" ("Revelation," 1771). Beale has a helpful summary of the parallels between the trumpets, the bowls, and the plagues (Beale, *Revelation*, 809–10).

While images of judgment and the subtheme of repentance dominate the second vision, the theme of salvation is also present.[13] Five scenes of celebration bring that theme to the foreground of the book.[14] The new song of 5:8–10 declares that the Lamb is worthy because he "purchased for God with [his] blood [some] from every tribe and tongue and people and nation." The verb "purchase" (*agorazō*) also occurs twice in 14:3–4 and highlights Jesus's sacrificial death on behalf of those who remain faithful to him. The mention of "every tribe and tongue and people and nation" is the first in the book, but it is not the last (cf. 7:9; 10:11; 11:9; 13:7; 14:6; 17:15). It highlights the universal audience of the message of mission. The celebration of Satan's downfall in 12:7–12 includes the statement that Jesus's followers "overcame . . . because of the blood of the Lamb" (12:11), highlighting both the victory that comes with salvation (*enikēsan*) and the sacrificial work that makes salvation possible. Those who were victorious (*tous nikōntas*) over the beast, his image, and his number stand on the sea of glass before God's throne (15:2; cf. 4:6) and sing the song of Moses and the Lamb immediately prior to the pouring out of the seven bowls of wrath (15:2).

The interlude between the sixth and seventh seals (7:1–18) is the longest of the five passages and pairs with a second passage that describes the 144,000 in 14:1–5. It also has the richest collection of rewards associated with salvation. The interlude begins with an angel delaying destruction of the earth and sea until the bondservants of God receive a divine seal on their foreheads (7:1–3). John then sees 144,000 individuals from the twelve tribes of Israel who have received the seal (7:4–8; cf. 14:1–5). Finally, he sees a countless multitude from every nation, people, tribe, and tongue (7:9–17). It is this latter group that John describes in detail. In addition to bearing God's name on their foreheads (7:3; cf. 2:17; 3:12; 14:1; 22:4), they wear white robes (7:9; cf. 6:11; 7:13, 14), carry palm branches (7:9), and celebrate the salvation (*sōtēria*) that God and the Lamb have bestowed on them (7:10).[15] Their robes are white because of the blood of the Lamb (7:14; cf. 5:9; 12:11; 19:8, 14). They neither hunger nor thirst (7:16). The Lamb guides them to

13 The twenty-four elders bring both themes together when they thank God for judging the dead and rewarding the saints (Rev 11:16–18).

14 The five scenes are Revelation 5:1–10; 7:1–18; 12:7–12; 14:1–6; 15:1–4.

15 The name on their foreheads most likely symbolizes possession and protection (cf. Ezek 9:4–6). The white robes likely symbolize righteousness and purity (see Beale's excursus, *Revelation*, 431, 436–38). The palm branches most likely symbolize victory (cf. 1 Macc 13:51; 2 Macc 10:7).

springs of the water of life (7:17; cf. 21:6; 22:4). God wipes away every tear from their eyes (7:17; cf. 21:6). Together, the five scenes make it clear that the saving message of mission leads to celebration because Jesus's sacrificial work results in victory over Satan, the forces of evil, tribulation, sorrow, and death.

## Judgment and Salvation in the Vision of the Coming of Christ (Rev 17:1-20:15)

The third vision consists of a series of events associated with Christ's victorious coming. The first section of the vision describes the fall of Babylon (17:1–18:24).[16] It depicts Babylon as a harlot seated on a scarlet beast, before recounting the judgment of the city. That judgment repays Babylon double for its deeds (18:6), among which the sin of immorality is foremost (17:2, 4; 18:3, 4, 5, 7, 9; cf. 19:2). It throws the city down violently (18:21) and lays waste to it (18:19). The means of judgment are plagues, pestilence, famine, and fire (18:8; cf. 17:16; 18:9, 18). The judgment is final (18:21–24), represents the Lamb's total victory over the beast and his kingdom (17:14–18), and is cause for great rejoicing among God's people (18:20; cf. 19:1–6).

The second section of the vision describes the victory of Christ, first ascribing salvation, glory, and power to God for his righteous judgment and giving him glory for the marriage of the Lamb (19:1–10), then depicting Christ as the King of kings and Lord of lords whose coming results in the defeat and doom of the beast, the false prophet, and their followers (19:11–21). The theme of judgment permeates the section. God's judgment is true, righteous, and faithful (19:2, 11) and is based on deeds, including immorality (19:2; cf. 17:2–4; 18:3–9) and causing the death of God's people (19:2). It is severe (19:15, 20; cf. 9:17–18; 14:10), deadly (19:17–18, 21), and eternal (19:3; cf. 9:11; 20:13). The theme of salvation is less prominent but is also present. It rests on God's righteous judgment (19:1–2), reflects Christ's righteousness and sacrifice (19:11–13; cf. 5:9; 7:14; 12:11), and results in the righteousness of his followers (19:8, 14).

The third section of the vision describes the judgment of Satan (20:1–3, 7–10) as well as the resurrections of the righteous and the unrighteous (20:4–6, 11–15). The judgment of Satan takes place in two stages. First, an

16 Babylon is best understood as the cultural, social, intellectual, and commercial capital of the beast's worldwide empire. See Tenney, *Interpreting Revelation*, 82. Beale comments, "In the Apocalypse Rome and all wicked world systems take on the symbolic name 'Babylon the Great'" (*Revelation*, 755). Ngundu takes a similar view, asserting that Babylon is "the embodiment of all entrenched worldly resistance to God . . . the total system of humankind that excludes God from what it does" ("Revelation," 1596).

angel locks him in the abyss for one thousand years (20:2–3).[17] Then, he joins the beast and the false prophet in the lake of fire and brimstone, where he suffers conscious eternal torment (20:10). The resurrections also take place in two stages. In the first resurrection, God raises the righteous to life (20:4), and they exercise judgment as a reward for their faithful perseverance in the face of deadly opposition (20:4). They are blessed and holy, and they reign as priests of God and Christ (20:6). In the second resurrection, God raises the unrighteous, and all of them experience judgment according to their deeds before his great white throne (20:11–13). Like Satan, the beast, and the false prophet, they take their places in the lake of fire, which is the second death (20:14–15). The destinies of the two groups stand in stark contrast to one another.

**Table 6.4. The Destinies of the Righteous and Unrighteous**

| Resurrection of the Righteous | Resurrection of the Unrighteous |
|---|---|
| Raised to life (20:4) | Raised to judgment (20:12) |
| Names written in book of life (20:15) | Deeds written in books (20:12) |
| Works of faithful perseverance (20:4) | Works worthy of judgment (20:13) |
| Reign as priests (20:6) | Thrown into the lake of fire (20:14) |

Taken together, the events of the third vision highlight the facts that judgment is severe and final (18:21–24; 19:20–21; 20:9–10, 13–15) and that deeds are the basis for judgment (18:6; 19:1–2; 20:12–13). Judgment, however, is also a cause for celebration, because it is the basis for salvation (18:20; 19:1–6). Both God's judgment and his salvation are true, righteous, and faithful (19:1–2, 11). Salvation rests on God's righteousness (19:1–2) and on Christ's sacrifice (19:11–13). Judgment and salvation, therefore, are interlocking elements of the message of mission.

17 There is, of course, extensive discussion over whether the thousand years are literal or figurative. Khatry argues that it is best to take the number "as literally as possible" ("Revelation," 1801). Ngundu argues that the number is symbolic of "an immense total . . . the complete time that God has determined since [Satan's] fall from heaven" ("Revelation" 1600). In either interpretation, Satan and his unrighteous followers experience eternal judgment, while the righteous followers of the Lamb experience eternal salvation.

## Judgment and Salvation in the Vision of the New Heaven and New Earth (Rev 21:1–22:5)

The fourth vision describes the post-judgment existence that the one who overcomes (*ho nikōn*) will inherit (21:7). Naturally, the theme of salvation is prominent.[18] Sections that itemize the blessings of salvation (21:1–8; 22:1–5) frame descriptions of the glory of the heavenly city of the new Jerusalem (21:9–21) and the glory of life in that city (21:22–27).[19]

The scope of the blessings of salvation is sweeping. God will dwell with his people (21:3; 22:3), who will see his face (22:4) and will have his name on their foreheads (22:4). They will not experience sorrow, death, mourning, crying, or pain (21:4). They will not experience night (22:5) or any of the results of the curse (22:3). They will have open access to the tree of life, its fruit, and its healing leaves (22:2). They will drink freely from the water of life (21:6; 22:1). They will serve God and the Lamb (22:3) and will reign with them for ever and ever (22:5). Those who experience these blessings come from all the nations (21:24, 26), because—as his bride (21:2, 9; cf. 19:7–10)—their names are written in the Lamb's book of life (21:27; cf. 3:5; 20:1, 15).

The ultimate good news of the message of mission in Revelation is that salvation far outshines judgment. Judgment will be severe and final, but salvation will be glorious and eternal. God will make all things new (21:5) as he dwells with his people in a heaven-on-earth paradise that echoes but transcends the original garden of Eden. In the new Jerusalem, those who overcome will enjoy constant refreshing from the water of life (22:1; cf. Gen 2:10), unhindered access to the tree of life (22:2; cf. Gen 2:9), total freedom from the curse that resulted from Adam's sin (22:3; cf. Gen 1:31; 3:14–19), intimate fellowship with God (22:3–4; cf. Gen 3:8), and sovereign authority to rule over creation with him forever (22:5; cf. Gen 1:28).[20]

---

18 References to judgment appear in two places: the statement that the cowardly, unbelieving, abominable, murderers, immoral, sorcerers, and idolators will experience the lake of fire and brimstone that is the second death (Rev 21:8), and the statement that no one who practices abomination and lies will ever enter the new Jerusalem (21:27).

19 The framing sections contribute more to a study of the themes of judgment and salvation than do the detailed descriptions of the city's glory (Rev 21:10–14), dimensions (21:15–17), wall, gates, and streets (21:18–21), and life (21:22–27).

20 Khatry has a helpful summary of the similarities between the opening chapters of Genesis and the closing chapters of Revelation. "Revelation," 1769, 1804–5.

**Table 6.5. The New Jerusalem and the Garden of Eden**

| New Jerusalem | | Garden of Eden | |
|---|---|---|---|
| Rev 22:1 | River of the water of life | Gen 2:10 | River to water the garden |
| Rev 22:2 | Tree of life | Gen 2:9 | Tree of life |
| Rev 22:3 | No longer any curse | Gen 1:31 | Everything very good |
| Rev 22:3-4 | See God's face | Gen 3:8 | God walked in the garden |
| Rev 22:5 | Reign forever | Gen 1:28 | Fill and subdue the earth |

Citizens of the new heaven and new earth can look forward with expectation to life with God as he always intended for his people.

## Judgment and Salvation in the Epistolary Conclusion (Rev 22:6–21)

The epistolary conclusion begins with the third instance of "to show what must soon take place" (cf. 1:1; 4:1). The section consists of a summary (22:6–11), a promise (22:12–15), an invitation (22:16–20), and a benediction (22:21). In light of the faithful and true word of prophecy the triune God has spoken (22:6, 16, 17), the conclusion calls readers to hear (22:17, 18) and keep (22:7, 9) the book's message.[21] In regard to the themes of judgment and salvation, Jesus's promise at his coming "to repay to each one as his or her work is" (22:12, my translation) captures both aspects and echoes previous statements that judgment and salvation are according to what a person does (cf. 18:6; 19:1–2; 20:11–13).

**Table 6.6. Judgment and Salvation in the Epistolary Conclusion**

| "to repay to each one . . ." | | | |
|---|---|---|---|
| 22:15 | no access to the city | 22:14 | access to the city |
| 22:19 | no access to the tree of life | 22:14 | access to the tree of life |
| ". . . as his or her work is" | | | |
| 22:11 | those doing unrighteousness | 22:11 | those doing righteousness |
| 22:11 | those being unholy | 22:11 | those being holy |
| 22:15 | those practicing sorcery, immorality, murder, idolatry, and lying | 22:14 | those washing their robes |

21 The calls to hear (*akouō*) and keep (*tēreō*) the things written in the book form an inclusio with the same verbs in the superscription (cf. 1:1–3).

The conclusion, therefore, addresses two groups: those who are unholy because they practice unrighteousness and those who are holy because they practice righteousness (22:11). The first group is excluded from the new Jerusalem and the tree of life (22:15, 19) because they practice sorcery, immorality, murder, idolatry, and lying (22:15; cf. 21:8, 27). The second group is included in the new Jerusalem and has access to the tree of life (22:14) because they have washed their robes and made them white by the blood of the Lamb (22:14; cf. 5:9; 7:14; 12:11; 19:8, 14). The choice is clear. Those who read the book and hear the message must decide whether they will follow the path of final judgment or the path of eternal salvation.

## The Message of Mission in Revelation

Bringing together evidence collected from the four visions and the epistolary closing makes it possible to identify the following essential elements of the message of mission in Revelation.

**Table 6.7. Essentials of the Message of Mission in Revelation**

| Essentials of the Message of Mission | |
|---|---|
| Nature | God's judgment and salvation are true, righteous, faithful, and cause for celebration. |
| Scope | Judgment and salvation apply to members of every tongue, tribe, people, and nation. |
| Criteria | The basis of judgment is human deeds; the basis of salvation is Christ's sacrificial work. |
| Call | Repentance frees from judgment; perseverance confirms salvation. |
| Result | Judgment results in severe consequences; salvation results in eternal blessings. |

Tracing the twin themes of judgment and salvation throughout Revelation leads to twin conclusions. On the one hand, God promises judgment to everyone who opposes him, his purposes, and his people. On the other hand, God promises salvation to everyone who repents of evil deeds, endures tribulation, overcomes by the blood of the Lamb, and holds fast to the testimony of Jesus Christ. Together, the themes of judgment and salvation form the message of mission in Revelation, both for John's original readers and for readers today.

## Bibliography

Beale, G. K. *The Book of Revelation*. New International Greek Testament Commentary. Eerdmans, 1999.

Collins, John J. "Toward the Morphology of a Genre." *Semeia* 14 (1979): 1–20.

Johnson, Alan F. "Revelation." In *The Expositor's Bible Commentary*, volume 12, edited by Frank E. Gaebelein. Zondervan, 1981.

Khatry, Ramesh. "Revelation." In *South Asia Biblical Commentary: A One-Volume Commentary on the Whole Bible*, edited by Brian Hintle. Zondervan, 2015.

Mounce, Robert H. *The Book of Revelation*. Rev. ed. Eerdmans, 1998.

Ngundu, Onesimus. "Revelation." In *Africa Bible Commentary: A One-Volume Commentary Written by 70 African Scholars*, edited by Tokunboh Adeyemo. Zondervan, 2010.

Tenney, Merrill C. *Interpreting Revelation*. Eerdmans, 1957.

# Chapter 7

# Subversive Suffering

## The Missional Message of the Two Witnesses in Revelation 11:3-13

*Andrea L. Robinson*

The author of Revelation presents an alternate vision of reality intended to galvanize hearers through a message of triumph. Yet, the message of the Apocalypse is as counterintuitive as it is countercultural. Victory is achieved paradoxically through suffering, and evil is overcome through self-sacrifice. The Lamb who is slain-yet-standing serves as a governing metaphor for the entirety of Revelation. Just as Christ accomplished the redemption of the world through his sacrificial death, so also Christ's followers become instruments of restoration through their own cruciform obedience and perseverance.

The missional vocation of the saints is portrayed most explicitly through the narrative of the two witnesses in Revelation 11:3–13. These two figures are armed with powerful "weapons" yet are slain despite their armament. Their apparent ill fate, however, transforms into victory as the enemies of God fall, and the fallen witnesses rise again. In addition, the cruciform mission of the two witnesses succeeds where past judgments alone failed. Many from among the nations begin to fear the Lord and glorify him.

Through his symbolic narrative, John conveys essential truths about God's people and their mission in the world. The church may seem weak and the saints may suffer, but John graphically reveals that the cruciform message of the gospel transforms suffering into salvation. The church is not, in fact, powerless but is armed with "weapons" formidable enough to defeat the evil in human hearts and the power structures such evil perpetuates.

John's message of victorious perseverance in the face of hostility was intended to reorient the identity and purpose of early Christians under the dominion of Rome. At the same time, the cruciform model of the two witnesses should inspire believers of every time and culture to persevere through opposition for the sake of every nation, tribe, people, and tongue.

In this chapter, we will thus discuss John's message in regard to victory, power, suffering, and the vocation of the saints. We will begin by examining the interpretive foundations of John's communicative strategy and message. We will then turn to Revelation 11:3–13 and first evaluate the identity, actions, and weapons of the two witnesses. Second, we will analyze the role of the nations and their response to the witnesses. Third, we will conclude with implications for the church and the saints.[1]

## The Gospel Message Through the Lens of Apocalyptic Literature

Possibly the most misused and abused book of Scripture, Revelation has been afflicted with a myriad of interpretations over the centuries. Somehow, when interpreters arrive at this final book, sound hermeneutical principles, like the sea in Revelation 21:1, disappear. However, when John's Apocalypse is interpreted in the context of first-century Asia Minor and the context of Scripture—a straightforward message arises, that of the gospel.

In Revelation, John presents the gospel message through the lens of apocalyptic literature. At a fundamental level, the apocalyptic genre relies on dramatic imagery and symbolism to unveil truths that lie beyond earthly perception. Such symbolism is derived and interpreted through the medium of concrete historical-cultural situations, but the inherent multivalence of symbolism renders the message accessible to readers of virtually any period of history.

Along such lines, Revelation doesn't offer a glimpse of the future so much as a glimpse of the world as it truly is, in every era of history and in every culture. As John unveils cosmic and spiritual truths, he reveals a creation in distress and a people in need of rescue. Yet, Christ's future return—his *second* coming—is not the primary focus of the Apocalypse. Instead, Christ's *first* coming is the central means of transformation and liberation, a process begun at Calvary and continued through Christ's followers. And though John does describe "the end," he does not point to the end of the world or the destruction of creation. He describes the end of oppression, destruction, and dehumanization, and more importantly, the powers and systems that perpetuate such abuses.[2]

More than a series of end-time events to decrypt, Revelation takes place in a "perpetual present."[3] At the same time, the Apocalypse looks to the past to guide hearers and readers. According to González, "History is important because it does not repeat itself; it is always new. And yet history is worth

1 All Scripture quotations are taken from the NASB.

2 Richard, "Reading the Apocalypse," 168.

3 Richard, 148.

studying, because there are patterns that appear repeatedly and because by looking at these patterns we may draw some guidance for our particular moment in history."[4] The churches, martyrs, and saints, the systems of power, and strategies for resistance, though based in first-century Rome, offer modern readers a mirror. What do we see of ourselves and our world in the text? How must we respond?

**A Call to Action**

Apocalyptic literature is sometimes viewed as a form of theodicy, offering an explanation for suffering, disappointment, or persecution and providing comfort through the hope of a better future. Yet, while Revelation does offer comfort to the oppressed and persecuted, John's Apocalypse is not a simple theodicy.[5] John confronts the saints and calls the church to action; he exhorts those who follow the Lamb to use the weapons at their disposal to defeat the powers of death, oppression, and dehumanization; he calls God's people to see reality from a different lens *and live accordingly*.

More than consolation, John calls the church to radical reformation and courageous witness. In Revelation 2–3, when John addresses the seven churches, he offers more correction and rebuke than comfort.[6] Indeed, John makes no mention of official persecution in his apocalypse. Kraybill suggests that the majority of Christians in Asia Minor experienced "more internal *desire* to conform to pagan society than external *pressure* in the way of persecution."[7] The yearning for "social acceptance and financial security" was a powerful motivator to compromise with the ideologies of Rome and its imperial cult.[8]

Almost certainly, followers of the Lamb in first-century Rome faced greater persecution than members of the modern Western church. The greatest threat faced by present-day believers in first-world countries is typically social ostracism or verbal criticism. The earliest believers in ancient Rome likewise endured social ostracism and verbal abuse while also suffering physical assault, unjust imprisonment, and execution.[9] Such violence, however, was sporadic and local, as the Roman Empire neglected

4 González, "Revelation," 51.

5 DeSilva, "Social Setting," 276; cf. Maier, "Coming Out of Babylon," 69.

6 Maier, "Coming Out of Babylon," 70.

7 Kraybill, *Imperial Cult*, 196 (emphasis original).

8 Kraybill, 197.

9 See Acts 5:18, 40; 7:57–60; 16:37; 2 Corinthians 11:23–25; Hebrews 10:32–33; Revelation 2:13; et al.

to maintain any official policy regarding the treatment of Christians. Along such lines, there is little evidence that the more extreme forms of persecution had extended into Asia Minor by the time John composed his apocalypse for the churches in that region.[10]

Most likely, the saints to whom John wrote were not victimized *because* they were Christians, but because their ideals, beliefs, and actions put them at odds with Rome. Such subversive perseverance reflects the work of Christ, who had also been slain by Rome. And in purposeful accord with the slain-yet-standing Lamb, the faithfulness of the saints, whether in the face of social osctracism or fully unto death, would become the primary means by which the world would be healed. In John's Apocalypse, the Great Commission is thus reaffirmed in the context of suffering and presented through the medium of apocalyptic literature.[11]

**Subversive Suffering**

In the Apocalypse, witness (μαρτυρία) is tied directly to victory. Overcoming (νικάω), often perceived as an attitude akin to emotional fortitude, is actually an efficacious and transformative action. The saints overcome the world *by means of* their cruciform witness and faithfulness in the midst of suffering. The power of the death, resurrection, and exaltation of Christ unfolds soteriologically through the verbal and embodied testimony of the saints. In fact, each of John's letters to the seven churches concludes with an exhortation to overcome, and the epistle to Laodicea ends with Christ's promise of reward for those who overcome *as he overcame* (Rev 3:21; cf. 5:5). By way of contrast, the enemies of the Lamb overcome through martial and political power (6:2; 11:7; 13:7).

On the surface, Revelation might seem to glorify violence. Along such lines, the violent and abusive practices of Rome are met with equally destructive measures by the forces of the Lamb. Yet, such an interpretation overlooks the essential truth that John's Apocalypse subverts the logic of dominion. Although military imagery is used to describe the weapons of Christ and his saints, the portrait of a lion-as-lamb who is slain-yet-standing signals that conquering will take a different form (5:5–6).[12]

10 Beale, *Revelation*, 12–16.

11 Holwerda, "Church," 148.

12 Slater, *Revelation*, 51. Cf. Koester, *Revelation*, 375–76.

Though John takes a nonviolent stance toward evil, he does not advocate a passive response.[13] John depicts a rescue mission, initiated by the Lamb and continued by his followers. Along such lines, the crucifixion of Jesus by the Roman Empire reveals the paradigm of redemption, the plot of the Apocalypse, and the mission of the church.[14] The slain-yet-standing Lamb demonstrates precisely *how* God carries out his missional intent, not through violence but through sacrificial love. According to Flemming, "This is a counter-imperial message. Rome rules by the power of violence and military conquest; Jesus vanquishes God's enemies through weakness and (self-) sacrificial death, in solidarity with the weak and oppressed."[15]

Yet, the story of the Lamb is incomplete. Satan and the self-deifying forces of empire continue to rebel against God and oppress his people.[16] Consequently, those who follow the Lamb must carry on Christ's mission, and John explicitly details how the saints overcome: through the blood of the Lamb and faithful witness unto death (Rev 12:11). Conquest is no longer defined by military action but by faithful testimony, which places the saints in direct conflict with the powers of the world. Moreover, the enemy's response is often vicious, as the devil lashes out with great wrath because he knows his time is short (12:12). Thus, victory requires a willingness to witness even when testifying leads to persecution and death. Such cruciform action catalyzes transformation that cannot be achieved through words alone.[17] As sacrificial witness brings an end to evil in human hearts and, ultimately, all creation, it may also result in an end of the earthly lives of those who testify. Yet, the saints will rise again, just as the crucified and risen Savior they emulate.[18]

## The Witnesses

On the surface, Revelation 11:3–13 appears to be a narrative about two prophets who are martyred for their testimony and resurrected by God. A closer reading, however, reveals a graphic parable about the mission of the church.[19] Though the connection is not immediately obvious, John has already provided the

---

13 Kraybill, *Imperial Cult*, 202.

14 Gorman, *Reading Revelation Responsibly*, 108; Thompson, "Reading What Is Written," 170.

15 Flemming, "Revelation," 165–66. Cf. deSilva, *Seeing Things John's Way*, 343.

16 Flemming, "Revelation," 165.

17 Blount, "Witness," 40–42.

18 Alkier, "Witness or Warrior," 137.

19 Aune, *Revelation 6–16*, 631; Bauckham, *Theology of the Book*, 85; Beale, *Revelation*, 573–74; Flemming, "Revelation," 173.

interpretive keys to his symbolism. In 11:4 the witnesses are identified as lampstands, but in 1:20 John identified lampstands as churches. In addition, the position of the witnesses, "before the Lord" (11:4), links them with the lamps that burn before God's throne, which are identified as God's Spirit (4:5). The witnesses, thus, bear God's Spirit just as the church is empowered by the Spirit to witness to the ends of the earth (Acts 1:8).[20] In sum, the two witnesses represent "a convergence of the activity of Jesus, the prophetic ministry of the Holy Spirit, and the ongoing witness of the church."[21]

In addition to lampstands, the witnesses are also identified as olive trees. Such imagery derives from Zechariah 4:2–10, in which the two olive trees represent Zerubbabel, the king, and Joshua, the priest, men anointed and empowered by God's Spirit to rebuild the temple.[22] Zechariah 6:12–13 merges the two roles with a prophecy of a coming Branch, one who is both priest and king, who will build the temple of the Lord. Although the prophecy is typically associated with Christ, John goes further and applies the imagery to the church (Rev 1:20; 3:12; 11:1–2).

That *two* witnesses are present is also significant. First, the plurality of bodies highlights the corporate nature of the church.[23] And though the figures have distinct bodies, the witnesses speak from one mouth, implying a unified testimony. Second, the presence of two witnesses likely reflects the Jewish requirement that at least two witnesses be present for legally valid testimony.[24] Indeed, the very term "witness" suggests an obligation to speak the truth, especially in situations under dispute. As such, the church continues the legacy of Christ, God's faithful "witness" (Rev 1:5; 3:14), by boldly testifying to the singular truth of the gospel.[25]

One final point should be noted regarding the identity of the witnesses, who are sometimes associated with Elijah and Moses. The correlation of the two prophets with Moses and Elijah largely derives from the powers they wield. Just as Elijah called down fire upon Mount Carmel, the witnesses are armed with fire from their mouths.[26] Just as Elijah prevented rain from

---

20 Beale, *Revelation*, 577.

21 Thomas and Macchia, *Revelation*, 203. Cf. Beale, *Revelation*, 576–77.

22 Holwerda, "Church," 156.

23 Beale, *Revelation*, 594.

24 Deuteronomy 19:15; John 8:13–18; Bauckham, *Theology of the Book*, 85; Beale, *Revelation*, 575; Holwerda, "Church," 157; Thomas and Macchia, *Revelation*, 201.

25 Bauckham, *Climax of Prophecy*, 273; Koester, *Revelation*, 110; Osborne, *Revelation*, 410, 418.

26 Revelation 11:5; 1 Kings 18:38; cf. 2 Kings 1:10–14.

falling upon Israel, the witnesses have the power to shut up the sky.[27] Just as Moses turned the waters of the Nile to blood and struck Egypt with plagues, the witnesses have the power to turn water into blood and strike the earth with every plague.[28]

While John almost certainly alludes to Moses and Elijah, he does not imply that the witnesses are reincarnated versions of the Old Testament prophets. Rather, John evokes the contexts in which Elijah and Moses ministered. Both men prophesied during periods of intense persecution and deception. Both men boldly spoke against the abuse of power, the oppression of people, and the depravity of idolatry. Such a religo-cultural milieu would have been familiar to John's first-century audience under the dominion of Rome.

**The Weapons**

Just as the allusions to Moses and Elijah evoke broader themes, the weapons of the witnesses convey potent truths. First, the authority the witnesses exercise over nature likely points more to the power of prayer than the ability to perform miraculous signs. Like John, James references the context of Elijah's miraculous ministry, but James specifically roots Elijah's power in prayer:

> The effective prayer of a righteous man can accomplish much. Elijah was a man with a nature like ours, and he prayed earnestly that it would not rain, and it did not rain on the earth for three years and six months. Then he prayed again, and the sky poured rain and the earth produced its fruit. (Jas 5:16b–18)

In the context of Revelation, John has already revealed that the prayers of the saints are a powerful catalyst for events that take place on the earth (Rev 5:8; 8:3ff.). Thus, John likely intends his readers to understand that the power of the witnesses is rooted in prayer.

Second, fire equates to the revelation of God's truth.[29] Depending upon an individual's response, the fire of the gospel will either result in purification leading to eternal life or destruction resulting in eternal death.[30] Considering John's frequent allusions to the Old Testament, he may draw upon Jeremiah 5:14: "Therefore, thus says the LORD, the God of hosts, 'Because you have

---

27 Revelation 11:6; 1 Kings 17:1.

28 Revelation 11:6; Exodus 7:14–24.

29 Flemming, "Revelation," 173.

30 Fire that destroys: Revelation 9:18; 14:10; 16:8; 17:16; 18:8; 19:20; 20:9–10, 14–15; 21:8; fire associated with the holiness/purity of God and his people: Revelation 1:14; 2:18; 3:18; 4:5; 8:5; 10:1; 11:5; 14:8; 15:2; 19:12.

spoken this word, behold, I am making My words in your mouth fire, and this people wood, and it will consume them.'"

Third, and closely related, the fire from the *mouth* of the witnesses evokes the larger context of opposing testimonies in Revelation. Stevens explains,

> If any war is pictured in Revelation that war is a war of words—a war of witness, of confession, of testimony, of obedience to God. The war is won on the paradigm of Jesus as presented in the four Gospels and, indeed, in the rest of the New Testament—faithful testimony, even to the point of death (Rev 21:11).[31]

Though the weapons of the witnesses are powerful, the men still follow the cruciform pattern of Christ as they die at the hands of their enemies.

Yet, the witnesses are killed only after their testimony is complete (Rev 11:7; cf. 13:7). That the beast rises up and overcomes (νικάω) the saints, who are, themselves, repeatedly exhorted to overcome (νικάω), threatens to undermine perceptions of victory.[32] Morales, however, suggests, "By use of the same verb for conquering (νικάω) here, John is signaling a rival ideology of what it means to conquer on earth. Whereas the beast conquers by killing, the Lamb and his followers conquer by dying. No more profound difference in ideology could be conceived."[33] As John demonstrates through the example of the witnesses and makes explicit in Revelation 12:11, the saints overcome "because of the blood of the Lamb and because of the word of their testimony, and they did not love their life even when faced with death."

**Standing Yet Slain**

Both the location and the duration of the witnesses' death indicate that the narrative isn't simply about the fate of two men. John identifies the location as "the great city . . . where their Lord was crucified," which, at a surface level, seems to point to Jerusalem. Yet, the city, also called "Sodom and Egypt," seems to be inhabited by people of every tribe, tongue, and nation (Rev 11:8–9). John further describes the "great city" as Babylon in 18:21, 24: "Babylon, the great city . . . in [whom] was found the blood of prophets and of saints" (18:21, 24). Accordingly, the "great city" is best identified as the system of the world that opposes God and his people.

---

31 Stevens, *Revelation*, 156. Cf. A "sword" in Jesus's mouth: Revelation 1:16; 2:16; 19:15, 21; "weapons" in the mouths of God's enemies: Revelation 9:17–19; 12:15–16; 13:2, 5–6; 16:13; truth in the mouths of the saints: Revelation 14:5.

32 Thomas and Macchia, *Revelation*, 205.

33 Morales, *Christ, Shepherd*, 81.

In addition, the period of time that witnesses lie dead in the street, 3.5 days, exudes theological significance. First, 3.5 *years*, the duration of the witnesses' ministry, represents a finite period of persecution and testing for God's people. The number arises from the Old Testament and is reflected in the 3.5-year drought of Elijah, to which John has already alluded, and in the period during which Antiochus IV desecrated the Jerusalem temple.[34] Thus, the 3.5 years does not refer to a specific length of time, but rather the nature of the time—a limited period of affliction for God's people.[35] Likewise, the 3.5 *days* takes on a similar meaning. The witnesses may be "dead," but the duration indicates that the affliction is temporary.

Just as the witnesses followed Jesus in ministry and death, they would likewise follow him in resurrection. With the use of 3.5, John cleverly converts the duration of Jesus's ministry (three years) and the duration of his death (three days) into conventional apocalyptic language of 3.5 years and 3.5 days.[36] John also draws a subtle comparison between the 3.5 *days* of shame and the 3.5 *years* of ministry. Beale explains that the "victory" of the beast "is brief and insignificant in comparison to the victorious testimony of the witnesses."[37]

Nonetheless, as the bodies of the witnesses lie in the street, the earth-dwellers rejoice, believing that they have conquered the saints (Rev 11:10). Further, "those from the peoples and tribes and tongues and nations" gaze upon the dead bodies and refuse them burial, an intentionally humiliating fate (Rev 11:9). That the bodies of the witnesses are visible to peoples from all over the earth does not imply that the citizens of the world watch the events on television. Rather, the universal formula (peoples, tribes, tongues, and nations) indicates that the mockers live throughout the earth, as do the saints they persecute.[38] As such, the fate of the witnesses reflects the experience of persecuted saints in every time and place.[39]

34 Daniel 7:25; 1 Kings 17:1; 18:1; Luke 4:25; Revelation 11:6.

35 Koester, *Revelation*, 108.

36 Bauckham, *Theology of the Book*, 85; Bauckham, *Climax of Prophecy*, 280; Beale, *Revelation*, 594.

37 Beale, *Revelation*, 595.

38 Beale, 574, 593–94.

39 Bauckham, *Theology of the Book*, 86; Beale, *Revelation*, 592; Koester, *Revelation*, 111.

After the witnesses follow Christ in death, they are subsequently resurrected by the Spirit (πνεῦμα) of God. According to Revelation 11:11–12,

> But after the three and a half days, the breath [πνεῦμα] of life from God came into them, and they stood on their feet; and great fear fell upon those who were watching them. And they heard a loud voice from heaven saying to them, "Come up here." Then they went up into heaven in the cloud, and their enemies watched them.[40]

Continuing to provide interpretive keys for his audience, John offers a clear reference to Ezekiel 37:5, by alluding to a passage that describes *corporate* resurrection. John reinforces his portrayal of the witnesses as a corporate entity.[41]

But does John describe a one-time eschatological resurrection of all God's people? While such an interpretation is possible, another option is more contextually probable. If the witnesses represent the church, might the resurrection of the witnesses represent the continual life of the church? In every age, the church faces persecution unto death. In certain regions of the world, the church may seem to be completely wiped out. Yet, the body of Christ always rises. Over and over, the church will seem to be defeated, but the Spirit-empowered, prayerful witness of the saints will carry on.

## The Nations and the Remnants

Upon the resurrection and ascension of the witnesses, terror falls upon the enemies of God. Such fear is validated as a great earthquake strikes the city. A tenth of the city falls, seven thousand people die, and "the rest were terrified and gave glory to the God of heaven" (Rev 11:13). Yet, whether the response of the survivors reflects genuine conversion is a matter of dispute. It will here be argued that a remnant from the nations does experience salvation, but not necessarily as a mass universal event at the eschaton. Rather, the conversion reflects the soteriological efficacy of the cruciform witness of the saints throughout history. The sacrificial witness of God's church brings about a salvific result among the nations that judgments alone do not accomplish.

---

40 That the witnesses ascend to heaven in a cloud doesn't imply a dispensational type of "rapture." The imagery is likely a continuing allusion to the ministry of Elijah, who was taken to God in a whirlwind at the conclusion of his ministry (2 Kgs 2:11), and to the ministry of Jesus, who ascended in a cloud after his resurrection (Acts 1:9–11). Cf. Aune, *Revelation 6–16*, 632; Beale, *Revelation*, 600.

41 Beale, *Revelation*, 597.

**Judgment, Witness, and Repentance**

Throughout the Apocalypse, John's portrayal of the nations is complex, especially in Revelation 11. Jon Morales, in his narrative analysis of the "nations" in Revelation, offers a helpful summary:

> The four appearances of the nations prior to Revelation 11 emphasized the actions of others towards them. They were to be shepherded and smashed by the church (Rev 2:27). Many, in fact an innumerable crowd, from (ἐκ) the nations would receive the benefits of the Lamb's death and be made into a kingdom and priests (Rev 5:9; 7:9, 14). Finally, Revelation 10:11 highlighted John's responsibility to prophesy about the nations. By contrast, in Revelation 11 the nations act. They trample the holy city and rage against God and his people, actions that, to put it prosaically, do not go well for them. God meets rage with rage, and judgment comes. As a character in John's overall drama, the nations achieve more characterization as the narrative develops. They appear in close relationship to the main characters, Jesus and the churches, even though in Revelation 10–11 the primary relationship is oppositional. Revelation 10 portrayed the nations in alliance with the kings of the earth (Rev 10:11), while Revelation 11 foregrounded their alignment with the beast and the earth-dwellers. However, it should also be noted that those so aligned are a group from (ἐκ) the nations, and not the nations in their totality. The ἐκ (in Rev 5:9, 7:9, and 11:9) is John's way of distinguishing a subgroup within the larger "nations" group. This nuance in all instances should be brought out in interpretation.[42]

In short, though the "nations" are often viewed as a cohesive whole, subgroups from within the nations may ally themselves either with the beast *or* with God. In Revelation 5:9 and 7:9, people *from* every nation worship God, whereas in 11:9 people *from* every nation celebrate the death of the witnesses. So, despite the antagonism of the nations toward God's people in Revelation 11:9, John has already foreshadowed in 5:9 and 7:9 that some from among the nations will experience salvation.[43] And the appearance of the nations in the new Jerusalem (21:24, 26) confirms that a conversion has taken place.

The immediate context of the conversion in 11:13 must also be considered to appreciate John's message. After the ascension of the witnesses, God sends judgment upon those who had persecuted his saints (11:13). God's faithfulness

42 Morales, *Christ, Shepherd*, 82–83.

43 Thomas and Macchia, *Revelation*, 198.

to his people and his creation necessitates divine judgment against those who seek to sabotage his redemptive mission.[44] Along such lines, Revelation 8–9 seems to offer an increasing and unstoppable crescendo of violence. Through the trumpet judgments, John describes various disasters falling upon a third of the earth, culminating in the death of one-third of humanity. As for the rest who are not killed, John explicitly notes that "they did not repent" (9:20–21; cf. 16:9).

Although the narrative thread of divine judgment seems to continue into Revelation 11, only one-tenth of the city falls, sparing nine-tenths of the population. In the face of God's judgment and a gospel testimony that is both spoken and embodied, the survivors in 11:13 give glory to God. Stevenson explains,

> What accounts for the difference between judgment *without* repentance (9:13–21) and judgment *with* repentance (11:13)? Sandwiched between these two is John's call to prophetic witness (10:1–11) and the prophetic witness of the community of God as represented by the two witnesses (11:1–12). Within the narrative flow of the sixth trumpet, judgment alone fails to generate repentance, but judgment coupled with the faithful witness of God's people does.[45]

God's judgment is not simply punitive; in conjunction with the witness of the saints, judgment evokes genuine repentance and faith. The cruciform testimony of the church has a soteriological impact on the nations that far exceeds the efficacy of judgments alone.

### Fear and Glory

Not all interpreters agree that genuine conversion takes place in Revelation 11. G. K. Beale argues that although the survivors fearfully acknowledge God's power, they do not experience true repentance or offer authentic worship.[46] He compares Revelation 11:13 to 6:15–17, in which those who survive the plagues fearfully pray to the mountains and the rocks, "Fall on us and hide us from the presence of Him who sits on the throne, and from the wrath of the Lamb" (6:16). Beale also appeals to the Old Testament, citing instances in which the fear of the Lord does not equate to true reverence, as when the peoples of Canaan are terrified in the face of God's power (Exod 15:16).[47]

44 Flemming, *Foretaste of the Future*, 53; Flemming, "Revelation," 166.

45 Stevenson, *Slaughtered Lamb*, 172. Cf. deSilva, *Seeing Things John's Way*, 76; Flemming, *Foretaste of the Future*, 123; Holwerda, "Church," 150; Koester, *Revelation*, 112.

46 Beale, *Revelation*, 602–7.

47 Cf. Psalm 105:38; Jonah 1:10, 16; et al.; Beale, *Revelation*, 604.

Yet, the Old Testament also offers examples in which the fear of the Lord is expressed in the context of genuine worship, especially in conjunction with the idea of glorifying God. For example, the psalmist calls all the peoples of the earth to fear and glorify the Lord in preparation for his eschatological return (Ps 96:3–13).[48]

Although various Old Testament passages do provide examples of people ascribing glory to God out of subjugation or fear, John clearly establishes the function of "glory" within his own narrative.[49] Most notably, in Revelation glory is never ascribed to God by an unbeliever.[50] Further, in 14:6–7, fearing God and giving him glory in the hour of judgment is associated with genuine worship.[51] Then, in 16:9, the inverse appears as the inhabitants of the earth "refused to repent and glorify him."

In the Old Testament and in Revelation, "glory" is often attributed to God in passages that anticipate the worship of God by peoples throughout the earth.[52] DeSilva explains,

> The hope of the psalmist that "all the nations" made by God would "come and worship before" God and "glorify his name" (Ps. 86:9) is proclaimed also by the redeemed beside the throne of God [Rev 15:4] . . . and made real as the kings of the earth bring their glory into the new Jerusalem and the nations walk in the light of God and the Lamb that illuminates the city (21:23).[53]

Clearly, the conversion of the nations and the means by which conversion takes place is central to the message of Revelation.[54]

The group from the nations who fears and glorifies God is described as "the remnant," οἱ λοιποί (Rev 11:13). The remnant is a theological concept, originating in Old Testament prophetic literature, which denotes the portion of the community that escapes death, judgment, or exile.[55] Though

---

48 Cf. Deuteronomy 10:12; 1 Samuel 12:14; 1 Kings 18:3; Psalms 22:23; 33:8; et al.

49 Morales, *Christ, Shepherd*, 80n27. Cf. Bauckham, *Climax of Prophecy*, 287–89; Flemming, "Revelation," 167.

50 Revelation 1:6; 4:9, 11; 5:12–13; 7:12; 19:1, 7.

51 Cf. Psalm 96:3–13.

52 Psalm 96:3–13; Isaiah 24:15–16; 42:10–12; Bauckham, *Climax of Prophecy*, 279.

53 DeSilva, *Seeing Things John's Way*, 76; Holwerda, "Church," 160.

54 Bauckham, *Climax of Prophecy*, 238.

55 H. Fendrich, "λοιπός," in *Exegetical Dictionary of the New Testament*, 2:360; Aune, *Revelation 6–16*, 628; Jeremiah 24:8; Ezra 9:13–15; Isaiah 10:20–22; 11:11–16; 28:5; 37:31–32; Romans 9:24–29; 11:5.

the term typically refers to those who remain faithful to God, some New Testament authors use λοιπός to describe a group of people who are outside of God's kingdom.[56]

John takes the remnant concept and develops it in a unique way. In Revelation 9 and 11, the remnant describes the group of people who are delivered from judgment or death. Yet, whereas the Old Testament remnant typically described a small minority, John's remnant constitutes the majority of humanity—two-thirds in 9:20–21 and nine-tenths in 11:13. And this remnant may choose whether or not to become part of God's kingdom. In 9:20–21, the remnant does *not* repent, but in 11:13 the remnant gives glory to God.

Old Testament allusions may support the assertion that the remnant in 11:13 does, in fact, experience conversion. In Amos 5:3 and Isaiah 6:13, God brings judgment upon cities that reject him, and only one-tenth of the population is spared, a portion Isaiah describes as a "holy seed." During Elijah's ministry, to which John has already alluded, God promises judgment over all Israel except the minority of seven thousand faithful individuals who have not worshiped Baal (1 Kgs 19:14–18; cf. Rom 11:2–5). In Revelation 11:13 John delivers a striking inversion: The majority are spared judgment. Only one-tenth of the people—seven thousand individuals—perish, while nine-tenths of the population gives glory to God. Rather than a small minority, the remnant is now a faithful majority.[57] Whereas the word of God delivered through the Old Testament prophets was effectual only among a small, mostly Jewish minority, and whereas the prophetic word was insufficient to spread the glory of God to the ends of the earth, the cruciform ministry of the living Word has the power to reach every people, tribe, tongue, and nation.[58]

It should be noted, once again, that John's numbers do not necessitate a universal end-time salvation. Because apocalyptic literature utilizes hyperbolic language, John is likely encouraging his hearers that their testimony will reap a great harvest—a harvest greater than that which resulted from the ministries of the Hebrew prophets, the plagues of the Exodus, or the famine of Elijah. Rather than a powerless minority, God's people hold the power to reach the entire world with the gospel message—and are guaranteed success.

56 Matthew 22:1–6; 25:1–13; Mark 16:13; Luke 8:10; 18:9–11; Acts 5:13; Romans 11:7; Galatians 2:13; Revelation 9:20.

57 Bauckham, *Theology of the Book*, 87; Bauckham, *Climax of Prophecy*, 282–83; Thomas and Macchia, *Revelation*, 209.

58 Bauckham, *Theology of the Book*, 87.

## The Church

John's graphic parable of the two witnesses exemplifies the message of the gospel and the mission of the church. The witness of faithful Christ-followers may appear futile and ineffective against multitudes that mock and deride God's people. Earthly powers may dominate and debase those who follow the Lamb. The church may suffer persecution to the extent that, at times, it will seem to be eradicated. Yet, the cruciform power of the gospel transforms suffering into triumph.

In the battle against the oppressive and destructive forces of the world, God's people are armed with prayer, the power of the Spirit, and the cruciform efficacy of the gospel. Through the ministry of the witnesses, John reveals that the prayers of the saints are just as effectual as those of the Old Testament prophets. In fact, as a result of Christ's work, all believers now have a greater power than the saints of the Old Testament—the indwelling presence of God's Spirit.[59] As such, the witness of the church is conveyed with supernatural power, and those who deliver the message are spiritually invincible. Though the body may die, whether corporately or individually, the same Spirit who vivified God's creation (Gen 1:2), the same Spirit who gave life to humanity (Gen 2:7), and the same Spirit who brought life to dry bones (Ezek 37:5) guarantees eternal life for all who follow the Lamb.

By illuminating the true nature of victory, John reveals that worldly notions of power perpetuate systems of oppression and debasement. Violence and military might only breed more death, resulting in a victory characterized by domination and subjugation. By way of contrast,

> John's utter reliance on God is the foundation of his strategic response to a situation of systemic evil. He longs for Rome's demise, but never issues a call for violent revolution. In contrast to the Zealot model of armed resistance, faithful Christians must respond with patient endurance rather than violence.[60]

The conquest strategies of God's kingdom—patient endurance, faithful testimony, and self-sacrifice—do not result in the death of one's "enemies." Rather, God's witnesses are the ones who face death. Yet, the death of the saints doesn't breed more death but eternal life, dignity, and freedom for the saints themselves and for every nation, tribe, and tongue.

---

59 Holwerda, "Church," 157.

60 Kraybill, *Imperial Cult*, 201.

Because resisting the ideology of empire often comes with a steep cost, John demands a complete reorientation of intellect, ideals, and purpose. As such, John's subversive strategy is, counterintuitively, to sharpen the boundaries between the church and the world.[61] Yet, the boundaries of God's kingdom don't serve the purpose of keeping people out. Whereas softening ideological boundaries and participating in the practices of the world (Rome/Babylon) mutes witness by upholding systems that oppose God, firm boundaries exclude earthly structures of power, prejudice, greed, and exploitation.[62] Indeed, the boundaries of God's kingdom create a safe and sacred space in which all peoples can enjoy unity in diversity.

In Revelation, John draws a stark boundary line as he polarizes all humanity into two groups: followers of the Lamb and followers of the beast.[63] The testimony of the witnesses, thus, offers each group an opportunity to affirm their place or step into a new group. In fact, as John describes the persecution of the witnesses, he simply identifies their antagonist as "anyone" (τις; 11:5). Morales explains,

> This "anyone" then becomes the two witnesses' "enemies" (Rev 11:5). It is as if John is breaking the fourth wall, so to speak, and giving the warning directly to the hearer. The hearer thus becomes an active participant in the drama and must answer the question: will he assume the stance of the church's narrated enemy? . . . The gentile hearer must decide to which kingdom he belongs before time draws to a close.[64]

Along similar lines, John never narrates the defeat of the beast in Revelation 11. He, perhaps, hints that as the church age continues, the beast will continue to war against God's people and deceive the nations. Accordingly, God's people must battle to remain faithful witnesses and reject every challenge that might hinder their ability to spread the gospel.[65] Further, as God's people "come out of Babylon" (Rev 18:4), they must embody the gospel by "working for peace, justice, and reconciliation within and among the nations."[66] As believers bear witness to the fullness of the gospel message, they likewise call others out of Babylon.[67]

---

61 Flemming, "Revelation," 171.

62 DeSilva, *Seeing Things John's Way*, 332.

63 Kraybill, *Imperial Cult*, 202.

64 Morales, *Christ, Shepherd*, 83.

65 Alkier, "Witness or Warrior," 136.

66 Flemming, "Revelation," 177.

67 DeSilva, *Seeing Things John's Way*, 71.

Though John offers a spiritual perspective on the world, it is not an otherworldly viewpoint. John doesn't call believers to leave their earthly circumstance but to bear witness to the truth within it. According to Fleming,

> Practically, if our hope lies in escaping a doomed world, then we might be tempted to think of *mission* simply in terms of getting people ready to leave this world for heaven. . . . In contrast, Revelation's picture of God as the Creator who is intensely committed to *this* world and its ultimate liberation calls God's people to become channels of compassion, healing, and *shalom* at every level of human need.[68]

Indeed, as John concludes the Apocalypse, he focuses on the splendor of God's kingdom and the healing of the nations (Rev 22:2) rather than the gory destruction of Rome/Babylon. John's scathing critiques from the earlier chapters of the Apocalypse must now be seen in light of the eschatological new Jerusalem. The inauguration of this "city" includes social and economic dimensions that rectify the failures and abuses of empire. Such a hope dominates John's vision of the future but also declares God's purposes for the present.[69] DeSilva emphasizes,

> It is a proclamation of God's purpose for creation, in light of which all human purposes and societies are judged, critiqued, weighed in the balance and found wanting. Christians are challenged not only to *wait* but also to *witness*, hence to proclaim and protest, to encourage and direct, in the light of God's vision.[70]

In Revelation 11, as John vividly depicts the church carrying out such a mission, he likewise reveals that they are supernaturally empowered and equipped to succeed. Through the treatment of the witnesses, John has not only allowed but encouraged his audience to be angry about the oppression, debasement, and exploitation of the earth and its people. Yet, God's saints aren't to direct their efforts toward violence or revenge; they are to become faithful witnesses and agents of redemption.

68 Flemming, *Foretaste of the Future*, 41 (emphasis original).

69 Kraybill, *Imperial Cult*, 196.

70 DeSilva, *Seeing Things John's Way*, 348 (emphasis original).

## Conclusion

Throughout his apocalypse, John delivers a message that is antithetical to human logic: Victory is attained through suffering and self-sacrifice. Rather than taking up arms against earthly forces of evil, believers are called to live sacrificially and offer witness that may result in social ostracism, financial hardship, bodily persecution, and even death. Just as the slain-yet-standing Lamb accomplishes the redemption of the world through his death, so also Christ's followers become instruments of restoration through their own cruciform witness. As exemplified by the graphic narrative of Revelation 11:3–13, suffering incurred through faithful testimony does not yield defeat but redeemed souls. Though the church may seem weak and the saints may suffer, God's people are actually armed with "weapons" formidable enough to defeat the evil in human hearts and the power structures such evil perpetuates. Those who follow the Lamb are not only called but supernaturally empowered to fight the oppression, debasement, and exploitation of the earth and its people. In doing so, the saints embody the message that God's kingdom is patently different from the systems of earthly power; violence only breeds further violence and death, but patient endurance, faithful testimony, and sacrificial witness yield eternal life, dignity, and freedom for every nation, tribe, and tongue.

Though John's message was originally directed toward believers in first-century Asia Minor, his words resonate throughout the history of the church. John exhorts God's people, past and present, to fight the enduring evil of "Babylon" by means of faithful testimony. Such sacrificial witness may result in temporary suffering, but John reminds believers of every age that eternal victory is guaranteed.

## Bibliography

Alkier, Stefan. "Witness or Warrior? How the Book of Revelation Can Help Christians Live Their Political Lives." In Hays and Alkier, *Revelation and the Politics of Apocalyptic Interpretation.*

Aune, David Edward. *Revelation 6–16.* Word Biblical Commentary 52B. Nelson, 1998.

Balz, Horst, and Gerhard Schneider, eds. *Exegetical Dictionary of the New Testament.* Vol. 2. Eerdmans, 1991.

Bauckham, Richard. *The Climax of Prophecy: Studies on the Book of Revelation.* T&T Clark, 1993.

Bauckham, Richard. *The Theology of the Book of Revelation.* Cambridge University Press, 1993.

Beale, G. K. *The Book of Revelation.* New International Greek Testament Commentary. Eerdmans, 1999.

Blount, Brian K. "The Witness of Active Resistance: The Ethics of *Revelation* in African American Perspective." In Rhoads, *From Every People and Nation.*

deSilva, David. *Seeing Things John's Way: The Rhetoric of the Book of Revelation.* Westminster John Knox, 2009.

deSilva, David. "The Social Setting of the Revelation to John: Conflicts Within, Fears Without." *Westminster Theological Journal* 54, no. 2 (1992): 273–302.

Flemming, Dean. *Foretaste of the Future: Reading Revelation in Light of God's Mission.* IVP Academic, 2022.

Flemming, Dean. "Revelation and the '*Missio Dei*': Toward a Missional Reading of the Apocalypse." *Journal of Theological Interpretation* 6, no. 2 (2012): 161–77.

González, Justo L. "*Revelation*: Clarity and Ambivalence: A Hispanic/Cuban American Perspective." In Rhoads, *From Every People and Nation.*

Gorman, Michael J. *Reading Revelation Responsibly: Uncivil Worship and Witness: Following the Lamb into the New Creation.* Cascade, 2010.

Hayes, Richard B., and Stefan Alkier, eds. *Revelation and the Politics of Apocalyptic Interpretation.* Baylor University Press, 2012.

Holwerda, David Earl. "The Church and the Little Scroll (Revelation 10, 11)." *Calvin Theological Journal* 34, no. 1 (1999): 148–61.

Koester, Craig R. *Revelation and the End of All Things.* 2nd ed. Eerdmans, 2018.

Kraybill, J. Nelson. *Imperial Cult and Commerce in John's Apocalypse.* Journal for the Study of New Testament Supplement Series. Sheffield Academic Press, 1996.

Maier, Harry O. "Coming Out of Babylon: A First-World Reading of *Revelation* Among Immigrants." In Rhoads, *From Every People and Nation.*

Morales, Jon. *Christ, Shepherd of the Nations: The Nations as Narrative Character and Audience in John's Apocalypse.* Library of New Testament Studies. T&T Clark, 2018.

Osborne, Grant R. *Revelation.* Baker Exegetical Commentary on the New Testament. Baker Academic, 2002.

Rhoads, David, ed. *From Every People and Nation: The Book of Revelation in Intercultural Perspective.* Fortress, 2005.

Richard, Pablo. "Reading the Apocalypse: Resistance, Hope, and Liberation in Central America." In Rhoads, *From Every People and Nation.*

Slater, Thomas B. *Revelation as Civil Disobedience: Witnesses Not Warriors in John's Apocalypse.* Abingdon, 2019.

Stevens, Gerald. *Revelation: The Past and Future of John's Apocalypse.* Pickwick, 2014.

Stevenson, Gregory. *A Slaughtered Lamb: Revelation and the Apocalyptic Response to Evil and Suffering.* Abilene Christian University Press, 2013.

Thomas, John Christopher, and Frank Macchia. *Revelation.* Two Horizons New Testament Commentary. Eerdmans, 2016.

Thompson, Marianne Meye. "Reading What Is Written in the Book of Life: Theological Interpretation of the Book of Revelation Today." In Hays and Alkier, *Revelation and the Politics of Apocalyptic Interpretation.*

# Chapter 8

# God and the Underside

## Revelation's Missional Political Theology: An Invitation to Emulate the Lamb

*Jessica Janvier*

### Locating Revelation's Political Theology

In our accounting of the Greek language and its surrounding culture, the term *theology* has from the beginning been associated with the political realm. From what we know, it makes its first appearance in a conversation between Adeimantus and Socrates concerning how the mythical literature about the Greek gods should influence the state didactically.[1] Hence, it should not be surprising that the Scriptures carry within them a political theology, on account of their evolution out of a wider cultural setting that tightly intertwined the religious and political realms.

This accounts for the traditional Christian readings of the Hebrew Bible and the New Testament, which have predominantly seen within the Scriptures a missional impulse at work that has a political aim seeking to encompass the whole world. Describing this impulse, theologian Richard Bauckham has said,

> The Bible itself embodies a kind of movement from the particular to the universal, which we as readers need to find ourselves inside. The Bible is a kind of project aimed at the kingdom of God, that is, towards the achievement of God's purposes for good in the whole of God's creation.[2]

Revelation seems to agree with this universal thrust, as the last book of the Christian canon portrays the goal of God's kingdom encompassing the world coming to fruition. It announces, "The kingdom of the world has become the kingdom of our Lord and of his Messiah, and he will reign forever and ever" (Rev 11:15).[3]

The announcement of a self-understood benevolent worldwide kingdom (or empire, as some hearers of βασιλεία [*basileia*] in this context have

1 Taubes, "Theology and Political Theory," 57.

2 Bauckham, *Bible and Mission*, 11.

3 All Scripture quotations are from the NRSV.

interpreted it) seeking to circumscribe the earth would have been nothing new to the world of the first century, from which Revelation would gain its initial audience. A geopolitical superpower vying for control of global affairs is all too familiar to many in contemporary times. Such political announcements, as Revelation reflects, have tended to elicit great trepidation or subservient joy, as incorporation has often been accompanied by the threat of violence. In the Roman world of the first century, in which many of the earliest Christians were located, the invitation to join the empire was nonnegotiable.

The death of Julius Caesar led to a two-decade-long civil war with different military leaders jockeying to inherit the power and territories he conquered. His adopted son, Octavian, came out on top and inherited the title *Augustus*. More importantly, he also inherited the title *divi filius* in Latin or υἱοῦ τοῦ Θεοῦ in Greek, both meaning "son of God." As the one who put an end to the civil war and heir to the expanding empire that had the world in its purview, it was his divine commission as the embodiment of divinity (son of god) to extend the peace of Rome or *Pax Romana* to the world. Ironically, this peace was spread mostly through conquest and coercion, though there were some municipalities that came into the fold with enthusiasm. Nonetheless, once a part of the empire, dissent was not tolerated, and obedience was enforced through draconian measures, such as crucifying dissidents.

Augustus Caesar and the subsequent Caesars set the theological, political, and missional tone of the empire, as the practice of emperor worship united the communities of the empire with the divine "peace"-bringing mission. On this, historian Christopher Kelly explains,

> It can . . . be difficult [for moderns] to conceive of a society with no firm division between religion and politics. Yet in the Roman empire, the religious rituals surrounding emperor-worship were not somehow secondary to the "real business" of rule (administration, justice, taxation, warfare). Rather, religious imagery and religious language were an inseparable part of Roman political vocabulary. For its enthusiasts, the worship of living emperors and their posthumous deification offered a means of understanding what it meant to be part of the Roman empire . . . It could provide a language for comprehending absolute power.[4]

Thus, those participating in the mission of the empire to widen its boundaries embodied a *missional political theology*, primarily through the power of

---

4 Kelly, *Roman Empire*, 30.

Rome's military apparatus. In other words, their political aims (i.e., their mission) were tied to a religious outlook (theology), and their outlook served as an empowering philosophy (political strategy) that helped to organize their thinking as to how they should engage the world around them with the power they had in order to accomplish their mission.

Revelation was written in this context; however, it had its own vision of a kingdom that it foresaw engulfing the world. Likewise, it had its own vision of a divine leader—the *Son of God* who was commissioned to oversee that kingdom and its spreading. If the *missio Dei* in Revelation is expressed by the "kingdom of this world" becoming the "kingdom of our Lord and his Messiah," then its way of calling Christians to participate in the spreading of that kingdom is an expression of the text's missional political theology.

Despite the overlap in setting between Revelation and the Roman Empire, their shared language and conceptual frameworks should not be mistaken as identical in meaning. The relationship between the two is best expressed in what Justin Meggitt calls "polemical parallelism."[5] This sort of parallelism was a way for the authors of the New Testament to utilize language familiar to people living within the empire while at the same time inverting it for their own purposes.[6]

To hear the missional political theology of Revelation, one must comprehend the text's political critique of the Roman Empire, its invitation to emulation, and warnings against conformity.

## A Word on Methodology of Interpretation

The missional political theology present in Revelation can only be heard with some sense of clarity when a proper hermeneutic is applied to its reading. Therefore, before we proceed, a word about interpretation is necessary.

Interpretive approaches to this text have been plentiful over the centuries, but among the most influential in the United States have been the preterist view and the futurist perspective. Regarding the preterist view, Craig Keener has said,

> Preterists read the book of Revelation the way they believe John's original audience in the seven churches would have. In other words, they seek to apply to Revelation the same interpretive method we apply to every other book of the Bible, namely that we should read

5 Meggitt, "Taking the Emperor's Clothes Seriously," 157.

6 For a more in-depth discussion on the use of parallelism in the New Testament, see Brooks-Janvier, "Essence of Antebellum Afro-Evangelicalism," 31–39.

> it in its historical context. Because the most radical preterists insist, however, that the events of Revelation were entirely fulfilled in the first century, they read it in a manner that John's original audience probably would not have.[7]

On the futurist approach, Keener has noted,

> Futurists are certainly right to claim that some events in the book await fulfillment, such as God's unchallenged eternal city supplanting the kingdoms of this world . . . But the futurist position, like the other ones, can be pressed too far; in its radical form, it "implies that the book had nothing to say to the many generations between John of Patmos and the interpreter."[8]

Falling in the category of extremes within the futurist approach are those who have used the text to foster wild speculation about current political events and world leaders, leading some to regrettable actions. Responding to this kind of interpretation, Michael Gorman in his book *Reading Revelation Responsibly* has asserted, "How one reads, teaches and preaches Revelation can have a powerful impact on one's own—and other people's—emotional, spiritual, and even physical and economic well-being."[9]

With this in mind, the most pervasive futurist interpretation is the dominant popular-level view of dispensationalism. Beyond its reading of Revelation, its theological approach to the Scriptures insists upon a sharp separation between Israel and the church and a literalism that does not always mesh well with the symbolism and hyperbolic language present in the ancient world's literature. Moreover, its invention of a rapture theology that decontextualizes the parousia has helped to create a distortion in the teleology of Christian eschatology. If the ancient church looked forward to "the resurrection of the dead and life of the world to come," dispensationalism has taught the church to look forward to escaping this world and its troubles.[10] Despite its popularity in conservative lay circles, its historical roots within Christian theology are quite shallow. Noting the history of dispensationalism and its provocative rapture theology, New Testament scholar Scot McKnight has recounted,

---

7 Keener, *Revelation*, 28.

8 Keener, 28.

9 Gorman, *Reading Revelation Responsibly*, 11.

10 Regarding "we look for the resurrection of the dead and the life of the world to come," see the Nicene Creed.

> The idea of *the rapture* first emerged, as we know it today, in the early nineteenth century from the spiritual vision of a teenage girl at a small revival in Glasgow, Scotland. The woman claimed to have had a vision of a *"pre-tribulation rapture"* at which time the church would be taken out of this world and swept up into heaven. British minister John Nelson Darby, having been present for the sharing of the vision, became convinced of its validity, and began sharing the vision as truth. Darby brought his rapture gospel to America, where he quickly encountered Dwight L. Moody, who soon became the worldwide disseminator of a *"pre-tribulation rapture."*[11]

Notwithstanding its populist appeal, McKnight has noted that this outlook has been at times "labeled a heresy because it was not fully formulated until the nineteenth century."[12] Regardless of the label given to this development in the history of Christian theology, its encouragement toward escapism is not particularly helpful for Christian political theology in general nor Revelation's missional political theology in particular, as will become apparent as this chapter unfolds. As Gorman has pointed out, this approach "has no ongoing ethic of life between the times, between the first and the second comings. There is no compulsion to love one's neighbor, practice deeds of mercy, work for peace and justice."[13] It is no coincidence that this view became popular in the pessimistic years after the United States Civil War and became a motivating factor for evangelicals to disengage from the civil rights struggles in the latter part of the twentieth century. Nevertheless, those within this perspective who have developed a political expression have tended to see in it an impetus for not working for peace in the Middle East, contributing to political strategies that discourage amity, especially between the state of Israel and the Palestinian people.[14]

In these readings of the text, what is missing is a reading that approaches Revelation from its *own* historical, literary, and cultural milieu. Additionally, what is missing from these approaches is a pastoral-theological interpretive lens that calls people toward Christlikeness in the public square. As Bauckham has noted, "Misinterpretations of Revelation often begin by misconceiving the kind of book it is."[15] The nature of the book of Revelation can be understood from

---

11 McKnight, *Revelation for the Rest of Us*, 314 (emphasis original).

12 McKnight, 301.

13 Gorman, *Reading Revelation Responsibly*, 116.

14 For more on this, see Gorman, 10. His footnote references there are helpful as well.

15 Bauckham, *Theology of the Book*, 1.

its genre. Revelation came into being as an expression of Jewish apocalyptic literature, a well-established genre at the time. To understand apocalyptic literature, John Collins helpfully explains. Defining the genre, he says,

> "Apocalypse" is a genre of revelatory literature with a narrative framework, in which a revelation is mediated by an otherworldly being to a human recipient, disclosing a transcendent reality which is both temporal, insofar as it envisages eschatological salvation, and spatial insofar as it involves another, supernatural world.[16]

One of the goals of apocalyptic literature was to give a heavenly perspective on temporal issues. By using narrative and symbols that the initial receiving audience would readily understand, apocalypses gave hope for the present and optimistic expectation about God's sovereign ability to transform this broken world into one that is imbued with the shalom of his kingdom. By reading Revelation as apocalyptic literature and utilizing the historical-critical method to ascertain the meaning of its symbolic world to its first listeners, its overall message can be heard, which will enable us to discern its missional political theology.

## Revelation's Critique of Rome

Critical to understanding Revelation's missional political theology is its critique of the Roman Empire. This should not be surprising, as much of the Jewish population ruled by Rome were not fans of it. The exception would have been those among their rich ruling class who worked in tandem with the empire. For the most part, Rome's way of spreading its "peace" was not admired by the Jewish people because it involved war, conquest, and subjugation against a people who had previously experienced a measure of autonomy under the Hasmoneans. A window into the empire's way of expanding can be seen through the description given by ancient historian Appian's depiction of Rome overtaking the Italian people. He wrote,

> The Romans, as they subdued the Italian people successively in war, used to seize a part of their lands and build towns there or enroll colonists of their own to occupy those already existing, and their idea was to use these as outposts, but of the land acquired by war, they assigned the cultivated part forthwith to the colonists, or sold or leased it.[17]

---

16 Collins, "Introduction: Towards the Morphology of a Genre," 9.

17 Appian, *Bell. civ.* 1.1.

Beyond dispossessing peoples of their lands and material resources, Appian went on to describe the connection between the coming of Rome and the devolution of autonomous people to peons.

> For the rich, getting possession of the greatest part of the undistributed lands, and being emboldened by the lapse of time to believe that they would never be dispossessed, absorbing any adjacent strips and their poor neighbour's allotments, partly by purchase under persuasion and partly by force, came to cultivate vast tracts instead of single estates, using slaves as labourers and herdsmen.[18]

Therefore, it is unsurprising that the author of Revelation, as Adela Yarbro Collins puts it, decided to write an apocalypse that was "a thorough-going attack on the authority of Rome."[19] This "attack" can be seen in the signifiers for Rome found in 13:1–4. There the author wrote,

> And I saw a beast rising out of the sea, having ten horns and seven heads; and on its horns were ten diadems, and on its heads were blasphemous names. And the beast that I saw was like a leopard, its feet were like a bear's, and its mouth was like a lion's mouth. And the dragon gave it his power and his throne and great authority. One of its heads seemed to have received a death-blow, but its mortal wound had been healed. In amazement the whole earth followed the beast. They worshiped the dragon, for he had given his authority to the beast, and they worshiped the beast, saying, "Who is like the beast, and who can fight against it?"

Expounding on how the beast would have been perceived as signifying Rome, Keener explains,

> Judeans (as well as an exile on Patmos or citizens of Ephesus) would perceive Rome as coming from "the sea" even geographically, and the sand of the seashore may represent "the nations" over whom the beast claims to rule (Rev. 20:8). . . . Besides ten horns . . . it is in some respects like a leopard, in others like a bear, and in others like a lion (Rev. 13:2). Composite descriptions can amplify the glory of a creature (Ezek. 1:10), but here they amplify its hideousness. Thus, though John makes his allusion by way of Rome, the point goes beyond Rome to the general threat of an "evil empire."[20]

---

18 Appian, *Bell. civ.* 1.1.

19 Collins, "Political Perspective of the Revelation to John," 252.

20 Keener, *Revelation*, 335–36.

Like Keener, many contemporary commentators who read Revelation as apocalyptic literature and with an eye to its historical setting have seen the appalling beast it describes as pointing to Rome.[21] This outlook also corresponds to other Jewish apocalypses of the time, which depicted Rome symbolically as a beast.[22] Despite the grandeur of Rome's power and authority, Revelation's author uses the descriptive symbol of a beast to portray Rome, along with a ghastly dragon, often thought to be a signifier for Satan, as its source of power. Furthermore, when Rome as the beast becomes clear, it does not take much of a leap to see the worship of the beast and dragon as a veiled critique of Rome's idolatrous demand for emperor worship. Its worshipers saying, "Who is like the beast?" (Rev 13:4), would have elicited a parallel in the minds of Revelation's first readers to the people of God in Exodus 15:11, singing, "Who is like you, O LORD, among the gods?" Rome's self-evaluation as the sovereign, all-powerful ruler of the world and its beastly character ravaging the world with its violence, fueled by its god-complex, is clear. Revelation is not a celebration of Rome as a powerful political entity but a denunciation of it. Moreover, Revelation's political critique does not limit itself to the Roman Empire alone, as Keener alludes to, but it is a political critique of the spirit behind *empire*.

History has shown that when imperial notions enter the minds of a people, their spread is accompanied by the very characteristics that Rome displays—beastly violence and a veiled desire for worshipful recognition of omnipotence. Depicting the beast in a similar piecemeal fashion to Daniel's four apocalyptic beasts (see Dan 7), the beast of Revelation, embodied through Rome in the first century, was just the latest iteration of imperialism. Underscoring this point, the author of Revelation is even able to use Babylon (14:6–20; 17:1–18), a foregone empire, as a symbol of Rome. On this, Brian Blount remarked, "For John, historical Rome wasn't new . . . it merely followed the mutinous human pattern already established by even more ancient powers like Babylon. Rome too, for all her claims to special status and unique imperial identity, was nothing more than a miserable, demonically driven mimic."[23]

---

21 For a sample of scholars who share this perspective, see Wright, *Revelation for Everyone*, 42; McKnight, *Revelation for the Rest of Us*, 39; Aune, *Revelation 6–16*, 714–82; Witherington, *Revelation*, 174–87.

22 For example, see 4 Ezra, which is sometimes called 2 Esdras (a document composed of 4, 5, and 6 Ezra).

23 Blount, *Can I Get a Witness?*, 117.

## Invitation to Emulation

The author of Revelation was giving a heavenly view of a political entity. Based on its power, miracles (13:11–18), and claim of having a divine mission, it elicited a form of worship from the masses. Additionally, it was a persecutor of God's people (6:9–10; 13:9–10). The natural questions to these circumstances were, *What were God's people to do about it?* and more importantly, *What was God going to do about it?*

The Jewish apocalyptic tradition relayed the clear answers that God would overcome the power of evil at work in the world through his Messiah and that his people, with his help, would do so too. These answers were often conveyed through the paradigm of a coming "holy war." Bauckham explains,

> In Jewish eschatological expectation, the theme of the holy war plays a prominent role. The future will bring the final victory of the divine Warrior over his people's and his own enemies. But the tradition of an eschatological or messianic holy war can be divided into two forms, in one of which the victory is won by God alone or by God and his heavenly armies and in the other of which his people play an active part in physical warfare against their enemies.[24]

Collins separates these two streams into what she calls "revolutionary" and "passive" resistance.[25] Revolutionary resistance could be seen in the likes of the Maccabean revolt, which called for an active military response in which the heavenly armies were thought to fight alongside the earthly army, guaranteeing success. This motif was the "dominant Old Testament tradition" and showed up in the ideology of the first-century Bar Kokhba revolt.[26] However, as Collins and Bauckham have recognized, the passive resistance approach was the dominant tradition in the Second Temple period.[27] Additionally, Collins further qualifies the passive resistance approach, noting,

> Within the model of passive resistance we can distinguish two types. One . . . opts for a purely passive role of the elect vis-à-vis the

24 Bauckham, "Christian War Scroll," 17.

25 Collins, "Political Perspective," 242–45.

26 Bauckham sees the revolutionary as the dominant tradition in the Old Testament. "Christian War Scroll," 18.

27 Bauckham qualifies his assertion by saying, "It is possible that in this respect the extant ancient apocalypses are not entirely typical of the apocalyptic literature of the period. It must be remembered that most of the ancient Jewish apocalypses have been preserved only by Christians, who in the early centuries largely repudiated apocalyptic militancy" (18).

> oppressive power. The stance recommended is one of endurance and waiting. A violent conflict leading to the destruction of the oppressive power is expected. The imagery used is that of holy war, but the elect will not participate in the final battle. The second type . . . is like the first with one important difference. The behavior of the elect vis-à-vis the persecutors is the same, but a synergistic understanding of righteous suffering is introduced.[28]

In this context, Revelation fits within the passive resistance approach because it rejects the notion of God's people overcoming evil by physical militarism. In 13:9–10, the Spirit instructs in this way, "Let anyone who has an ear listen: If you are to be taken captive, into captivity you go; if you kill with the sword, with the sword you must be killed. Here is a call for the endurance and faith of the saints." While passive resistance meant a rejection of militarism, in Revelation it did not mean there was no call for God's people to participate in and partner with God in conquering the power of evil. In this apocalypse, conquering is modeled after the way God's Messiah overcame all the ungodly forces plaguing God's world.

As the idea of God's people participating in a militaristic exhibition decreased in the Second Temple period, what was prevalent was the idea of the promised Messiah militarily overcoming the persecuting empire. For instance, in Psalms of Solomon 17:22, this expectation is clear. The author's prayer was for God to "Undergird him [the Messiah] with the strength to destroy the unrighteous rulers, to purge Jerusalem from the Gentiles who trample her down to destruction." At first glance, the entrance of the Messiah into Revelation's first scene of the heavenly throne room seems to accord with the sentiments of the Psalms of Solomon.

Jesus is first introduced into John's hearing in this part of the narrative as the "Lion of the tribe of Judah, the Root of David, [who] has conquered" (5:5). Keenly, the author is invoking the anticipation of a militaristic conquering Messiah with these titles. But, in a reversal of expectations, what John sees is not what he hears. "Then I saw between the throne and the four living creatures and among the elders a *Lamb standing as if it had been slaughtered*, having seven horns and seven eyes, which are the seven spirits of God sent out into all the earth" (5:6, emphasis mine). Bauckham eloquently portrays the significance of this moment in saying,

---

28 Collins, "Political Perspective," 243.

> Insofar as 5:5 expresses Jewish hopes for messianic conquest by *military violence*, 5:6 replaces those hopes; and insofar as 5:5 evokes narrowly nationalistic expectations of Jewish triumph over the Gentile nations, 5:6 replaces those expectations. But insofar as the Jewish hopes, rooted in Old Testament scriptures, were for the victory of God over evil, 5:6 draws on other Old Testament scriptures to show *how* they have been fulfilled in Jesus. Jesus the Messiah has already defeated evil by sacrificial death. He has won a victory, but by sacrifice, not military conflict, and has delivered God's people.[29]

Revelation presents Jesus as the faithful witness par excellence (1:5). Through his faithfulness to God, even to the point of death, he overcame the real enemies of God's people, which Paul refers to—and certainly the author of Revelation would agree with—as "rulers," "authorities," and "cosmic powers of this present darkness," and "spiritual forces of evil in heavenly places" (Eph 6:12). The dragon—a dark spiritual entity—fuels Rome's debauchery, and ultimately it is the dragon that must be defeated if humanity is to be freed from its sinful enslaving power and allurement. This early articulation of the Christus Victor soteriological outlook anticipated God's people following the path of Jesus in the way that they conquer, as reflected in Revelation 12:11: "But they have conquered him [the dragon] by the blood of the Lamb and by the word of their testimony, for they did not cling to life even in the face of death." In the theology of Revelation, it is the people of the Lamb, following the way of the Lamb in being faithful witnesses, even to the point of death, who defeat the power of evil and not the taking up of arms. The faithful witness of the church, characterized by its allegiance to the kingdom of God and his Messiah, reveals the lame grandiosity of Rome and any other imperial pretender. In this light, the beauty and truth of the Lamb can be seen.

A part of the counterintuitive message that Revelation offers is that it is a faithful witness that defeats the antihuman, anti-God forces that stand behind human malevolent actors in a way that militaristic violence never can. The two witnesses from 11:1–14 personify this point. As they remain faithful even unto death, their persecutors turn into those who "gave glory to the God of heaven." On this pericope, N. T. Wright has explained,

> Now—this is the part which many find particularly difficult—it appears that the "two witnesses" of verses 3–13 *are a symbol for*

29 Bauckham, "Christian War Scroll," 20–21 (emphasis original).

> *the whole church in its prophetic witness, its faithful death, and its vindication by God.* The church as a whole is symbolized by the "lampstands," as in 1.20. The church is to prophesy, "clothed in sackcloth" as a sign of mourning for the wickedness of the world and the evil that it will bring on itself.[30]

Going on, he notes the impact that is "the result will be that the world, looking on, will at last be converted."[31] McKnight, in agreement, puts it this way: "John sees a vision that paints the story of persecution as one leading to *gospeling* and *conversions* of the church's oppressors."[32]

The missional invitation of Revelation is clear. Following the way of the slaughtered Lamb, even unto death, as faithful witnesses is the corporal means that God's people are invited to partner with him to bring in the nations until he ushers in the time of the new heavens and the new earth. It is an invitation to emulate the Lamb.

## Warnings Against Conformity

Once one is able to hear Revelation's political critique of Rome and its invitation to emulation, its *missional political theology* also becomes clear. The missional political aim of Revelation is for the kingdom of this world, which was represented by the corrupt, violently oppressive, and blasphemous Roman Empire, to become the kingdom of our Lord. The theology that is supposed to shape the strategy of that mission is the life of Jesus, who performed his duty as Messiah, taking on and defeating the enemies of God's people, not as a lion but as a lamb. In other words, the church's mission toward an all-encompassing kingdom should not resemble Rome's way of pursuing that mission. Revelation, in this respect, is a religiopolitical critique of a strategy that seemed very reasonable, effective, and powerful to all other empires of the world that have come, gone, and are at work now.

The earliest centuries of the church took up this challenge, imperfectly, of course. Nonetheless, they grasped at the counterintuitive missional political vision from a kingdom not of this world, articulated a gospel that reflected it, and perplexed outsiders by it. Articulating this perplexity with a poignant political nod, Origen explained early in the second century, "At the coming of [Joshua], the walls of Jericho were overthrown; at the coming of my

30 Wright, *Revelation*, 38.

31 Wright, 38.

32 McKnight, *Revelation for the Rest of Us*, 163 (emphasis original).

Lord Jesus, the world is overcome."[33] For Origen and the earliest Christians, the cross was still a symbol of the Lamb overthrowing the dragon in an unexpected way, as it was in Revelation. Reflecting this understanding, he preached,

> The cross of our Lord Jesus Christ was twofold. Perhaps to you it seems an astonishing and novel word that I say, "The cross was twofold," that is, it is twofold and for a double reason. For the Son of God was indeed visibly crucified in the flesh, but invisibly on that cross the Devil "with his principalities and authorities was affixed to the cross."[34]

Alas, this was not to last. The cross became a symbol that was incorporated into the Roman way of conquest. This is perhaps best illustrated by Eusebius's account of Constantine's vision of conquest that involved the cross. Eusebius recounted, "Around noontime, when the day was already beginning to decline, he saw before him in the sky the sign of a cross of light. He said it was above the sun and it bore the inscription, 'Conquer with this.'"[35] The form of conquest that Constantine engaged in involved bloody warfare, which led Christian theology down a path of developing missiologies that tried to blend the salvation of the Lamb with the methods of the beast and the dragon. As Wright has noted, "There have been, down the years, plenty of lion-Christians. Yes, they think, Jesus died for us; but now God's will is to be done in the lionlike fashion, through brute force and violence, to make the world come into line, to enforce God's will."[36]

Much of Western Christianity has suffered from this blended missiology. As the number of Christians has decreased in the United States and is on the decline in the Western world, it could lead one to wonder if Jesus is standing at our door, warning that he will remove our lampstand if we don't repent of a conformed-to-this-world missiology at home, which trusts more in political power than emulating the Lamb as faithful, true witnesses.

To believe that God desires to convert the nations through faithful lamblike witness is a test of faith for those who are seated in the heart of empire with incredible power at their disposal. The method of engagement seems like tools appropriate for the weak and those experiencing life from the "underside"

---

33 Magree, "Nonviolent Christ at the Apocalyptic Center," 516.

34 Magree, 518.

35 Eusebius, *Essential Eusebius*, 184.

36 Wright, *Revelation*, 26.

of history. However, Revelation asks us to take on the garb of the lowly, the posture of the weak, and a missiological perspective that flows more naturally from the underside in order to experience the power of the Lamb to convert the nations. In counterintuitive fashion, Bauckham reminds us,

> There is, therefore, a sense in which Revelation takes a view from the "underside of history," from the perspective of the victims of Rome's power and glory. It takes this perspective not because John and his Christian readers necessarily belonged to the classes that suffered rather than shared Rome's power and prosperity. It takes this perspective because if they are faithful in their witness to the true God, their opposition to Rome's oppression and their dissociation of themselves from Rome's evil will make them victims of Rome in solidarity with other victims of Rome. The special significance of Christian martyrdom is that it makes the issue clear. Those who bear witness to the one true God, the only true absolute to whom all political power is subject, expose Rome's idolatrous self-deification for what it is.[37]

The power of the Lamb to conquer is located among the underside of history where few would think to look for the powerful; yet Revelation reveals that following the path of the Lamb leads to an everlasting kingdom—a kingdom with an actual omnipotent power source that Rome and all its progeny could only wish for.

## Bibliography

Appian. *The Civil Wars*, vol. 3 of *Roman History*. Translated by Horace White. Loeb Classical Library 4. Harvard University Press, 1913.

Aune, E. David. *Revelation 6–16*. World Biblical Commentary 52B. Zondervan, 1998.

Bauckham, Richard. *Bible and Mission: Christian Witness in a Postmodern World*. Baker Academic, 2003.

Bauckham, Richard. "The Book of Revelation as a Christian War Scroll." *Neotestamentica* 22, no. 1 (1998): 17–40.

Bauckham, Richard. *The Theology of the Book of Revelation*. Cambridge University Press, 1993.

Blount, Brian K. *Can I Get a Witness? Reading Revelation Through African American Culture*. Westminster John Knox, 2005.

37 Bauckham, *Theology of the Book*, 39.

Brooks-Janvier, Jessica. "The Essence of Antebellum Afro-Evangelicalism: A Reading of the Evangelical Tradition Through the Paradigm of African American Religion." PhD diss., Columbia International University, 2023. ProQuest Dissertations & Theses Global.

Christopher, Kelly. *The Roman Empire: A Very Short Introduction*. Oxford University Press, 2006.

Collins, Adela Yarbro. "The Political Perspective of the Revelation to John." *Journal of Biblical Literature* 96, no. 6 (1977): 241–56.

Collins, John. *Semeia 14: Apocalypse; The Morphology of a Genre*. Society of Biblical Literature, 1979.

Eusebius. *The Essential Eusebius*. Translated by Colm Luibheid. New American Library, 1966.

Gorman, Michael J. *Reading Revelation Responsibly: Uncivil Worship and Witness; Following the Lamb into the New Creation*. Wipf & Stock, 2011.

Keener, Craig. *Revelation*. NIV Application Commentary. Zondervan, 2000.

Magree, Michael C. "The Nonviolent Christ at the Apocalyptic Center of Origen's Homilies on Joshua." *Theological Studies* 83, no. 3 (2023): 501–18.

McKnight, Scot. *Revelation for the Rest of Us: A Prophetic Call to Follow Jesus as a Dissident Disciple*. Zondervan, 2023.

Meggitt, Justin. "Taking the Emperor's Clothes Seriously: The New Testament and the Roman Emperor." In *The Quest for Wisdom: Essays in Honour of Philip Budd*. Orchard Academic, 2002.

Taubes, Jacob. "Theology and Political Theory." *Social Research* 22, no. 1 (1955): 57–68.

Witherington, Ben, III. *Revelation*. New Cambridge Bible Commentary. Cambridge University Press, 2003.

Wright, N. T. *Revelation for Everyone*. Westminster John Knox, 2011.

Part 3

# The Missionary Methods of Revelation

# Chapter 9

# Worship, Discipleship, and Politics in Revelation

## Asian Perspectives

*Kwa Kiem-Kiok*

### Introduction and Framing the Issues

Revelation does not seem to be an obvious source for guidance on how Christians can engage in politics and the public square today.[1] To find such answers, one could more obviously look at the Old Testament prophets or how Jesus related to the Roman authorities. After all, politics is about our lives in this world here and now, the activities of governing lives in this world, and how our societies are organized and run. In Asia where I am situated, few Christians would be involved in the grubby world of politics because that would mean compromising one's Christian principles. Revelation, as is popularly thought, is otherworldly, addressing only matters of the distant future. The fantastic imagery replete in the book, as well as its nonlinear narrative style, make it difficult to understand, let alone apply meaningfully in our context today. Reading through Revelation, themes such as worship or suffering may come more readily to mind. Hence, Revelation and the world of politics are far apart. While much can be drawn from other parts of Scripture to inform us on the topic of Christians and politics, in this chapter we shall seek to bridge the gap between Revelation and politics with three interconnected themes—context, worship, and discipleship.

While generally defined as an apocalypse, which refers to what is to happen at the end of time, Revelation is also an epistle, a letter written to the believers in the seven churches in Asia Minor (Rev 1:9–3:22).[2] That audience and context shall thus guide our reading and application today. Since the Christian community exists in time and space, the location of the community will affect the reading and interpretation of the text, just as Revelation was written to a specific audience at a particular time.[3] A guiding principle for what the book means today will flow from John's vision as a "clarion call to

---

1 We shall draw out the difference between politics and the public square later in this chapter. For now, we will use the terms somewhat interchangeably.

2 Scripture from NIV unless otherwise stated.

3 See, for example, Lee, "Fire from Their Mouths," 207–37.

the followers of Jesus to live their lives as faithful citizens of New Jerusalem in the midst of their fallen Babylon world."[4]

Scenes of heavenly worship (chs. 4, 7, 19, 21) dominate John's vision, and all that happens in the vision centers around God's throne room. The worship of the one who sits on the heavenly throne must certainly affect and impact the daily lives of believers, the first readers then, and us today. Therefore, reading Revelation enables us to know how to live out our faith and deepens our understanding of discipleship. More than merely needing to "read the Bible and pray every day"[5] we shall see that discipleship includes involvement in the wider society, including the political realm. That does not necessarily mean standing for political office, but the context and our worship of God should determine how that political or public involvement will look for our faith communities.

Hence, the three areas of context, worship, and discipleship will be explored in this chapter. These are not three neat and discrete categories; they overlap and influence one another.

This is where a missional reading of the text guides us. A missional hermeneutic sees the Bible as a whole story of God's mission in and for the whole world.[6] Christopher Wright likens a missional hermeneutic to a map of the Bible that sets out the major features of the story of God's mission as well as connects that larger panorama with some of the less-trodden paths.[7] As Dean Fleming writes specifically with reference to this book, "Revelation beckons God's people to embrace God's great purposes for God's creation (God's mission) and to bear prophetic witness to that redeeming mission, with our lips and with our lives."[8] The *missio Dei*, the mission of God, starts with God's self-revelation as the one who loves the world and "is the nature and activity of God, which embraces both church and the world. . . . *Missio Dei* enunciates the good news that God is a God-for-people."[9] God is always reaching out to his people—even in the garden of Eden when Adam and Eve hid from God after eating the prohibited fruit, he reached out to them, and asked "Where are you?" (Gen 3:9). The local Christian community is those who are then "called into and caught up in" that *missio Dei.*[10]

4 Mulholland, "Revelation," 413.

5 The words of a popular children's Sunday school song.

6 See Hunsberger's helpful description and outline of missional hermeneutics in his "Proposals for a Missional Hermeneutic," 309–21.

7 Wright, *Mission of God*, 68–69.

8 Fleming, *Foretaste of the Future*, 22.

9 Bosch, *Transforming Mission*, 10.

10 Michael Barram as quoted in Hunsberger, "Proposals for a Missional Hermeneutic," 314.

In Revelation, John sees a vision of a great multitude who gather to worship God (7:9–17). There will be judgment of the devil and the dead when the book of life is opened (20:7–15), the marriage supper of the Lamb, which is the union between Christ and the church, and a new heaven and a new earth (21). This is the culmination of the *missio Dei* as God brings all creation to himself in the new heaven and new earth. The missiological task from now until then is to partner with God in that task.

Revelation was written in the first century to the seven churches in what we now call Asia Minor. What does the book say to believers today, especially those in Asia, particularly in the twenty-first century, regarding political engagement?

## The Context of the Audience and the Social Milieu of Revelation

John is writing specifically to the believers in "the seven churches in the province of Asia" (1:4). These first-century believers were small faith communities in the Roman Empire. And yet John sees a vision of "a great multitude that no one could count, from every nation, tribe, people and language, standing before the throne and before the Lamb" (7:9) worshiping God. For those small numbers of believers in the first century, that vision of a great multitude would be beyond imagining.

Furthermore, John sees this multitude as multicultural—from "every nation, tribe, people, and language." On the day when all believers throughout time will worship before the throne of God, human cultures, without their sinful dimensions, will be seen. Language, physical characteristics such as skin color, hair texture, shibboleths, and costume are among the cultural features that will be there. Therefore, in mission and ministry today, we do not seek to erase local cultures but rather affirm the good in them. Our discipleship should both reflect our cultural forms as well as challenge them, and that discipleship includes Christian witness in the public square.[11]

The affirmation of culture comes from our Lord himself. When "the Word became flesh and made his dwelling among us . . . full of grace and truth" (John 1:14), God, in Jesus, became a first-century Jewish male, bound in that culture. In the incarnation, God affirmed the worth of human culture. The incarnation is thus a model for us today to embody God's love concretely and specifically in mission and ministry. However, that does not mean that

11 As suggested by Hwa's definition of contextualization in *Mangoes or Bananas?*, 13–14.

every aspect of cultures is good and God-honoring; rather, Christians need to do, as Hiebert suggests, critical contextualization, that is Christians need to exegete their culture, exegete scripture, and then build hermeneutical bridges between the two.[12]

Today, Asian Christians in this diverse continent do such contextualizing when they grapple with the theological, ethical, and practical issues that we face. Recent publications from the Asia Theological Association reflect the diversity of issues and concerns. For example, the Asia Bible Commentary Series is written by Asian scholars for this context, while *Asian Christian Ethics: Evangelical Perspectives*[13] discusses issues such as family relationships, corruption and bribery, and creation care. All these are steps taken to contextualize the faith and will help the maturing of the Asian Christian church.

One area that Asian Christians need to grapple with is their role in the public or political realm. In this regard, Peñamora suggests that when we see God as Lord over our public spaces, the kingdom "must be characterized by certain values and performative actions, such as those displayed by Jesus in the Markan account of the temple-cleansing incident."[14] When building bridges between the text and the context, those actions will be different when carried out in India or Indonesia. But all believers everywhere are challenged in their worship and discipleship to work out what would be meaningful in their situations.

## Worship

Today, we have reduced the concept of "worship" to a few hours spent in church on Sundays. Sometimes we are even more narrow and refer to congregational singing as worship. Revelation 4 and 7 challenge such thin definitions. John sees a vision of God full of symbolism. Kraybill writes, "Human experience of the divine usually involves symbol or icon, since that is the primary way mortals apprehend transcendent reality."[15] John's vision is of God who sits on a glorious throne in heaven with a rainbow shining like an emerald encircled and from which came flashes of lightning and rumblings (4:2–6). He is surrounded by twenty-four elders with crowns of gold on their heads. There are also four fantastical living creatures who give glory, honor, and thanks to him, and elders who bow down and worship him and sing his glory (4:6b–11): "You are worthy, our Lord and God, to receive glory and honor and power, for you created all

12 Hiebert, "Critical Contextualization," 1–13.

13 Peñamora and Wong, *Asian Christian Ethics.*

14 Peñamora, "God's Basileia in Asia's Res Publica," 260.

15 Kraybill, *Apocalypse and Allegiance*, 85.

things." The Lamb who is seated on the throne is worthy to be praised and worshiped; he was slaughtered and reveals the

> paradox of God's plan to redeem creation. God's fullest self-revelation has not come with brawn and bluster to match the muscle of Rome, but with the seeming weakness and vulnerability of a Lamb. . . . This Lamb is worthy of praise, not just by the heavenly court, but also all of creation.[16]

In Revelation 7, there is the symbolic number of 144,000 people who were sealed, who are from the tribes of Israel (v. 4), gathered with a great multitude that no one could count from "every nation, tribe, people, and language" (v. 9), singing praise to God and the Lamb for their salvation. Since this God is the one enthroned and sovereign, everything else pales. God's throne is in heaven and therefore over all that God has created.

The throne is a symbol of authority and power, which is still meaningful and relevant today. That God is on the throne is a strong emphasis of his rule and sovereignty. This is especially seen in God's relationship to the rebellious realm. In Revelation, God is always pictured as sovereign over fallen Babylon, the beast and false prophet, Satan, and the whole realm of evil; in the same way, by faith Christians today affirm that God is over rulers, tyrants, and even oppressive systems.

Therefore, true worship inculcates a sense of awe and wonder in the worshiper, that is, a sense of both distance from and proximity to God. Worship in church should therefore reflect all the truths about God. Before this portrait of the most majestic throne room of all, "the emperor's claims fade into absurdity, and worshipping Christians find the strength to withstand the falsehood of the emperor's claims."[17] That is, when we fully worship God this way, we are saying that we do not pay allegiance to Caesar. These political perspectives flow from the worship of God because "worship is inherently political."[18]

The challenge for all churches is to build that excitement, awe, and worth of God in the weekly worship services, whether in a megachurch in Singapore or in a rural house church in China. Furthermore, God's sovereignty means his justice prevails, if not in the present age, then in the age to come. That knowledge gives believers today who are facing injustice or persecution comfort and hope.[19] In John's vision, for justice to be truly done, it must be

16 Kraybill, 98–99.

17 Keener cited in Witherington, *Revelation*, 123.

18 Flemming, *Foretaste of the Future*, 163.

19 Witherington, *Revelation*, 124–25.

seen to be done in or at the end of human history. Kraybill rightly points out that "heartfelt worship is vital in order to maintain hope amid adversity, and praise builds allegiance to the God who provides salvation."[20]

Josh Butler argues that worship in Revelation 4 is also a "theopolitical encounter."[21] By this he means that "worship thus orients the worshipping community's vision for the public life of the world around the kingdom reign of God."[22] God's throne in heaven affirms, against the powers of Rome, that the earth is the Lord's and all that is in it. God's throne is not just about the reality of his reign but his character as well. This means that when Christians proclaim God's character—his justice, mercy, love, and compassion—they worship him. And then, flowing out of worship of this God, we live out these qualities in our everyday lives. Those actions would have wider social repercussions. For example, by caring for and including the disabled within our faith communities, Christians are challenging the prevailing societal norms that marginalize the disabled and give them little human worth and dignity.

## Discipleship

Even as God is worshiped in the heavens, Jesus Christ is portrayed as walking in the midst of the churches, walking among the lampstands that are the churches.[23] He is near. Jesus Christ is the center of the book: It is "the revelation from Jesus Christ" (1:1), the one "who is and who was, and who is to come" (1:4), and who is among the golden lampstands that are the seven churches (1:13). He is the Alpha and Omega who is coming again soon (22:20). It is Christ's death that is the "fulcrum and turning point in human history and in particular between good and evil."[24] As followers and worshipers of this Christ, then, discipleship is following Christ in all aspects of our lives. As Mulholland puts it, the basic thrust of the vision is not orthodoxy but orthopraxy.[25]

The themes of discipleship are seen not only in the worship scenes but also in and through what God has done, is doing, and will ultimately consummate in and through Jesus, and God's action through the Messiah in and through the new Jerusalem, which is John's image for the realm of God's

20 Kraybill, *Apocalypse and Allegiance*, 106.

21 Butler, "Politics of Worship," 7–12.

22 Butler, 7.

23 Witherington, *Revelation*, 124–25.

24 Witherington, 125–26.

25 Mulholland, "Revelation," 413.

people and a synonym for God's kingdom of priests.[26] Therefore, Christians today can live as faithful members of God's realm in the midst of a world in rebellion against God. It is by holding right beliefs and manifesting the fruits of faithful discipleship.

In many Asian churches today, discipleship is largely a private matter—it is seen as my personal salvation and walk with God; and there is little concern for how that discipleship influences my life in general and the issues facing society. A missiological reading of Revelation emphasizes that discipleship must encompass all of life, because Jesus is Lord over all aspects of life, including commerce and politics. This is depicted in worshipers casting their crowns before God (4:10), acknowledging that human achievements are nothing before God. Christians may be wary of consciously participating in politics, but living out their Christian faith in the day-to-day would have public and political implications. Faithful discipleship entails missional engagement with the prevailing culture, the need to at times follow cultural movements and at other times be countercultural (Matt 5:16–17).

The reality is that discipleship is costly and may lead to martyrdom, because John saw "under the altar the souls of those who had been slain because of the word of God and the testimony they had maintained. They cried out in a loud voice, 'How long, Sovereign Lord, holy and true, until you judge the inhabitants of the earth and avenge our blood?'" (Rev 6:9–10). Church history attests to this; to this day, believers are persecuted for their faith. Martyrdom is a reality faced by believers in some parts of Asia. Martyrdom can also be a form of witness. Lee suggests that the two witnesses in Revelation 11:3–13 are witnesses in a time of persecution, and their public witness "encourages the church that they are able to complete their task of witnessing to the world despite severe opposition and persecution, because *God will protect and empower them*."[27] This is an encouraging word for all Christians in that situation today.

Though right now we live in a broken and sinful world, Revelation looks forward to the fulfillment of the kingdom of God, the wedding supper of the Lamb and his bride, the new heaven and the new earth. This "New Jerusalem is a realm in which human beings find cleansing from sin, liberation from destructive bondages, healing of woundedness, wholeness for their brokenness, and transformation from death to life."[28]

---

26 Mulholland, 412.

27 Lee, "Fire from Their Mouths," 221 (emphasis original).

28 Mulholland, "Revelation," 412–23.

## Missional Reading

A missional reading of the text can be the glue that brings worship and discipleship together. As mentioned above, the *missio Dei* is God's mission of drawing all people to himself. He does that in many ways, supremely through the sending of Jesus Christ, his Son: "God so loved the world that he gave his one and only Son, that whoever believes in him shall not perish but have eternal life" (John 3:16). The assurance of God's throne in heaven and his presence and salvation through Jesus Christ is the impetus for Christian engagement in politics and the public sphere.

Flemming writes: "Mission in a biblical understanding represents the very opposite of cultural imperialism. It is about getting caught up in God's healing, reconciling, and liberating purposes for all the peoples of the world."[29] This means that mission in each context will have its unique flavors, though there may be some commonalities across different contexts. For example, in Asia, many schools and hospitals of good repute and standing today were started by Christian missionaries in the nineteenth century. The Christian Medical College, Vellore in Tamil Nadu, India, was founded in 1900 by American missionary Dr. Ida Scudder when she heard that three women died in childbirth in one night because there was no woman doctor for them. She became a doctor and first practiced out of her father's bungalow. She eventually started training for nurses and later doctors and setting up roadside dispensaries.[30] This may seem like merely providing needed medical care. But such action, at a time when women had little dignity and worth, giving them medical care and eventually medical training certainly disrupted the status quo and changed their standing at home and in the community. Here is an illustration of God's liberating purpose in that society with political implications.

## Public, Political, and Prophetic Dimensions

The public sphere refers to all matters that happen in the public square, ranging from caring for shared communal facilities in a neighborhood to discussing ideas on public platforms. In this space, Christians, as individuals or a local church, seek to build the common good and a robust and mature public theology that will help Christians engage meaningfully in their context. Such involvement is necessary as a means for Christians to bear witness to

29 Fleming, *Foretaste of the Future*, 7.

30 Wilson, "Scudder, Ida Sophia."

their faith. It is also a public proclamation, by word and deed, and so must be in language and forms that are understandable to the wider society. For example, when Christians take part in caring for the environment, they are proclaiming the worth of the creation, their worship of a Creator, and that they are stewards of creation. All these are usually proclaimed indirectly, but that may be necessary and appropriate in societies where there cannot be direct or overt speaking of Christian values in public. Such actions can then be a platform for further conversation about Christian worldviews.

Christian discipleship has a public dimension. That is, as believers live out their faith where they are, their faith will make an impact in the wider society. That is the effect of being salt and light (Matt 5:13–16). Public engagement is contextual: Christians in secular South Korea can do more in public spaces than Christians in Thailand because they have larger numbers and more clout. But Christians in both countries seek to live out their faith in their own cultures and sociopolitical and economic realities and to transform society and individuals.[31] In many contexts, public engagement is also prophetic in the sense that it means speaking Christian truth and values into that society, what German theologian Johannes Reimer would call "participatory involvement" in a context.[32] Creation care in a wasteful, throwaway consumeristic culture would be an example of such prophetic proclamation.

Political involvement can be more narrowly defined. The *Oxford Learner's Dictionary* defines politics as "the activities in getting and using power in public life to influence decisions that affect a society or country."[33] More than engaging in public spaces, in politics there is the added dimension of power; and Christians and the church have a complex relationship with power.[34] Political involvement includes voting in an election, joining a political party, and standing for political office. Indeed, for Christians who live in functional democracies, where the wishes of the citizens are respected, the simple act of casting a vote is powerful. All Christians everywhere should exercise their right to vote and do so wisely and prayerfully. The opportunity to vote in clean and fair elections is a privilege that should not be taken lightly.

31 Hwa, *Mangoes or Bananas?*, 13–14.

32 Reimer, *Missio Politica*, 85–89.

33 *Oxford Learner's Dictionary*, "Politics," accessed October 16, 2024, https://www.oxfordlearnersdictionaries.com/definition/english/politics?q=politics.

34 See, for example, Wright and Bird, *Jesus and the Powers*, where the authors, both biblical scholars, address the question of how Christians can engage with politics while remaining true to the teaching and example of Jesus.

**Public Engagement in the Asian Context**

The Constantinian model of the Western church has influenced many churches in Asia. Thus, some Christians believe that when a Christian holds high political office, they can influence society with Christian values, however those values are defined. This is seen as an ideal way to build a Christian society. However, as the church in Asia matures, it is more aware of the Asian geopolitical and sociocultural contexts and realizes that a different approach is needed. In Asia, the call is for a church that is numerically small and weak with little public influence to be salt and light in a society where another religion dominates; and it is possibly also where the public square is perceived to be corrupt and hence should be avoided. There is a growing realization that the Asian church needs to develop its own models and principles for public engagement. Scripture and the Christian tradition must certainly guide the Asian church in this task.

The praxis circle, first developed by South African theologian J. N. J. Kritzinger, illustrates how these dimensions of context, worship, and discipleship flow together into a *missio politica* as Reimer suggests.[35] Reimer uses this cycle to illustrate how to develop a contextual theology of political involvement. I have added in uppercase the themes of context, worship, and discipleship discussed here to show the overlap of ideas and how these themes have a public and political dimension.

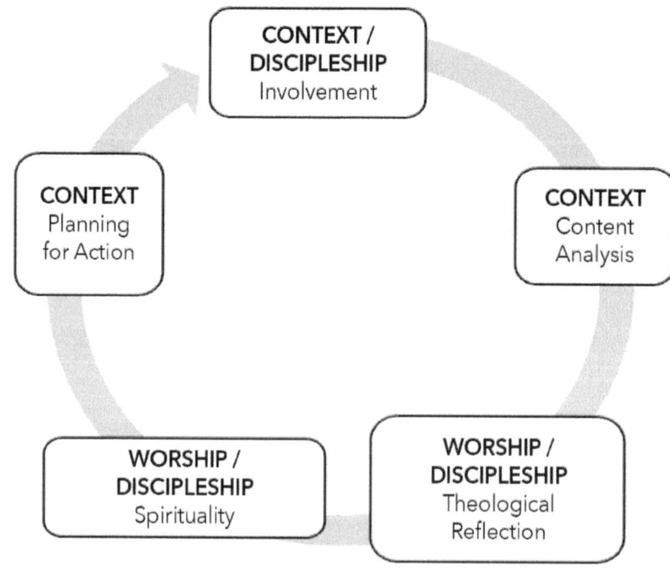


**Figure 9.1. Reimer's *Missio Politica Cycle***

35 Reimer, *Missio Politica* (my words overlay the model in uppercase letters).

**Politics and Public Engagement**

The public square in many Asian societies presents some unique challenges for Christian engagement. Many societies have a religious overlay—Islam in Malaysia and Indonesia, and Hinduism in India—which affects the place and position of Christians and the church and hence their engagement. Other countries, like South Korea, Taiwan, Singapore, and Japan, are secular societies with more or less functional democracies where adult citizens can vote. In some parts of Asia, there is overt persecution of Christians, where injustice and a culture of violence are part of the Asian lived experience. Peñamora suggests that in Jesus's act of cleansing the temple (Mark 11:15–17), his "defense of the rights of Gentiles in the sacred public space of the Jerusalem temple, . . . [shows] that for him, God is not only Lord of our private places, but he is also Lord over all that is public, and, indeed, over all creation."[36]

In those Asian societies that are more open, Agnes Chiu's suggestions of three principles for public theology could be helpful.[37] In practicing public theology, she suggests that Christians should be open to pluralism, be open to scrutiny, and speak a common language of shared values with others in their community. To these I would add that Christians need to have a clear idea of what they seek to achieve by such engagement. Is it to present a Christian voice and worldview on the issue, whatever the outcome? Or is it to endeavor to make the policy more aligned with Christian principles? If it is the latter, then how far will they go to make that happen? These call for a mature discipleship that can be reflexive and flexible. For example, in the casino debate in Singapore in 2005–2006, Christians and other civil society groups spoke up against building a casino in Singapore. Eventually, despite the opposition, the government decided to build two casinos, so, in one sense, Christians lost the debate. But in another sense, Christians had opportunities to articulate their vision for the public good and welfare of society.

The Malaysian movement Bersih (a Malay word meaning "clean"), which lobbied for clean and fair elections in that country, is one example of knowing what the issues are that citizens wish to fight for and not campaigning for any political party. In November 2007, its objectives led thousands of Malaysians to demonstrate for justice in the electoral process. Many Christians took part in this movement, even though it was not overtly Christian.

36 Peñamora, "God's Basileia in Asia's Res Publica," 260.

37 Chiu, "Prophetic Voice in the Wilderness," 217–34.

In many Asian countries, engagement takes the form of providing social services such as schools or hospitals, sometimes to particular groups like women or migrant workers, who are generally overlooked by society. These ideas tie in well with the point that when Christians worship Yahweh, they will act in ways that demonstrate his character and the values of his kingdom.

There could be a difference in whether individual Christians engage, for example, in their personal capacity or whether the institutional church engages publicly. Where the Christian church is not a legal entity, such as in Pakistan or Laos, it will be up to individual Christians to be witnesses where they are. In other societies, like South Korea and Indonesia, Christians may join a political party, and the church may make statements or engage actively in the public square. Where they have it, Christians should always exercise their right to vote and do so wisely and prayerfully, voting for those who stand for justice and decency for all.

**Religion in the Public Square**

In many societies in Asia, the question whether religion should be in the public square is a thorny one. When religion and politics mingle, political leaders use religion to achieve their political objectives. For example, in Malaysia and Indonesia, Islam is woven into politics and government, while in India, the present prime minister heads a Hindu nationalist political party. Since there is not always a separation of religion and politics, Christian witness in the public square has to be "shrewd as snakes and as innocent as doves" (Matt 10:16). Often, since other religions are present in the public spaces, Christianity is excluded. Even so, Christians can still be a witness, for example, by providing social services that are open to all but reflect Christian virtues of love, kindness, and generosity in ways that could be a profound witness.

In some secular democracies, like Singapore, religion is assiduously kept out of the secular public square. This is to ensure that public space is not influenced by religious views, which are sometimes perceived to be arbitrary. And yet, even in Singapore, about 80 percent of the population follows a religion, and it is not fair to completely exclude religious perspectives from the public square. After all, religion shapes worldviews and will be brought to bear in how citizens engage in the public square. Following the character of Jesus, who lived in this world full of grace and truth, Christians should find ways to engage gracefully and truthfully in their contexts. In some situations, it could mean speaking a language that is commonly accessible to people so that they are persuaded by our arguments. In other contexts, it may mean that one's faith is not directly seen but perceived through our words, actions, and attitudes. Mature Christian discipleship means that we need to discern what the best approaches are in the context and for that situation.

## Conclusion

Discipleship involves living out our Christian faith. When we face uncertainties, questions, or challenges in life, we can be tempted to either ignore them or bury our heads in the sand and wish they would go away. Reading Revelation challenges these stances. Indeed, as we have shown, in Revelation, Christians who wholeheartedly worship God in word and deed will find that they are witnesses in this bleak and volatile world with wars, a crumbling world order, and the pressures brought on by climate change. We suggest here that cultivating deep roots in our context, deepening our worship, and broadening our understanding of discipleship will equip Christians and our faith communities today to better live out the public dimensions of our faith. And as we embody that hope, we are bearing witness to the Christ "who is and was and who is to come."

## Bibliography

Bosch, David J. *Transforming Mission: Paradigm Shifts in Theology of Mission*. Orbis Books, 1991.

Butler, Josh. "The Politics of Worship: Revelation 4 as Theopolitical Encounter." *Culture Encounters* 5, no. 2 (2009): 7–23.

Chiu, Agnes. "A Prophetic Voice in the Wilderness: Church, Political Engagement, and Public Theology." In *Asian Christian Ethics: Evangelical Perspectives*, edited by Aldrin Peñamora and Bernard K. Wong. Langham Global Library, 2022.

Flemming, Dean. *Foretaste of the Future: Reading Revelation in Light of God's Mission*. IVP Academic, 2022.

Hiebert, Paul G. "Critical Contextualisation." *International Bulletin of Missionary Research* 11, no. 3 (1987): 104–12.

Hunsberger, George R. "Proposals for a Missional Hermeneutic: Mapping a Conversation." *Missiology* 39, no. 3 (2011): 309–21.

Hwa, Yung. *Mangoes or Bananas? The Quest for an Authentic Asian Christian Theology*. Regnum Books, 1997.

Kraybill, Nelson J. *Apocalypse and Allegiance: Worship, Politics, and Devotion in the Book of Revelation*. Brazos, 2010.

Lee, Chee-Chiew. "'Fire from Their Mouths': The Power of Witnessing in the Face of Hostility and Suffering (Rev 11:3–13)." *CTTS Journal* 4 (2013): 207–37.

Mulholland, M. Robert, Jr. "Revelation." In *James, 1–2 Peter, Jude, Revelation*, edited by Philip W. Comfort. Cornerstone Biblical Commentary. Tyndale House, 2011.

Peñamora, Aldrin M. "God's Basileia in Asia's Res Publica: Situating the Sacred in Asia's Public Sphere." In *Asian Christian Theology: Evangelical Perspectives*, edited by Timeteo D. Gener and Stephen T. Pardue. Langham Global Library, 2019.

Peterson, Eugene H. *Reversed Thunder: The Revelation of God and the Praying Imagination*. HarperSanFrancisco, 1988.

Reimer, Johannes. *Missio Politica: The Mission of Church and Politics*. Langham Global Library, 2017.

Wilson, Dorothy Clarke. "Scudder, Ida Sophia." In *Biographical Dictionary of Christian Missions*, edited by Gerald H. Anderson. Accessed October 16, 2024. https://www.bu.edu/missiology/missionary-biography/r-s/scudder-ida-sophia-1870–1960/.

Witherington, Ben, III. *Revelation*. New Cambridge Bible Commentary. Cambridge University Press, 2003.

Wright, Christopher J. H. *The Mission of God: Unlocking the Bible's Grand Narrative*. IVP Academic, 2006.

Wright, Tom, and Michael F. Bird. *Jesus and the Powers: Christian Political Witness in an Age of Totalitarian Terror and Dysfunctional Democracies*. SPCK, 2024.

# Chapter 10

# Exploring the Role of God's People as Witnesses to the Nations and Its Missiological Implications for Today

*Narry F. Santos*

God has called his people to become his witnesses to all the nations.[1] Revelation showcases rich expressions of this call for the church. In this chapter, we will explore the role of God's people as witnesses using the fourfold formula (i.e., every nation, tribe, language, and people) that represents all the nations as the scope of Christian witness. We will also reflect missiologically on the church's role as it relates to our mission today.

## Overview of the Fourfold Formula in Revelation

John's use of the fourfold formula of "nation [*ethnos*], tribe [*fulē*], language [*glōssa*], and people [*laos*]" occurs seven times in Revelation (5:9; 7:9; 10:11; 11:9; 13:7; 14:6; 17:15).[2] Five of these instances refer to the same four terms but in different order, as seen in the following usage: (1) every "tribe and language and people and nation"[3] in 5:9c; (2) every "nation, tribe, people and language" in 7:9b; (3) every "people, tribe, language and nation" in 11:9a; (4) every "tribe, people, language and nation" in 13:7b; and (5) every "nation, tribe, language and people" in 14:6b.

For the other two instances, the formula is also fourfold, but one word is exchanged for another; thus, we see the following: (1) many "peoples, nations, languages and kings [*basileusin*]"[4] in 10:11b; and (2) "peoples, multitudes [*ochloi*], nations and languages"[5] in 17:15b. These last two instances also employ a different word order and replace a different term for the word "tribes." Despite the differences in word order and the replacement of one word, what remains unchanged is the repeated use of a fourfold formula. John's use of this formula throughout Revelation (occurring seven times, which

1 For global perspective on God's mission, see Ott, *Church on Mission*.

2 Osborne uses the phrase "fourfold formula" as a reference to the nations (*Revelation*, 26). However, although Miller recognizes the inclusive elements in the use of the four terms together, he does not see their use as formulaic ("Mission in Revelation," 237).

3 Unless otherwise specified, the Scripture quotations in this chapter are from the NIV.

4 In Revelation 10:11, the term "kings" replaces the word "tribes."

5 In Revelation 17:15, the term "multitudes" replaces the word "tribes."

may connote the concept of completeness[6]) stresses the idea of universality[7] and the inclusive scope of the formulaic expression as a reference to "all the nations."[8] Such inclusion directly relates to the global nature of God's people as global witnesses who are on mission from a global God.[9]

In addition to the fourfold formula, the different terms in the formula are also used separately and with varying frequency ("nation/s" [fifteen times];[10] "tribe/s" [sixteen times];[11] "people" [two times];[12] "language" [none];[13] "king/s" [twenty times];[14] and "multitude/s" [two times].[15] The separate use of these different terms reinforces the universal scope of the church's role as witnesses to all the nations.

## Implications of the Global Nature of God's Mission

There are two implications regarding the global nature of God's mission in Revelation. First, God's people are designed to come from every nation, tribe, language, and people. As Grant R. Osborne comments, "The church is constituted by people drawn from all the nations of the earth."[16] In fact, the number of God's people to be gathered from the nations will be countless:

---

6 Two verses that contain the picture of completeness (through the verb *teleō* [to complete or finish]) being juxtaposed with the number "seven" (i.e., "seven angels" and "seven plagues") are found in 15:1 and 15:8. In addition, the idea of completeness is included in the words "it is done" (16:17b) after the seventh angel poured the seventh bowl into the air (16:17a).

7 Mounce, *Revelation*, 318.

8 Bauckham, *Climax of Prophecy*, 326.

9 For an intercultural perspective on Revelation, see Rhoads, *From Every People and Nation*.

10 The fifteen occurrences when "nation/s" is used separately (i.e., not as part of the fourfold formula) are in 2:26; 11:2, 18; 12:5; 14:8; 15:4; 16:19; 18:3, 23; 19:15; 20:3, 8; 21:24, 26; 22:2.

11 The sixteen occurrences in the separate use of "tribe/s" are in 1:7; 5:5; 7:4, 5 (three times), 6 (three times), 7 (three times), 8 (three times); 21:12. Of these sixteen instances, all but one (1:7 as a reference to the "tribes of the earth") refer to the tribe/s of Israel.

12 The two occurrences in the separate use of "people" are in 18:4 and 21:3, both referring to God's people.

13 Though glossa also occurs in 16:10, its use does refer to "language" but to "tongue" as the physical part of the body.

14 The twenty occurrences in the separate use of "king/s" are in 1:5; 6:15; 9:11; 15:3; 16:12, 14; 17:2, 10, 12 (two times), 14 (two times), 18; 18:3, 9; 19:18 (two times), 19; 21:24. In addition, the related term "kingdom" (*basileia*) occurs eight times (1:6, 9; 5:10; 11:15; 12:10; 16:10; 17:12; 17:17), and the verb "reign" (*basileuō*) occurs eight times (5:10; 11:15, 17; 17:8; 19:6; 20:4, 6; 22:5).

15 The two occurrences in the separate use of "multitude/s" are in 7:9 and 19:1, which refer to a great number of believers standing before the throne and in front of the Lamb (7:9) and a great multitude in heaven (19:1).

16 Osborne, *Revelation*, 260.

"After this I looked, and there before me was a great multitude that no one could count, from every nation, tribe, people and language" (7:9a). In this verse, we see the combination of the fourfold formula ("nation, tribe, people and language") and the word "multitude," emphasizing the innumerability of God's people in the eschaton. The multitude will be gathered from every nation, tribe, language, and people of the earth. Robert H. Mounce highlights this combination of "multitude" and the fourfold formula this way: "The universality of the multitude is stressed by the fourfold division into nations, tribes, peoples, and tongues."[17] In addition, two occurrences in the separate use of "multitude/s" refer to a great number of believers standing before the throne and in front of the Lamb (7:9b) and a great multitude in heaven shouting: "Hallelujah! Salvation and glory and power belong to our God" (19:1).

The second implication of God's global mission is the role of the church from every nation to become witnesses to all the nations in light of God's revelation through Jesus Christ. As Johnny V. Miller states, "The plan of God is to redeem some from every tongue, tribe, people, and nation to his own glory and in praise of his Son."[18] This plan of God is to be fulfilled by the global church. Osborne also emphasizes the value of God's global mission for the church in Revelation through these words: "Every nation continues the stress in the book on the universal mission of the church to the nations."[19] The responses to the testimony of Jesus Christ through the church will be different—some will be converted while others will rebel against God and reject God's people—but the church still needs to proclaim the eternal gospel "to those who live on the earth—to every nation, tribe, language and people" (14:6b).

In John's use of the word "nations" fifteen times throughout the book (aside from its seven occurrences in the fourfold formula), we see the ongoing need for more witnesses among the nations, as seen in the nine occasions when the nations are described negatively: They trample the Holy City (11:2); they are in rage and anger (11:18); they drink the "maddening wine" of Babylon (14:8; 18:3); they collapse (16:19); they are led astray (18:23); they are stricken down (19:15); and they are deceived (20:3, 8). Yet, the witness to the nations is not in vain because the nations are also described positively on four occasions: They worship God (15:4); they are present in the new heaven

17 Mounce, *Revelation*, 171.

18 Miller, "Mission in Revelation," 238.

19 Osborne, *Revelation*, 319.

and new earth,[20] walking by the light of God's glory (21:24) with their glory and honor being brought into the new city (21:26); and they experience the "healing of the nations"[21] (22:2). In two other occasions, we see the visions of the one who overcomes being given "authority over the nations" (2:26b) and of the "male child" (a reference to Christ) ruling "all the nations with an iron scepter" (12:5a; cf. 2:27a). These tensive visions for the negative and positive destinies of the nations[22] highlight the need for the global church to keep holding "fast their testimony about Jesus" (12:17b) through "the word of their testimony" (12:11b) as God's witnesses.[23]

## The People of God in Revelation

Before we survey the seven occurrences of the fourfold formula, it is important to understand the nature of God's people, whose role is to become witnesses to all the nations, tribes, languages, and peoples. Having such understanding is crucial in gaining perspective on their presence and witnessing role among all the nations. In a nutshell, God's people in Revelation are identified as the "church" (*ekklēsia*) and the "saints" (*hagios*).

### "Churches" as the People of God

The word "church" or "churches" occurs nineteen times as the common expression for God's people.[24] The first instance appears in the greetings of the letter: "To the seven churches in the province of Asia" (1:4). The locations of these seven Asian churches are named to John by a loud voice: "Write on a scroll what you see and send it to the seven churches: to Ephesus, Smyrna, Pergamum, Thyatira, Sardis, Philadelphia and Laodicea" (1:11). Other instances mention the word "churches" as a reference to the seven stars (i.e., "the angels of the seven churches" [1:20b]) and the seven lampstands (i.e., "the seven churches" [1:20c]). Other occurrences address the angel[25] in each of the seven churches (2:1, 8, 12, 18; 3:1, 7, 14) and use the same statement at

---

20 For Majority World views on this new heaven and new earth, see Green, Pardue, and Yeo, *All Things New*.

21 For more details on the healing of the nations, see Burnett, *Healing of Nations*; Gonzalez, *For Healing of Nations*.

22 For these tensive visions on the destiny of the nations, see Matthewson, "Destiny of the Nations," 121–42; and McNicol, *Conversion of the Nations*.

23 To read Revelation in light of mission, see Flemming, *Foretaste of Future*.

24 The nineteen times that "church" appears in Revelation are in 1:4, 11, 20 (two times); 2:1, 7, 8, 11, 12, 17, 18, 23; 3:1, 6, 7, 13, 14, 22; 22:16.

25 For the different uses of "angel" (*angelos*) in Revelation, see Munger, "Rhetoric and Function of Angels," 206–7.

the end of all messages to them: "Whoever has ears, let them hear what the Spirit says to the churches" (2:7a, 11a, 17a, 29; 3:6, 13, 22). The last occurrence of "church" is found in the words of Jesus at the epilogue of the book: "I, Jesus, have sent my angel to give you this testimony for the churches" (22:16a). All these instances affirm that John wrote to the seven churches in Asia Minor (or modern-day Turkey), which experienced distinct situations, strengths, weaknesses, calls, and challenges from Jesus (chs. 2–3).[26] Despite their unique situations, all the churches were given the same call to listen ("let them hear") and the challenge to "overcome" (2:7b, 11b, 17b, 26a; 3:5a, 12a, 21a).

The common call to listen and challenge to overcome are given in the context of the churches going through hardship, suffering, and persecution that require perseverance. Here is a sampling of their difficulties and endurance: "I know your deeds, your hard work and your perseverance. . . . You have persevered and have endured hardships for my name and have not grown weary" (2:2a, 3); "I know your afflictions and your poverty—yet you are rich! I know about the slander of those who say they are Jews and are not but are a synagogue of Satan" (2:9); "I know where you live—where Satan has his throne. You did not renounce your faith in me" (2:13b); and "I know your deeds. . . . I know that you have little strength, yet you have kept my word and have not denied my name" (3:8). In Ephesus, we see endurance in hardship and perseverance in battling false teachers. In Thyatira, we see perseverance in doing the works of service. In Philadelphia, we see perseverance in enduring persecution. Because of such suffering, the churches need to listen to the message of Christ and obey the challenge to overcome their suffering and persecution (though some churches like Pergamum and Thyatira were not faithfully resisting some false teachers ["teaching of Balaam" in 2:14, "teaching of the Nicolaitans" in 2:15, and teaching of "Jezebel" in 2:20]).

### "Saints" as the People of God

Aside from the use of the word "church," the term "saints" also describes the people of God in thirteen instances[27] that all occur in the time of judgment and the arrival of the eschaton (chs. 4–20). Three instances refer to the "prayers of the saints" (5:8; 8:3, 4 [ESV]) who were martyred. Osborne comments on these prayers of the saints, "The prayers are not only worship but probably also petitions brought before God by the martyred saints for vindication and

26 For an updated and detailed monograph on the seven churches in Asia Minor, see Hemer, *Letters to the Seven Churches*.

27 The thirteen instances of "saints" occur in Revelation 5:8; 8:3, 4; 11:18; 13:7, 10; 14:12; 16:6; 17:6; 18:20, 24; 19:8; 20:9.

justice."[28] The outpouring of judgments (seals, trumpets, and bowls) will be part of God's answer to these prayers, especially in answer to this question: "How long, Sovereign Lord, holy and true, until you judge the inhabitants of the earth and avenge our blood?" (6:10).

Moreover, the martyrdom of the saints is expressed in the spilling of their blood ("blood of the saints, the blood of the martyrs of Jesus" [17:6 ESV]) and of the prophets' blood (16:6; 18:24), in the beast's war against and conquest of the saints (13:7a)—thus, triggering the call "for patient endurance and faithfulness on the part of God's people"[29] (13:10b) and "for patient endurance of the people of God who keep his commands and remain faithful to Jesus" (14:12). God's people who obey these calls are to be rewarded (11:18b; 22:12b). Like the description for "church," the "saints" are described as suffering from God's enemies, including the earth-dwellers or "inhabitants of the earth" (11:10a), the beast (13:5–7a), and the "great city of Babylon" (18:21b).

Thus, the description above of the "churches" and "saints" as God's people shows their "embattled"[30] nature in Revelation. M. Eugene Boring explains the embattled church this way: "The people to whom John wrote had lived through tumultuous times, and many of them perceived their own time as being fraught with crisis."[31] As a result of experiencing much crisis, the role of God's people as witnesses in Revelation "takes place in the context of conflict, a struggle that may easily escalate to the point of persecution and suffering for faithful believers."[32]

## Survey of the Seven Occurrences of the Fourfold Formula

Having seen God's embattled people in Revelation (as "church" and "saints"), let us now proceed to the seven instances of the fourfold formula and see how God's people are to relate to all the nations as witnesses. The first two occurrences (5:9; 7:9) directly relate to the saints who come from every nation, language, people, and nation and who are found in the throne room of God in heaven, while the last five instances (10:11; 11:9; 13:7; 14:6; 17:15) refer to the people from all the nations who do not belong to God's family. As we briefly look at these seven occasions, we will also note who else is present

28 Osborne, *Revelation*, 259.

29 NIV translates *hagios* as "God's people" instead of "saints."

30 Rissi, *Time and History*, 109.

31 Boring, *Revelation*, 10.

32 Miller, "Mission in Revelation," 234.

in these instances and what their presence signifies to God's people and their role in God's mission for all the nations.

**"Every Tribe, Language, People, and Nation" (Rev 5:9)**

The first fourfold formula ("every tribe and language and people and nation" [5:9]) appears when the four living creatures and the twenty-four elders in the throne room of God (5:2) sing a new song (5:8–10). The song is in reply to the earlier question, "Who is worthy to break the seals and open the scroll?" (5:2). The one worthy to do it is "the Lion of Judah, the Root of David [who] has triumphed" (5:5), who is described as "the Lamb, who was slain" (5:11b). The new song that contains the first fourfold formula is as follows:

> You are worthy to take the scroll and open its seals, because you were slain, and with your blood you purchased for God persons from every tribe and language and people and nation. You have made them to be a kingdom and priests to serve our God, and they will reign on the earth. (5:9–10)

The persons in this first fourfold formula are part of God's people, because the blood of the Lamb who was slain purchased them for God. They are also described as a kingdom and priests to serve God in worship and witness and as those who will reign on the earth as royalty in the new kingdom of God. Ben Witherington III explains what the Lamb did for the believers: "The Lamb has paid the price of redemption for believers by his death and has created a worldwide people of God, not just from one tribe or nation."[33] We observe that the eschatological community is an inclusive community made up of believers from every tribe and nation.[34] This inclusive community is in the company of God on the throne, the Lamb, the four living creatures, the twenty-four elders, and the great multitude of angels. Such an eschatological view in heaven is meant to encourage the embattled churches, so they can be strengthened and "have an effective role in the work of God and a full reward at its consummation."[35]

**"Every Nation, Tribe, People, and Language" (Rev 7:9)**

The second fourfold formula ("every nation, tribe, people, and language" [7:9b]) also occurs in the heavenly realm—this time after the episode (7:1–8) with the "144,000 from all the tribes of Israel" (7:4b) who were sealed "on the

33 Witherington, *Revelation*, 121.

34 Wall, *Revelation*, 104.

35 Miller, "Mission in Revelation," 238.

foreheads of these servants of God" (7:3b). In addition to this specific number, the next episode involves "a great multitude that no one could count" (7:9a) that comes from the second fourfold formula "standing before the throne and before the Lamb" (7:9c). This great multitude from all the nations cries out in loud praise, "Salvation belongs to our God, who sits on the throne, and to the Lamb" (7:10). Moreover, this multitude is accompanied by God on the throne, the Lamb, and the 144,000, along with the angels, elders, and four living creatures (7:11). They populate God's throne room with the whole eschatological community.

When John was asked where the great multitude in white robes came from (7:13), one of the elders informed him that they came out of the "great tribulation; they have washed their robes and made them white in the blood of the Lamb" (7:14b). As a result, they are to serve God day and night (7:15a) and are given the promise: "'Never again will they hunger; never again will they thirst. The sun will not beat down on them,' nor any scorching heat. For the Lamb at the center of the throne will be their shepherd . . . and God will wipe away every tear from their eyes" (7:16–17). This promise assures the embattled churches that they will eventually become a "victorious community of saints,"[36] who will not anymore be hungry, thirsty, or beaten down because of God's protection and care. These eschatological realities make their present hardship and suffering worth going through, despite much cost and consequence.

**"Many Peoples, Nations, Languages and Kings" (Rev 10:11)**

In the first two instances of the fourfold formula (5:9; 7:9), we see that they refer to believers converted from all the nations. From the third instance onward, we observe that they shift reference to unbelievers who rebel against God and his people (10:11; 11:9; 13:7; 17:15) and yet are objects of God's redemptive mission (14:6).[37]

The third fourfold formula ("many peoples, nations, languages and kings" [10:11]) is found in the context of the first six trumpet judgments (8:6–9:21) and during the interlude (chs. 10–11) when John was asked by an angel to take the little scroll and eat it (10:9). After doing so, John was also told, "You must prophesy again about many peoples, nations, languages and kings" (10:11). Mounce comments that in this verse, "those that dwell on the earth are further specified as every nation, tribe, tongue, and people."[38]

36 Wall, *Revelation*, 118.

37 Osborne, *Revelation*, 405.

38 Mounce, *Revelation*, 273.

These earth-dwellers (*katoikeō*) are variously rendered as "inhabitants of the earth" (NIV), "those who dwell on the earth" (ESV), and "those (who) live on the earth" (NASB)—occurring eleven times in Revelation.[39] They are those upon whom the Sovereign Lord is to judge and upon whom the blood of the martyrs is to be avenged (6:10), upon whom a triple "woe" is pronounced (8:13), who gloat over the murdered bodies of the two witnesses (11:10), who worship the beast (13:8, 12), who are deceived by the beast (13:14), who are intoxicated with the wine of adulteries from the great prostitute (17:2), and whose names are not written in the book of life (17:8). These negative descriptions of the earth-dwellers confirm their identity as unbelievers, who are "from many peoples, nations, languages and kings" (10:11).

John was tasked by the angel to prophesy about them, implying positively that they are to be recipients of prophetic witness[40] rather than simply pronouncing negatively that they are objects of judgment.[41] Despite the presence of these unbelievers from many nations, we still see the presence of John, the angel holding the little scroll who referred to the Creator God, "who created the heavens and all that is in it, the earth and all that is in it, and the seas and all that is in it" (10:6). The presence of these friends of God in the midst of many foes of God still keeps the door open for prophetic witness through calls of repentance, despite the presence of judgment proclamation through the trumpet warnings.

**"Every People, Tribe, Language, and Nation" (Rev 11:9)**

The fourth fourfold formula ("every people, tribe, language, and nation" [11:9b]) shows up after the two witnesses prophesy for 1,260 days (11:3) with great power (11:5–6) and after the beast comes up from the abyss and attacks, overpowers, and kills them (11:7). As their bodies lie in the public square (11:8), the fourth fourfold formula appears: "For three and a half days some from every people, tribe, language and nation will gaze on their bodies and refuse them burial" (11:9). Then this formula is directly identified with the earth-dwellers in the following verse: "And those who dwell on the earth will rejoice over them and make merry and exchange presents, because these two prophets had been a torment to those who dwell on the earth" (11:10). Note the framing of the expression "those who dwell on the earth" in the beginning

39 The eleven occurrences of "earth-dwellers" are found in 3:10; 6:10; 8:13; 11:10 (two times); 13:8, 12, 14 (two times); 17:2, 8.

40 Bauckham, *Climax of Prophecy*, 264.

41 Schnabel, "John and Future of Nations," 7–8.

and end of this verse, emphasizing that they live only for the things of this earth and worship the earthly gods (9:20–21).[42] These unbelieving earth-dwellers, who are indeed focused on the things of this earth, refer to "every people, tribe, language, and nation" (11:9b).

As in the third fourfold formula, the identification of the fourth fourfold formula with the earth-dwellers reinforces that those who view the dead bodies of the two witnesses and rejoice are unbelievers from all the nations. However, despite the undeniably hostile presence of these unbelievers, we see the presence of the believing two witnesses who are later resurrected by God (11:11) and who ascend to heaven in a cloud while their enemies look on (11:12). What comes as a twist in this episode is this: After the earthquake that brought much calamity and death (11:13a), "the survivors were terrified and gave glory to the God of heaven" (11:13b). The words "gave glory to the God of heaven" can be seen as true conversion and repentance,[43] not so much as forced homage by a defeated foe.[44] The language of fear and giving glory to God also signifies the offer of salvation in two other verses: (1) "Fear God and give him glory" (14:7a); and (2) "Who will not fear you, Lord, and bring glory to your name?" (15:4a; 16:9). In the context of the fourth fourfold formula, we see that conversion and repentance can still happen among earth-dwellers from all the nations, as anticipated in these words: "All nations will come and worship before you" (15:4b). Moreover, the succeeding context of this fourfold formula attests to the upcoming change of allegiance from a worldly kingdom to Christ's kingdom: "The kingdom of the world has become the kingdom of our Lord and of his Messiah" (11:15b).

### "Every Tribe, People, Language and Nation" (Rev 13:7)

The fifth fourfold formula ("every tribe, people, language and nation" [13:7b]) occurs after the beast unleashes its power (13:1–5), blasphemes God, and slanders his name and the inhabitants of heaven (13:5–6). Then the fifth fourfold formula is seen: "Also it was allowed to make war on the saints and to conquer them. And authority was given it over every tribe and people and language and nation" (13:7 [ESV]). Note that the power given to the beast is now power over all the nations, leading "all"[45] earth-dwellers to worship the

42 Osborne, *Revelation*, 428.

43 For this view, see Giblin, "Revelation 11.1–13," 458; Holwerda, "Church and Little Scroll," 156.

44 For this view, see Schnabel, "John and Future of Nations," 9.

45 Of the eleven times the earth-dwellers appear in Revelation, only the occurrence in 13:8 includes the word "all" to describe them.

beast (11:8). The emphasis on "all" earth-dwellers stresses the universal nature of the beast worship.[46] Another way to refer to all earth-dwellers is through the use of the term "whole world" (3:10; 12:9; 16:14), which is involved in the worship of the beast, opposition to God, and persecution of the saints. The most appropriate description of all unbelieving earth-dwellers in the whole world is this: "all whose names have not been written in the Lamb's book of life, the Lamb who was slain from the creation of the world" (13:8b; cf. 17:8).

Despite the pervasive presence of the unredeemed nations in the fifth fourfold formula, we see the presence of the saints against whom the beast wages war and conquers (13:7a) and the presence of the Lamb that was slain (13:8b). The presence of both the saints and the Lamb in this episode assures the believers that the authority of the beast extends only to the nations who worship him. "His power over the saints is physical, not spiritual."[47] The Lamb that was slain has ultimate power because, through his blood, victory over the beast and all his cohorts has been won for all the nations.

**"Every Nation, Tribe, Language and People" (Rev 14:6)**

The sixth fourfold formula ("every nation, tribe, language and people" [14:6]) is found after the vision of "the Lamb, standing on Mount Zion with the 144,000 who had his name" (14:1b), who have been "redeemed from the earth" (14:3b), and who have kept themselves pure (14:4–5). After this, the sixth fourfold formula is given: "Then I saw another angel flying in midair, and he had the eternal gospel to proclaim to those who live on the earth—to every nation, tribe, language and people" (14:6). Again, like the last three instances of the fourfold formula, the occurrence here refers to the unbelievers in all the nations.

However, to these unbelievers the gospel (*euangelion* [good news]) is proclaimed (*euangelizomai* [to speak the good news]) by an angel.[48] Though this proclamation can be taken as a pronouncement of judgment (given the immediate context of judgment on the nations [14:8–11, 14–20]), the description "eternal" gospel seems to go beyond the message of judgment to include a call for repentance (16:9). The proclamation, which is given in midair (for maximum impact and the "widest possible range of people"[49]),

---

46 Osborne, *Revelation*, 502.

47 Osborne, 502.

48 The use of the same root word for both the noun and its cognate gives special emphasis to the concept of preaching the good news.

49 Witherington, *Revelation*, 190.

can be likened to a last effort to preach the gospel to all the nations. David E. Aune argues that this proclamation is "an appeal for repentance and conversion to the God who created heaven and earth in the context of impending judgment."[50] This final appeal occurs in the earlier presence of the Lamb and the redeemed 144,000 (14:1–5), the succeeding presence of three angels (14:6–13a), and the mention of the Spirit (14:13b).[51] The presence of this eschatological community again highlights their influence not just to bring about God's judgment and wrath but also to provide an opportunity for more persons from all the nations to be "purchased from among mankind and offered as firstfruits to God and to the Lamb" (14:4b).

**"People, Multitudes, Nations and Languages" (Rev 17:15)**

The seventh and final fourfold formula ("peoples, multitudes, nations and languages" [17:15b]) occurs after the episode of an angel showing John "the punishment of the great prostitute, who sits by many waters" (17:1b). The great prostitute is "Babylon the great, the mother of prostitutes and of the abominations of the earth" (17:5). Then in the angel's statement to John, we see the last fourfold formula: "The waters you saw, where the prostitute sits, are peoples, multitudes, nations and languages" (17:15). The waters where Babylon sits are a metaphor[52] for all the nations, as Witherington asserts: "The waters themselves represent nations and groups of people. The harlot sits on them, which suggests heavy-handed ruling or squashing of local autonomy."[53] The rule of this harlot is over the "kings of the earth" (17:2, 18; 18:9; 19:19) and the earth-dwellers whose names were not written in the book of life (17:8b).

In the midst of the destruction of the great prostitute amid all the nations (chs. 17–18), the presence of the angel, the Lamb who is identified as the triumphant "Lord of lords and King of kings" (17:14a), the saints who are described as the Lamb's "called, chosen and faithful followers" (17:14b), and the mention of God whose words are fulfilled (17:17b) all affirm the victorious presence of God and the Lamb that prevails over the great prostitute, whose "doom has come" (18:10b), whose "wealth has been brought to ruin" (18:17b), and whose city "will be thrown down, never to be found again" (18:21b).

50 Aune, *Revelation 6–16*, 825.

51 For details on the witness of the Spirit, see Yong, *Mission After Pentecost*, 249–72.

52 Beale contends that "waters" (*hudōr*) is a common metaphor for inhabitants in the Old Testament (Isa 8:7; 17:12–13; 47:2). *Revelation*, 882.

53 Witherington, *Revelation*, 224.

This survey of the seven instances of the fourfold formula shows that every nation, tribe, language, and people refer both to God's people from all the nations who are called, chosen, and faithful followers of Christ (5:9; 7:9) and to the unbelieving earth-dwellers from all the nations who reject God and his people (10:11; 11:9; 13:7; 14:6; 17:15). The saints will be rewarded, while the inhabitants of the earth will be judged (11:19). This tensive use of the fourfold formula reveals two identities (saints and unbelievers) and two destinations (new heaven and new earth [21:1] and lake of fire [20:15]). Dave Matthewson recognizes the value of this tension: "The tension between the judgment and salvation of the nations must be allowed to retain its full force. The tension functions in a rhetorical manner: to present the options available to the nations, and to highlight the reversal of power structures and the absolute sovereignty of God."[54]

Though the last five instances of the fourfold formula refer to the unbelieving nations, their contexts allow for the nations to respond to John's prophesying to them (10:11), to fear God and give glory to the God of heaven (11:13b; 13:7a), to align with the Lamb that was slain (13:8), to believe the eternal gospel (14:6a), and to submit to the Lord of lords and King of kings (17:14b). In other words, John presents tensive visions of salvation and judgment. He calls all the nations to choose: Will you repent (11:13b) and be converted, or will you continue in rebellion (16:9b, 11) and face judgment?

## The Role of God's People as Witnesses to the Nations

Having surveyed the seven occurrences of the fourfold formula, we now reflect on the role of God's people (the church/es and saints) as witnesses for all the nations, tribes, languages, and peoples. They are to fulfill this role so that these nations can also be part of God's family. The first two instances in Revelation (5:9; 7:9) show the multinational, multicultural, and multiracial identity of God's people as witnesses. The last five instances (10:11; 11:9; 13:7; 14:6; 17:15) show the global scope of the witness of God's people. As we reflect missiologically on this role of God's people today, we need to see the implications of witness in three pairs: (1) the witness of Christ and the church in mission; (2) the witness through suffering and perseverance; and (3) the urgency of witness and hope in God.

54 Matthewson, "Destiny of Nations," 121.

### Witness of Christ and the Church in Mission

The witness of the church is not anchored in its own testimony but in the witness[55] and testimony[56] of Christ. "Jesus Christ is the faithful witness" (1:5a) and "the Amen, the faithful and true witness" (3:14b), whose testimony is the spirit of prophecy (17:6b), and who sent an angel to give "his testimony for the churches" (22:16a). Because of Christ's witness and testimony, God's people are to also bear witness for Christ—like John, who bore "witness to the word of God and to the testimony of Jesus Christ" (1:2a [ESV]) while in Patmos (1:9b), like Antipas, who became a "faithful witness" (2:13), like the two witnesses who were able to "prophesy for 1,260 days" (11:3), like the saints who triumphed over Satan "by the blood of the Lamb and by the word of their testimony" (12:11) and who could "hold to the testimony of Jesus" (12:17b; 19:10b), and like the martyrs who bore witness by giving up their lives (6:9; 17:6) and who were "beheaded for the testimony of Jesus" (20:4b).

In other words, "ecclesiology corresponds to Christology,"[57] which leads to missiology. God's people are to become witnesses to all the nations because of the witness that Jesus modeled for the sake of all the nations. This close connection of the witness of Christ and the church in mission is highlighted by Stephen Pattemore: "The fact that the identity of the people of God is so closely associated with the 'slaughtered lamb' carries the implication that their response to their circumstances should be like his, the sacrificial offering of their lives."[58] Allan McNicol also concurs with the importance of this Christ-church connection: "But even as Christ attained his victory only after suffering and horrors, so the people of the kingdom must undergo a similar journey."[59]

### Witness and Perseverance in Suffering

The close link between the witness of Christ and the church leads us to the need for God's people to suffer and to sacrifice as faithful witnesses for the

55 The word "witness" (*martus*) is found in five instances in Revelation: 1:5; 2:13; 3:14; 11:3; 17:6.

56 The "testimony" (*marturia*) is found in ten instances in Revelation: 1:2, 9; 6:9; 11:7; 12:11, 17; 15:5; 19:10 (two times); 20:4.

57 Boring, *Revelation*, 78. For an Asian understanding of Christology, see Poobalan, "Christology in Asia," 83–100; Santos, "Multifaceted Portrayals of Jesus," 7–33. For an Asian understanding of ecclesiology, see Chan, "Asian Evangelical Ecclesiology," 139–56. For an African understanding of ecclesiology, see Ngaruiya, *Ecclesiology in Africa*.

58 Pattemore, *People of God*, 218.

59 McNicol, *Conversion of Nations*, 15.

sake of Christ. Their testimony includes the witness of suffering.[60] Michael Gorman describes the witness of the suffering pilgrim church: "This is the story of a faithful, missional people on earth who have been redeemed by the Lamb and empowered by the Spirit to worship and bear witness to God and the Lamb in spite of danger and persecution."[61]

Because of their witness in the midst of suffering and persecution,[62] God's people are exhorted to endure and persevere: "This calls for patient endurance and faithfulness on the part of God's people" (13:10b); and "this calls for patient endurance on the part of the people of God who keep his commands and remain faithful to Jesus" (14:12). When they endure and remain faithful, they are able to experience what it means to be blessed,[63] as seen in these verses: "blessed are the dead who die in the Lord from now on" (14:13b); "blessed is the one who stays awake" (16:15a); and "blessed are those who are invited to the wedding supper of the Lamb" (19:9a). Blessedness comes with witness in suffering and perseverance.

**Urgency of Witness and Hope in God**

In light of the witness of Christ and the church in suffering and perseverance, God's people are also called to become witnesses with a sense of urgency. Urgency in witness is emphasized throughout Revelation with the word "soon" (*tachu*):[64] Christ is coming soon (2:16; 3:11; 22:7, 12, 20); the promised woe will come soon (11:14); and what has been revealed will take place soon (1:1; 22:6). Rhetorically, the word "soon" frames the whole book, along with the intentional acts of both showing (*deiknuō*) and sending (*apostellō*) from God. At the beginning of Revelation, we see this statement: "The revelation from Jesus Christ, which God gave him to show his servants what must soon take place. He made it known by sending his angel" (1:1). At the end of the book, we see this statement: "The Lord, the God who inspires the prophets, sent his angel to show the servants things that must soon take place" (22:6b). In addition, the sense of urgency is further emphasized through another framing

60 For a theology of witness in suffering for the Asian church, see Lim, "Theology of Suffering and Mission," 181–98. For an African understanding of suffering, see Dau, "Following Jesus in Suffering," 105–24.

61 Gorman, *Reading Revelation Responsibly*, 38.

62 For global understandings of suffering and persecution from all continents, see Theocarous, *Suffering and Persecution*.

63 The word "blessed" (*makarios*) appears seven times in Revelation: 1:3; 14:13; 16:15; 19:9; 20:6; 22:7, 14.

64 The word "soon" appears eight times in Revelation: 1:1; 2:16; 3:11; 11:14; 22:6, 7, 12, 20.

of an important reality, "the time is near," at the start and end of the book (1:3b; 22:10b), with the added truth in the middle of the book that "time is short" (12:12b). The global mission of God's people as witnesses—who are called to show the eternal gospel and sent to all the nations—is short because the time is near, and Jesus is coming soon. Thus, God's people are not to waste their time and witness in suffering amid this difficult and polarizing time.

Together with this sense of urgency in mission, God's people are also called not to lose hope in God,[65] knowing that their reward is at hand "for rewarding your servants, the prophets and saints, and those who fear your name, both great and small" (11:18b ESV). Christ also gives this encouragement to his people: "I am coming soon! My reward is with me, and I will give to each person according to what they have done" (22:12). Moreover, in the eschaton, their blessed hope in finishing their task as witnesses will be fully realized when "a great multitude that no one could count, from every nation, tribe, people and language" (7:9a) will cry out in a loud voice: "Salvation belongs to our God, who sits on the throne, and to the Lamb" (7:10). Fulfilling their mission until the end is not in vain.

## Conclusion

This chapter investigated the fourfold formula of "nation, tribe, language, and people" in all its seven occurrences in Revelation and in the context of suffering and persecution. The study led us to see a twofold conclusion: (1) the nature of God's people is global (multinational, multicultural, and multiracial); and (2) the role of the church is to serve as God's witness to all the nations in view of God's revelation through Jesus Christ and in the midst of suffering. Thus, Revelation serves as an encouragement to God's people today across the globe to continue their mission from God despite being an embattled and persecuted church.[66] In his book, John's "supreme concern is to strengthen the faith of Christian people and their will to persist in obedience to God."[67] May the church today endure hardship and persevere as faithful witnesses until the end because of "Jesus Christ, who is the faithful witness, the firstborn from the dead, and the ruler of the kings of the earth" (1:5).

---

65 For more perspective on vision for Christian hope, see Chia, *Hope for the World*.

66 For mission in persecuted context, see Adeney and Aalish, *Afghan Mountain Faith*; Hampton, *Facing Danger*. For embattled mission in North America, see Santos and Naylor, *Mission Amid Global Crises*; Moon and Ott, *Against the Tide*.

67 Beasely-Murray, *Revelation*, 44. To see how obedience is applied as disciples, see McKnight, *Revelation for the Rest of Us*.

## Bibliography

Adeney, Miriam, and Rashid Aalish. *Afghan Mountain Faith: Stories of Justice, Beauty, and Relationships*. William Carey Publishing, 2023.

Aune, David E. *Revelation 6–16*. Word Biblical Commentary 51B. Nelson, 1998.

Bauckham, Richard. *The Climax of Prophecy: Studies on the Book of Revelation*. T&T Clark, 1993.

Beale, G. K. *The Book of Revelation*. New International Greek Testament Commentary. Eerdmans, 1999.

Beasley-Murray, G. R. *Revelation*. New Century Bible Commentary. Eerdmans, 1974.

Boring, M. Eugene. *Revelation*. Interpretation. Westminster John Knox, 1989.

Burnett, David. *The Healing of the Nations: The Biblical Basis of the Mission of God*. Paternoster, 1996.

Chan, Simon. "Toward an Asian Evangelical Ecclesiology." In Gener and Pardue, *Asian Christian Theology*.

Chia, Roland. *Hope for the World: The Christian Vision*. Langham Global Library, 2012.

Dau, Isaiah Majok. "Following Jesus in a World of Suffering and Disaster." In Reed, *Christianity and Suffering*.

Flemming, Dean. *Foretaste of the Future: Reading Revelation in Light of God's Mission*. IVP Academic, 2022.

Gener, Timoteo D., and Stephen T. Pardue, eds. *Asian Christian Theology: Evangelical Perspectives*. Langham Global Library, 2019.

Giblin, C. H. "Revelation 11.1–13: Its Form, Function and Contexual Integration." *New Testament Studies* 30 (1984): 433–59.

González, Justo L. *For the Healing of the Nations: The Book of Revelation in an Age of Cultural Conflict*. Orbis Books, 1999.

Gorman, Michael J. *Reading Revelation Responsibly: Uncivil Worship and Witness; Following the Lamb into the New Creation*. Cascade, 2011.

Green, Gene L., Stephen T. Pardue, and Khiok-Khng Yeo, eds. *All Things New: Eschatology in the Majority World*. Langham Global Library, 2019.

Green, Gene L., Stephen T. Pardue, and Khiok-Khng Yeo, eds. *The Church from Every Tribe and Tongue: Ecclesiology in the Majority World*. Langham Global Library, 2018.

Hampton, Anna. *Facing Danger: A Guide Through Risk*. William Carey Publishing, 2023.

Larkin, William J., Jr., and Joel F. Williams, eds. *Mission in the New Testament: An Evangelical Approach*. Orbis Books, 1998.

Lim, Kar Yong. "A Theology of Suffering and Mission for the Asian Church." In Gener and Pardue, *Asian Christian Theology*.

Matthewson, Dave. "The Destiny of the Nations in Revelation 21:1–22:5." *Tyndale Bulletin* 53, no. 1 (2002): 121–42.

McKnight, Scot, with Cody Matchett. *Revelation for the Rest of Us: A Prophetic Call to Follow Jesus as a Dissident Disciple*. Zondervan, 2023.

McNicol, Allan J. *The Conversion of the Nations in Revelation*. Library of New Studies 438. Bloomsbury, 2011.

Miller, Johnny V. "Mission in Revelation." In *Mission in the New Testament: An Evangelical Approach*, edited by William J. Larkin, Jr., and Joel F. Williams. Orbis, 1998.

Moon, W. Jay, and Craig Ott, eds. *Against the Tide: Mission Amidst the Global Currents of Secularization*. William Carey Publishing, 2020.

Mounce, Robert H. *The Book of Revelation*. The New International Commentary of the New Testament. Eerdmans, 1977.

Munger, Marcia Alice. "The Rhetoric and Function of Angels in Revelation." PhD diss. Trinity Evangelical Divinity School, 1998.

Ngaruiya, David K., and Rodney L. Reed, eds. *Ecclesiology in Africa*. Langham Global Library, 2024.

Osborne, Grant R. *Revelation*. Baker Exegetical Commentary on the New Testament. Baker Academic, 2002.

Ott, Craig. *The Church on Mission: A Biblical Vision for Transformation Among All People*. Baker Academic.

Pattemore, Stephen. *The People of God in the Apocalypse: Discourse, Structure, and Exegesis*. Society for the New Testament Studies Monograph Series 128. Cambridge University Press, 2004.

Poobalan, Ivor. "Christianity in Asia: Rooted and Responsive." In Gener and Pardue, *Asian Christian Theology*.

Reed, Rodney L., ed. *Christianity and Suffering: African Perspectives*. Langham Global Library, 2017.

Rhoads, David M. *From Every People and Nation: The Book of Revelation in Intercultural Perspective*. Fortress, 2005.

Rissi, Mathias. *Time and History: A Study on the Revelation*. John Knox, 1966.

Santos, Narry F. "Multifaceted Portrayals of Jesus: The Fourfold Gospel and Contextual Christologies." In Uytanlet and Lawrence, *Exploring the New Testament in Asia*.

Santos, Narry F., and Mark Naylor, eds. *Mission Amid Global Crises: Academy, Agency, and Assembly Perspectives from Canada*. Wipf & Stock, 2020.

Schnabel, E. "John and the Future of the Nations." Paper presented at the fifty-first annual gathering of the Evangelical Theological Society, Boston, MA.

Theocharous, Myrto, ed. *Suffering and Persecution: Rethinking Church in the 21st Century*. Langham Global Library, 2024.

Uytanlet, Samson L., and Bennet Lawrence, eds. *Exploring the New Testament in Asia: Evangelical Perspectives*. Langham Global Library, 2024.

Wall, Robert W. *Revelation*. New International Biblical Commentary. Hendrickson, 1995.

Witherington, Ben, III. *Revelation*. New Cambridge Bible Commentary. Cambridge University Press, 2003.

Yong, Amos. *Mission After Pentecost: The Witness of the Spirit from Genesis to Revelation*. Baker Academic, 2019.

# Chapter 11

# The Suffering Church

## God's Instrument for the End-Time Harvest

*Sigurd Grindheim*

Like most books of the New Testament, Revelation is not about mission in the sense that I prefer to use the term: the crossing of ethnic and linguistic boundaries in order to proclaim the gospel in word and deed. The recipients of the book were suffering severe persecution, and they were hardly in a position to engage in boundary-transcending ministry.

Nevertheless, the book has a message with great implications for the church's mission. As I will argue below, Revelation gives us a vision of a spectacular end-time harvest, and it shows the means by which this harvest will become reality, namely the faithful witness of the suffering church, even to the point of martyrdom.

Following a brief survey of the understanding of power in Revelation, this chapter focuses on the account of the two witnesses in Revelation 11:1–13. Against competing interpretations, it will be argued that this account does indeed envision a mass movement of people turning to God in genuine repentance. This turn of events is triggered not by the many judgments and disasters befalling the world but by God's vindication of the suffering church.[1] Finally, some implications for the contemporary church will be drawn.

### Power in Revelation

Revelation is highly paradoxical. In John's vision of the heavenly throne, Jesus is announced as the triumphant "Lion of the tribe of Judah, the Root

1 I approach Revelation based on the presupposition that the message would have been intelligible and directly relevant to the original readers, the churches in the province of Asia (Rev 1:4). That means that the symbols should be interpreted in light of the Old Testament and the contemporary Jewish and Greco-Roman culture. As the word of God, the message of the book is also always relevant to the church. At the same time, the book's message concerns the future, "what must soon take place" (1:1). Therefore, I find in the book references to the situation of the churches in Asia in the first century, a picture of the church and a message that remain relevant throughout church history, as well as a prophecy that especially concerns the return of Christ and the end of the present world order. In other words, I combine preterist, idealist, and futurist approaches to the book, as I understand the end times to refer to the whole period from the earthly ministry of Christ until his return. For an instructive overview of how the terms "preterist," "idealist," and "futurist" are used in scholarship on Revelation, see especially Hoskins, *Commentary on the Book of Revelation*, 29–35.

of David" (Rev 5:5).[2] Alluding to the prophecy regarding Judah in Genesis 49:9, the lion is a symbol of power that is well known to this day. For example, Ethiopia's Emperor Haile Selassie identified himself as the Lion of Judah to project an image of strength. The impressive lion statues he erected in Addis Ababa still inspire awe to this day. In Norway, the nation's center of political power, the Parliament, is located at Lion Hill, named after the lion sculptures that flank the building.

It comes as something of an anticlimax, then, when John proceeds to describe what he saw when he was introduced to the mighty Lion of Judah: "Then I saw a Lamb, looking as if it had been slain" (Rev 5:6). The announcement of power and victory gives way to a picture of a slaughtered lamb, a proverbial symbol of weakness and defeat. Apparently, this lion wins his victory through defeat.[3]

The picture of Christ's followers is no different. They are promised that "they will reign on the earth" (5:10). Nonetheless, they "have endured hardships for [Jesus's] name" (2:3), they "are about to suffer" (2:10), and individuals among them are put to death (2:13).

Like their Savior, so too does this people emerge triumphant through defeat: "They triumphed over [the accuser] by the blood of the Lamb and by the word of their testimony; they did not love their lives so much as to shrink from death" (12:11). As they suffer and die, their victory is secured.[4]

Indeed, their power is considerable. The antichrist, portrayed as a terrifying beast, was enabled to "exercise its authority for forty-two months" (13:5). In contrast, the martyrs "reigned with Christ a thousand years" (20:4), even though the beast "was given power to wage war against God's holy people and to conquer them" (13:7).

## The Two Witnesses (Rev 11:1–13)

The paradoxical nature of the church's power is dramatically on display in the account of the two witnesses. This account concludes the extended narrative following the sounding of the sixth trumpet, keeping the audience in suspense until the sounding of the seventh trumpet and creating a delay in the narrative of God's judgments.

---

2 All translations of the Bible are from the NIV.

3 Bauckham, *Climax of Prophecy*, 183.

4 On the believers' victory through defeat in Revelation, see Stewart, "Triumph of the Lamb." For an application of Revelation's paradoxical theology of power to church leadership, highlighting the need for humility patterned after the humility of Christ, see Choi, "Theology of Missional Leadership."

This passage is rich in symbolism, beginning with the picture of measuring, which represents protection (Zech 2:1–5; cf. Ezek 40:3–42:20).[5] The temple stands for the people of Christ, some of whom have previously been promised the position as pillars in the temple (Rev 3:12).[6] It is more difficult to know what to make of the outer court, but in light of the contrast between true and false Christ-followers that runs through Revelation, it may represent the unfaithful members of the church.[7]

The time period of forty-two months or 1,260 days (according to a lunar calendar) is the time the enemies of God's people exercise their power (cf. 12:6, 14; 13:5).[8] It is a time of persecution for the witnesses of Christ, a time that is also associated with Christ's ascension into heaven (12:5–6). These three and a half years are, therefore, most likely symbolic of the time of the church.[9]

During this time, God appoints two witnesses to proclaim repentance, symbolized by their sackcloth attire (cf. Jer 4:8; Matt 11:21 par.). While some commentators insist they are historical persons, a symbolic interpretation

---

5 Bauckham, *Climax of Prophecy*, 269; David Aune, *Revelation 6–16*, 604; Beale, *Revelation*, 559; Koester, *Revelation*, 483–84.

6 Bauckham, *Climax of Prophecy*, 272; Beale, *Revelation*, 562, 571; Koester, *Revelation*, 484. Dalrymple suggests that the phrase "the altar, with its worshipers" functions epexegetically, clarifying what is meant by "the temple of God." More specifically, he takes "the altar" as a reference to the martyrs (cf. 6:9) and "its worshipers" as pointing to the righteous who faithfully worship the Lord ("Use of *καί* in Revelation 11,1," 387–94).

7 Similarly, Kistemaker, *Exposition of the Book of Revelation*, 326; Ford, *Revelation*, 177; Boxall, *Revelation of Saint John*, 162. Bauckham reads the outer court as the outward experience of the church, in contrast to its inner, spiritual reality. In the sense that the church suffers persecution, it does not enjoy protection, while the church is kept safe from spiritual harm (*Climax of Prophecy*, 272; similarly, Caird, *Commentary on the Revelation*, 132; Mounce, *Revelation*, 568–69; Osborne, *Revelation*, 412; Koester, *Revelation*, 485). In the following, however, the two witnesses also enjoy physical protection until their testimony has been completed (vv. 5–7).

8 It is probably modeled after the time of roughly three and a half years from 167 to 164 BCE when Antiochus IV Epiphanes controlled the Jerusalem temple and used it for Zeus-worship, corresponding to the last half of Daniel's seventy weeks (Dan 7:25; 9:27; 12:7, 11–12), a paradigmatic time of ungodly forces oppressing the people of God.

9 Similarly, Beale, *Revelation*, 565–66. Aune, reading the book from a preterist perspective, situates the period in the time of Roman oppression of the church (*Revelation 6–16*, 609). In contrast, more futurist-oriented scholars situate the three and a half years toward the end of the church's witness (Mounce, *Revelation*, 221). Within a dispensationalist framework, McLean identifies this period as the second half of Daniel's seventy weeks, the time of tribulation following the rapture of believers ("Chronology of the Two Witnesses," 460–71; followed by Tan, "Futurist View of the Two Witnesses," 259). Dismissing such an understanding, Bauckham urges those who insist on a literal interpretation of the time periods in Revelation to consider 2:10 and 17:12 (*Climax of Prophecy*, 263).

is to be preferred.[10] They are called "two lampstands," a symbol that has previously been interpreted as referring to the seven churches to which the book is addressed (1:20).

The twin identification of the witnesses as "the two olive trees" and "the two lampstands" that "stand before the Lord of the earth" alludes to Zechariah 4:3, 11, 14, where the two olive trees flanking the lampstand represent "the two who are anointed to serve the Lord of all the earth," referring to Zerubbabel, the Davidic leader of the exiles, and Joshua, the high priest. If so, the two witnesses probably stand for the church in its role as kings and priests, proclaiming the gospel of Jesus Christ to the world and ruling over sin (cf. Rev 1:6; 5:10; 20:4, 6).[11] Their ministry is modeled after that of Elijah, who brought fire down from heaven (2 Kgs 1:10–14; cf. Sir 48:3; Luke 9:54) and who stopped the rain (1 Kgs 17:1), as well as that of Moses, who turned the water into blood (Exod 7:14–24) and "struck the Egyptians with all kinds of plagues" (1 Sam 4:8).

God's protection ensures the continuation of their ministry, but when their witness is complete, their enemies appear to get the better of them. Their protection does not apparently involve escape from all harm but from the ultimate harm of falling under the wrath of God. The beast, the manifestation of the enemy persecuting Christ-followers introduced in 13:1–10, is able to kill them. Their defeat and humiliation appear to be complete when they are denied a burial and left on public display. Such disgrace was unheard of,

---

10 While opting for a literal interpretation, Wong lists twenty-five different interpretations, which he classifies as symbolic, corporate, and literal. The most notable options are to identify the witnesses as the church, the martyr church, Israel or faithful Israel, Moses and Elijah (or two persons performing their role), Elijah and Enoch, and the preterist interpretations that refer to James and John or Peter and Paul ("Two Witnesses in Revelation 11," 344–54).

More recently, Tan has argued for the literal interpretation ("Futurist View," 460–63). Most of her arguments could also be applied to the vision of the beast (Rev 13:1–8), but the symbolic interpretation of the beast is not in doubt. One of her stronger arguments is taken from Seiss, who maintains that the use of the word "figuratively" (πνευματικῶς) indicates that "only the names 'Sodom and Egypt' are to be spiritualized, or taken in a sense different from the letter" (*Apocalypse*, 234). However, as there is no evidence that Jerusalem was called "Sodom and Egypt," the qualifier "figuratively" (πνευματικῶς) is necessary to give an account of the vision, regardless of its interpretation.

11 Similarly, Aune, *Revelation 6–16*, 631; Beale, *Revelation*, 578; Osborne, *Revelation*, 421. Bauckham understands the two olive trees and the two lampstands in light of the requirement that a testimony be accepted on the words of two witnesses (Num 35:30; Deut 17:6; 19:15), and he identifies the two witnesses as the church in its function as witness (*Climax of Prophecy*, 274). Strand argues instead that the olive trees symbolize the Holy Spirit ("Two Olive Trees," 258–60).

as even crucified victims were buried on the same day.[12] Indeed, not to be buried was a curse (Deut 28:25–26; 1 Kgs 14:10–11; Jer 16:4).

Their humiliation took place in the proverbially ungodly Sodom and Egypt, now also associated with Jerusalem, the scene of the ungodly powers' apparent triumph over Christ. With this symbolic geographical information, the witnesses' activity is associated with and modeled after that of their Lord.[13]

The narrative in the Gospel of John includes three distinct references to the Passover during Jesus's public activity (2:13; 6:4; 11:55), corresponding to a ministry spanning about three years. Similarly, the ministry of the two witnesses also lasted for three and a half years.[14] More importantly, the witnesses imitate Christ in ministering by giving their lives.[15] Like his, their death appears to be the ultimate humiliation and defeat. Yet, they return to life after three and a half days, much like Jesus, who was resurrected on the third day.[16] The witnesses' resurrection is also in fulfillment of the prophecy from Ezekiel 37:1–14, portraying the eschatological resurrection of Israel.[17]

Finally, the witnesses are made like Christ in their ascension to heaven in a cloud. As Christ's ascension was his heavenly enthronement and ultimate vindication (Acts 2:33–36), so must the witnesses' ascension represent their vindication by God.

Their vindication is followed by God's judgment of their enemies; as a result of a severe earthquake, a tenth of the city collapsed, and seven thousand people died. The number reminds us of the remnant at the time of Elijah, when God promised to "reserve seven thousand in Israel—all whose knees have not bowed down to Baal and whose mouths have not kissed him" (1 Kgs 19:18). Now, however, the proportions are reversed. It is no longer a minority that is saved but a minority that is punished and killed, just as only a tenth of the city was destroyed. In contrast with the time of Elijah, the survivors now represent the majority.[18]

---

12 Mark 15:42–47; Matthew 27:57–61; Luke 23:50–56; John 19:38–42; Josephus, *Jewish War* 4.317.

13 This humiliation also involves extensive gift-giving in a fashion that recalls the account of the Purim festival in Esther 9:19, 22 (v. 10). Unlike the Purim, however, the gifts are traded by the enemies of God's people. In a further reversal of the Purim, the giving of gifts does not succeed but precedes the vindication of the righteous (Bauckham, *Climax of Prophecy*, 281–82).

14 Beale, *Revelation*, 584.

15 Bauckham, *Climax of Prophecy*, 280; Beale, *Revelation*, 590.

16 Bauckham, *Climax of Prophecy*, 280; Beale, *Revelation*, 594.

17 Note the quotation from Ezekiel 37:5, 10 in Revelation 11:11.

18 Bauckham, *Climax of Prophecy*, 282–83.

**"The Survivors Were Terrified and Gave Glory to the God of Heaven" (11:13)**

Scholars are divided on the significance of the expression "the survivors were terrified and gave glory to the God of heaven" in 11:13. Some take it as an indication that the survivors genuinely turn to God and are saved.[19] Others take it to mean that nonbelievers are also forced to acknowledge the majesty of God, somewhat like the prediction found in Philippians 2:10–11: "At the name of Jesus every knee should bow, in heaven and on earth and under the earth, and every tongue acknowledge that Jesus Christ is Lord, to the glory of God the Father."[20]

The Greek term that is translated "terrified" (ἔμφοβος) occurs only once in Revelation, but its root (φοβ-) is an ambiguous term. In a positive sense, fear of God and his name characterizes his people (11:18; 14:7; 15:4; 19:5). On the other hand, fear in itself, fear that is not an expression of a healthy relationship with God, is a negative quality. Accordingly, the faithful are encouraged not to fear (1:17; 2:10). Conversely, it is characteristic of those who witness God's judgment that they are struck by fear, as they do not turn to God but experience deep sorrow (18:10, 15; cf. 11:11).

However, giving glory to God is an exclusively positive concept in Revelation. It is what his servants do, both in heaven and on earth.[21] What is more, in 14:6–7, an angel, proclaiming "the eternal gospel," is calling "those who live on the earth—to every nation, tribe, language and people"—to do exactly what the survivors did: "Fear God and give him glory."

In the narrative, the survivors represent the crowd from "every people, tribe, language and nation" (11:9), an expression that echoes the vision of the heavenly multitude, a crowd that comes "from every nation, tribe, people and language" (7:9; cf. 5:9). In other words, the multitude constituted by those who are saved corresponds to the multitude that repents as a result of the two witnesses' testimony.

These observations should tip the balance in favor of the interpretation that the survivors are in view as genuinely turning to God following the divine judgments they have experienced and following God's vindication of

19 E.g., Swete, *Apocalypse of St. John*, 138; Charles, *Revelation of St. John*, 291; Caird, *A Commentary on the Revelation of St. John the Divine*, 140; Beasley-Murray, *Book of Revelation*, 187; Bauckham, *Climax of Prophecy*, 278–79; Roloff, *Revelation of John*, 134; Aune, *Revelation 6–16*, 628; Osborne, *Revelation*, 433–35; Boxall, *Revelation*, 167; Blount, *Revelation*, 218.

20 E.g., Mounce, *Revelation*, 224; Schnabel, "John and the Future of the Nations," 256; McNicol, *Conversion of the Nations in Revelation*, 123–29.

21 In heaven: Revelation 4:9, 11; 5:12, 13; 7:12; 15:4; 19:1, 7. On earth: 14:7. Failure to repent is also failure to give glory to God (16:9). On fearing and giving glory to God as an expression of repentance, see also Isa 24:15; 42:12; Jer 13:16; Mal 2:2.

the suffering church. Nevertheless, many scholars dismiss this interpretation, sometimes because it is associated with the work of Richard Bauckham. Capitalizing on the language of Revelation 21:3, "God's dwelling is now among the people," Bauckham finds a universalist vision in the last chapters of the book. As the interpretation outlined above serves as one of Bauckham's arguments, some scholars also reject the idea of an expansive end-time harvest reflected in this interpretation.[22]

Taken on its own, however, the account of the two witnesses does not lead to the conclusion that all people will be saved, only that people from all nations will be. Consistent with the outlook throughout the book, some people are judged and some are saved. The good news of this vision is to show a scenario in which the condemned only constitute a minority.

That this group constitutes the majority should not be taken in an overly literal sense, as if it were a promise that the majority of the world's population will escape God's wrath. The relative numbers function as a commentary on the significance of the two witnesses and their ministry. Their suffering, followed by the demonstration of their vindication by God, will eventually prove to be the most effective means to bring people to faith.

By the same token, it is also futile to try to trace the chronology of this highly symbolic account and make it correspond to a historical outline. The point of the vision is not to make a statement about chronology but to illustrate that the

22 Bauckham concludes, "The history of the covenant people—both of the one nation Israel and of the church which is redeemed from all the nations—will find its eschatological fulfilment in the full inclusion of all the nations in its own covenant privileges and promises" (*Climax of Prophecy*, 313). A sustained critique of Bauckham's position has been presented by Schnabel ("John and the Future of the Nations"; cf. McNicol, *Conversion of the Nations*, 123–29). Regarding the passage in Revelation 11:1–13, his argument is partly based on the Old Testament background of the terms "were terrified" (ἔμφοβοι ἐγένοντο) and "gave glory" (ἔδωκαν δόξαν), especially the parallel in Daniel 4:34 (LXX) describing Nebuchadnezzar's repentance, which was only temporary. However, what is decisive for the interpretation is the context in Revelation (see above). Schnabel's strongest point is that the account of the two witnesses is set in a context of judgment. The unfolded little scroll carried by the angel in 10:2 provides the basis for a command that "you must prophesy again about many peoples and nations and languages and kings" (10:11). Based on the other uses of the expression προφητεύω ἐπί ("prophesy about"), Schnabel argues convincingly that it should be translated "prophesy against" ("John and the Future of the Nations," 250–54). However, as in the prophets cited by Schnabel (Jeremiah and Ezekiel), a prophecy of judgment is not an end in itself. God brings salvation through judgment, and the harsh words of judgment in Jeremiah and Ezekiel's prophecies are followed by assurances of salvation. This salvation is announced precisely to those who have experienced God's judgment. In the case of Jeremiah and Ezekiel, God's salvation is promised to the exiles, those who have suffered the covenant curse of being banished from the land. The same dynamic is on display in Revelation 11:1–13 as well. The judgment proclaimed by the two witnesses eventually leads to the salvation of those who were put under judgment when they repent and turn to God.

ministry of the two witnesses is more effective in bringing people to God than all the divine acts of judgment recorded in the book.[23] In contrast to the ministry of the witnesses, all the acts of God's judgment do not lead to repentance. Time and time again, we read that those who witness these spectacular disasters "did not repent and give him glory" (16:9; cf. 9:20, 21; 16:11).

Indeed, the account of the two witnesses is the only account describing the repentance of the ungodly in Revelation. Apparently, these witnesses could do what the angels could not: bring about the repentance of the ungodly. In other words, God has made himself dependent on his church in order to bring salvation to the nations.

Just as Christ's victory was won through suffering and death, so was that of the witnesses. The ungodly repented as a result of their humiliating death, followed by their vindication by God. It should be noted, however, that suffering in and of itself did not have this outcome, but suffering followed by vindication.[24] The ungodly do not turn to Christ simply because they see Christians suffer. They turn to Christ when this suffering provides a glimpse of how God is working through his witnesses.

## Implications for the Contemporary Church

For an illustration, we may turn to church history. Reading Revelation 11:13 as a prediction of "a general movement towards Christianity," H. B. Swete observed that it has been "fulfilled more than once in ecclesiastical history."[25] We may be more specific. It is the witness of the suffering church that has this effect, as in the dictum attributed to Tertullian, "the blood of the martyrs is the seed of the church."[26]

Many examples of this principle could have been mentioned. From my personal experience, I am most familiar with the history of the Protestant church in Ethiopia. Missionaries from Europe and America came in large

23 Caird aptly observes, "Where retributive punishment had failed to bring men to repentance, the death of the martyrs would succeed." *Commentary on the Revelation*, 140; similarly, Bauckham, *Climax of Prophecy*, 279.

24 In his critique of G. B. Caird, Mounce correctly observes that "it was not the death of the martyrs, but their being brought back to life that struck terror to the hearts of their enemies and caused them to give glory to God" (*Revelation*, 224). Mounce makes too much of his critique, however, when he dismisses the interpretation that the survivors genuinely repented. Nevertheless, he is right to insist that it was not the witnesses' suffering alone, but also their divine vindication, that resulted in the mass conversion of the survivors.

25 Swete, *Apocalypse of St. John*, 138.

26 The form in which the dictum is quoted has been modified from Tertullian's words: "The oftener we are mown down by you, the more in number we grow; the blood of Christians is seed." *Apology* 50.13.

numbers in the twentieth century and brought the gospel to areas in which the name of Jesus was previously unknown. They planted many churches and saw encouraging growth.

When the Communist Dergue regime took power in 1977, Protestant Christianity was viewed as an enemy of Ethiopia. The authorities sought to eradicate the church through harsh persecution. Church property was confiscated. Pastors and elders were arrested, beaten, and tortured. Some of them were killed. Young church members were harassed. If they continued to be involved in Christian activities, they were threatened with being sent as soldiers in the war with Eritrea. In the Wollega region, the Ethiopian Evangelical Church Mekane Yesus (EECMY) saw the number of open churches reduced from 377 to 22. Most of the missionaries had to leave the country, and they feared that the persecution would snuff out the light of the gospel before it had caught fire in Ethiopia.

They could not have been more wrong. In 1959, the EECMY counted twenty thousand members. In 2000, that number had grown to 3.6 million.[27] Much like its Savior, and as predicted in Revelation, the church in Ethiopia emerged triumphant through apparent defeat.

## Conclusion

The church is always tempted to rely on material resources, money, great buildings, and impressive development programs for its success. While these things may have their role to play, Revelation shows us that what matters to God is not the same as that which matters to humans. The book may serve as an illustration of the oracle from 1 Samuel 16:7: "The LORD does not look at the things people look at. People look at the outward appearance, but the LORD looks at the heart." When it comes to changing people's hearts, God's most powerful weapon is the faithful witness of the suffering church.

27 Eide, *Revolution and Religion in Ethiopia.*

## Bibliography


Aune, David. *Revelation 6–16*. Word Biblical Commentary 52B. Nelson, 1998.

Bauckham, Richard. *The Climax of Prophecy: Studies on the Book of Revelation*. T&T Clark, 1993.

Beale, G. K. *The Book of Revelation*. New International Greek Testament Commentary. Eerdmans, 1999.

Beasley-Murray, George R. *The Book of Revelation*. New Century Bible. Eerdmans, 1974.

Blount, Brian K. *Revelation: A Commentary*. New Testament Library. Westminster John Knox, 2009.

Boxall, Ian. *The Revelation of Saint John*. Black's New Testament Commentaries 18. Hendrickson, 2006.

Caird, G. B. *A Commentary on the Revelation of St. John the Divine*. Black's New Testament Commentaries. Black, 1966.

Charles, R. H. *A Critical and Exegetical Commentary on the Revelation of St. John*. Vol. 1. International Critical Commentary. T&T Clark, 1920.

Choi, Gyeongchun. "A Theology of Missional Leadership in the Book of Revelation." PhD diss., Andrews University, 2016.

Dalrymple, Rob. "The Use of καί in Revelation 11,1 and the Implications for the Identification of the Temple, the Altar, and the Worshippers." *Biblica* 87, no. 3 (2006): 387–94.

Eide, Øyvind M. *Revolution and Religion in Ethiopia: The Growth and Persecution of the Mekane Yesus Church, 1974–85*. 2nd ed. Eastern African Studies. James Currey, 2000.

Ford, J. Massyngberde. *Revelation: Introduction, Translation, and Commentary*. Anchor Yale Bible. Doubleday, 1975.

Hoskins, Paul M. *Commentary on the Book of Revelation*. CreateSpace, 2017.

Kistemaker, Simon J. *Exposition of the Book of Revelation*. New Testament Commentary. Baker, 2001.

Koester, Craig R. *Revelation: A New Translation with Introduction and Commentary*. Anchor Yale Bible 38A. Yale University Press, 2014.

McLean, John A. "The Chronology of the Two Witnesses in Revelation 11." *Bibliotheca Sacra* 168, no. 672 (2011): 460–71.

McNicol, Allan J. *The Conversion of the Nations in Revelation*. Library of New Testament Studies 438. T&T Clark, 2011.

Mounce, Robert H. *The Book of Revelation*. New International Commentary on the New Testament. Eerdmans, 1977.

Osborne, Grant R. *Revelation*. Baker Exegetical Commentary on the New Testament. Baker Academic, 2002.

Roloff, Jürgen. *The Revelation of John*. Translated by John E. Alsup. Continental Commentaries. Fortress, 1993.

Schnabel, Eckhard J. "John and the Future of the Nations." *Bulletin for Biblical Research* 12, no. 2 (2002): 243–71.

Seiss, J. A. *The Apocalypse: A Series of Special Lectures on the Revelation of Jesus Christ with Revised Text*. Vol. 2. Philadelphia, 1865.

Stewart, Quentin D. "The Triumph of the Lamb and His Followers Through 'Defeat' and 'Sacrifice' in St. John's Apocalypse." MA thesis, Trinity Evangelical Divinity School, 1998.

Strand, Kenneth A. "The Two Olive Trees of Zechariah 4 and Revelation 11." *Andrews University Seminary Studies* 20, no. 3 (1982): 257–61.

Swete, H. B. *The Apocalypse of St. John: Introduction and Notes*. Macmillan, 1907.

Tan, Christine Joy. "A Futurist View of the Two Witnesses in Revelation 11." *Bibliotheca Sacra* 171, no. 684 (2014): 452–71.

Wong, Daniel K. K. "The Two Witnesses in Revelation 11." *Bibliotheca Sacra* 154, no. 615 (1997): 344–54.

# Chapter 12

# Hospitality as the End and Means for Mission

## Reflections on the Wedding Supper of the Lamb

*Edward L. Smither*

What will heaven look like? Growing up in a church tradition steeped in American Southern gospel music, I first imagined heaven as walking on streets of gold. Later, during my college and young adult years, as I served in discipleship and worship ministries, I thought of heaven as a never-ending Hillsong worship concert in a football stadium (I wondered if we would get tired and need to sit down). In more recent years, after studying the motif of hospitality in Scripture, I've become convinced that a prevailing picture of heaven is table fellowship with our Lord.[1]

In his 1996 painting "Das Mahl" ("The Meal"), German priest and artist Sieger Köder (1925–2015) captures this heavenly meal hosted by the risen Lord. Still bearing the marks of suffering on his hands, our Lord sits at the head of the table and breaks bread for a diverse group of guests—poor, tired, and broken sinners representing every tribe and nation now redeemed and welcomed because of Christ's gracious saving work. The images of fish and bread remind us of how Jesus miraculously fed the crowds in the Gospels. As Jesus breaks the bread, we also remember the Last Supper he shared with his disciples—a meal that became a model for the Eucharist. Köder's work also shows us that a significant part of our heavenly occupation will be enjoying fellowship with our Savior.

In Revelation 19:1–10, John invites us to imagine heaven as a wedding banquet hosted by Christ.[2] John sees a "great multitude" (19:1)—heaven dwellers from "every nation, tribe, people and language" (7:9)—seated at the "wedding supper of the Lamb" (19:9).[3] This picture of heaven—the outcome of God's missionary dealings with the nations—is a feast where the redeemed (the bride and the guests) enjoy fellowship with the eternally embodied Lord Jesus Christ (the bridegroom).

While Revelation 19 reveals the end of God's mission, the wedding supper also points back to many meals in Scripture where nonbelievers

---

1 See further Smither, *Mission as Hospitality*.

2 For more on an imaginative reading of Revelation, see McKnight, *Revelation for the Rest of Us*, 26–33.

3 Unless otherwise noted, all Scripture is from the NIV.

"Das Mahl" aus dem Misereor-Hungertuch "Hoffnung den Ausgegrenzten" von Sieger Köder © MVG Medienproduktion, 1996.

encountered the living God around tables and in hospitable spaces. In this chapter, following an initial interaction with Revelation 19:1–10, I show that God's hospitality is not only the outcome of his mission but the means for it in the Old and New Testaments.

## The Wedding Supper as the End of Mission

After the final defeat of Babylon (17:1–18:24) and just before the establishment of the new Jerusalem (19:11–22:5),[4] John paints this jubilant picture of heaven amid rounds of hallelujahs:

4 See further McKnight, *Revelation for the Rest of Us*, 93; Fanning, *Revelation*, 472; and Beale, *Revelation*, 926.

After this I heard what sounded like the roar of a great multitude in heaven shouting:

"Hallelujah!
Salvation and glory and power belong to our God,
  for true and just are his judgments.
He has condemned the great prostitute
  who corrupted the earth by her adulteries.
He has avenged on her the blood of his servants."

And again they shouted:

"Hallelujah!
The smoke from her goes up for ever and ever."

The twenty-four elders and the four living creatures fell down and worshiped God, who was seated on the throne. And they cried:

"Amen, Hallelujah!"

Then a voice came from the throne, saying:

"Praise our God,
  all you his servants,
you who fear him,
  both great and small!"

Then I heard what sounded like a great multitude, like the roar of rushing waters and like loud peals of thunder, shouting:

"Hallelujah!
  For our Lord God Almighty reigns.
Let us rejoice and be glad
  and give him glory!
For the wedding of the Lamb has come,
  and his bride has made herself ready.
Fine linen, bright and clean,
  was given her to wear."

(Fine linen stands for the righteous acts of God's holy people.)

Then the angel said to me, "Write this: Blessed are those who are invited to the wedding supper of the Lamb!" (19:1–9a)

The first three rounds of hallelujahs rejoice at the destruction of Babylon, but the fourth points to the wedding supper of the Lamb.[5] What is the wedding supper? Who is the host and who are the guests? What happens at the supper, and what does this tell us about Christian mission?

### The Wedding Supper

John's "wedding supper" (*gamos*) is a banquet or feast following the Hebrew tradition (19:7, 9).[6] John uses the same term in his Gospel for the wedding feast at Cana where Jesus worked his first miracle (John 2:1). Though John's Gospel describes a literal wedding, Matthew and Luke have Jesus using the term as a metaphor for the kingdom of heaven or kingdom of God (Matt 22:2; Luke 14:15).[7]

The wedding supper in Revelation 19:6–9 seems to celebrate the betrothal period, which is followed by the completed marriage celebration two chapters later. John writes, "I saw the Holy City, the new Jerusalem, coming down out of heaven from God, prepared as a bride beautifully dressed for her husband" (21:2). Buist Fanning notes that the wedding supper in 19:6–9 is "the picture of God's communion with his people in the . . . New Jerusalem to come."[8]

### The Host

The living God hosts this feast. As in the broader witness of Scripture, God's attributes are multifaceted. First, he is the "Lord Almighty" who "has begun to reign" (19:6). The refrains of "hallelujah" in the passage acknowledge God's sovereign rule over the earth.[9]

Second, God the Son is the Lamb who was slain. Unlike his enemies in Revelation (e.g., Babylon, the dragon, and the sea and earthly beasts), the Lamb is sacrificial, gracious, giving, and gentle. Having defeated the powers of darkness through his death, burial, and resurrection, the Lamb "purchased for God persons from every tribe and language and people and nation" (5:9).[10]

Finally, God is the bridegroom. In the prophets, God is depicted as Israel's husband even when his bride is unfaithful (Isa 50:1; 54:4–8; Jer 3:20; Hos 2:16–20). In the New Testament, Jesus assumes the role of the bridegroom, and his bride is the church (Mark 2:19–20; 2 Cor 11:2). In his

---

5 See further Mounce, *Revelation*, 346.

6 See further Kistemaker, *Revelation*, 514.

7 See further Osborne, *Revelation*, 674.

8 Fanning, *Revelation*, 477.

9 See further Fanning, *Revelation*, 473.

10 See further McKnight, *Revelation for the Rest of Us*, 38–39, 70–71, 78.

exposition on the church in Ephesians 5:25–32, Paul expands upon Christ as the bridegroom.[11]

**The Guests**

How can we describe the guests at the wedding supper of the Lamb? First, the bridegroom's guest is his bride—the people of God and the body of Christ. Because of the saving work of Christ, the "bride has made herself ready," and she is dressed in "fine linen, bright and clean" (19:7–8). Like Hosea's wife returning to him to be "betroth[ed] . . . forever" (Hos 2:19), she is the bride in Isaiah who proclaims:

> I delight greatly in the LORD; my soul rejoices in my God. For he has clothed me with garments of salvation and arrayed me in a robe of his righteousness, as a bridegroom adorns his head like a priest, and as a bride adorns herself with her jewels. (Isa 61:10)

Unlike Babylon, the "mother of prostitutes" (17:5), the bride of Christ is made pure and chaste.[12]

Second, the guests include "a great multitude" (19:1). As John has already described them, they are "a great multitude that no one could count, from every nation, tribe, people and language" (7:9). In the wedding supper imagery, the bride and the guests are the same. They are the saints, "God's universal people,"[13] gathered around the throne in worship.[14]

Third, they have been "invited" (*kaleo*) to the feast (19:9). Their invitation or calling has been secured by God's sovereignty and the work of Christ in his death, burial, and resurrection.[15]

Finally, as John describes the redeemed people of God throughout Revelation (1:3; 14:13; 16:15; 20:6; 22:7, 14), the wedding guests are "blessed" (*makarios*) in 19:9. Like Israel returning from exile to the promised land, the people of God are being restored to full communion with him. In this passage, John seems to remember Jesus's similar words and promise: "Blessed is the one who will eat at the feast in the kingdom of God" (Luke 14:15).[16] The

11 See further Fanning, *Revelation*, 480.

12 See further Fanning, 481; Kistemaker, *Revelation*, 513–14; Osborne, *Revelation*, 673; Beale, *Revelation*, 938–39; and Blount, *Revelation*, 345–47.

13 Blount, *Revelation*, 344.

14 See further Kistemaker, *Revelation*, 512–14; Osborne, *Revelation*, 663; and Blount, *Revelation*, 347.

15 See further Aune, *Revelation 17–22*, 1034; and Tabb, *All Things New*, 182.

16 See further Fanning, *Revelation*, 480; Osborne, *Revelation*, 674; Aune, *Revelation 17–22*, 1032; and Mounce, *Revelation*, 348.

blessing in Revelation 19:9 also points to the eternal blessedness sketched out in the final chapters of Revelation.

**The Activity**

Since the wedding supper is a picture of the beginning of God's eternal rule, the primary activity at the feast is praise and worship. As shown, the celebration's announcement is preceded by three rounds of hallelujahs, which hearken back to Israel's habit of singing psalms of praise during its feasts and celebrations. This jubilant posture is captured in the repeated exhortation, "rejoice and be glad" (19:7).[17]

The wedding guests are jubilant because of the final victory over evil and sin. In what David Aune calls "judgment doxology,"[18] God's people celebrate the final defeat of Babylon, which represents the worldly systems of evil. This rejoicing provides a final answer to the psalms of lament prayed by the people of God through the centuries: "How long, LORD?" (Ps 13:1).[19]

As John envisions this jubilation over evil, he is probably thinking about both ancient and contemporary Babylon. On one hand, the wedding supper of the Lamb condemns the likes of Belshazzar and his decadent banquet (Dan 5). Using the golden cups stolen from the Jerusalem temple, Belshazzar praises the gods of gold, silver, bronze, iron, wood, and stone. When a message appears on the wall that the king cannot understand, Daniel arrives to interpret the message and announce the end of Belshazzar's reign, his death, and the end of the Babylonian Empire.[20] On the other hand, the wedding supper also condemns John's Babylon—the Roman Empire. In addition to largely rejecting the gospel and persecuting followers of Christ, the Romans demonstrated their decadence through lavish banquets that featured gluttony, drunkenness, and sexual immorality.[21]

As the wedding guests worship and rejoice, they enjoy intimate communion with God. The highlight of their salvation is experiencing "the personal presence of God and the Lamb with the saints in the renewal of all things."[22] This is the happy outcome for the Laodiceans who heeded the voice

17 See further Beale, *Revelation*, 926–27; Mounce, *Revelation*, 342, 347; Osborne, *Revelation*, 664–65; and Fanning, *Revelation*, 480.

18 Aune, *Revelation 17–22*, 1022.

19 See further Beale, *Revelation*, 928; and Mounce, *Revelation*, 342.

20 See further Edward L. Smither, *Mission in the Way of Daniel*, 51–52, 94.

21 See further Beale, *Revelation*, 929; McKnight, *Revelation for the Rest of Us*, 53–54; and Smither, *Mission as Hospitality*, 30.

22 Fanning, *Revelation*, 481; see also Beale, *Revelation*, 945.

of the Lord: "Here I am! I stand at the door and knock. If anyone hears my voice and opens the door, I will come in and eat with that person, and they with me" (3:20). The outcome of faith is an intimate relationship with God captured by the image of table fellowship.[23]

Finally, the wedding feast signifies the full participation of God's people in the renewal of all things.[24] So much of sin and idolatry in the Scriptures is connected to ingratitude expressed through disordered loves and appetites. This was true of Adam and Eve in the garden when they consumed the forbidden fruit. It also characterized the Israelites when they attempted to gather manna on the Sabbath day and hoard what they collected one day for the next (Exod 16:20–28). Before giving a list of human "wickedness, evil, greed and depravity" (Rom 1:29), Paul states that the heart of the problem was ingratitude: "For although they knew God, they neither glorified him as God nor gave thanks to him, but their thinking became futile and their foolish hearts were darkened" (Rom 1:21). On the contrary, in John's vision, the great multitude worships with grateful hearts: "We give thanks to you [*eucharisteō*], Lord God Almighty, the One who is and who was, because you have taken your great power and have begun to reign" (11:17; also 4:9; 7:12). At the wedding supper of the Lamb, the outset of the renewal of all things, the guests eat with thankful hearts and give glory to God.

**Summary**

The end of mission is that the redeemed people of God from every tribe, language, and nation sit down to intimate table fellowship with the Lord. It is a place of rest, thanksgiving, and celebration. Being blessed, the bride and guests look forward to the final blessedness described in Revelation 21–22. The wedding supper also looks back on Israel's history where God likens the redemption of his people to a banquet.[25] Isaiah prophesied:

> On this mountain the LORD Almighty will prepare a feast of rich food for all peoples, a banquet of aged wine—the best of meats and the finest of wines. On this mountain he will destroy the shroud that enfolds all peoples, the sheet that covers all nations; he will swallow up death forever. The Sovereign LORD will wipe away the tears from all faces; he will remove his people's disgrace from all the earth. (Isa 25:6–8)

23 See further Fanning, *Revelation*, 190.

24 See further Fanning, 482.

25 See further McKnight, *Revelation for the Rest of Us*, 98–99.

Isaiah's vision also resembles the picture given by David in his psalm of praise to the Good Shepherd:

> You prepare a table before me in the presence of my enemies. You anoint my head with oil; my cup overflows. Surely your goodness and love will follow me all the days of my life, and I will dwell in the house of the LORD forever. (Ps 23:5–6)

## Hospitality as the Means for Mission

The outcome of mission is God dwelling with his people in intimate fellowship, captured by the image of a wedding feast. But hospitality is also a means for mission throughout Scripture. Let us make this case by exploring one representative example of missional hospitality in the Old and the New Testaments. In the New, we limit our focus to John's Gospel.

### Hospitality and Mission in the Old Testament (Ruth 1–4)

Arguably, the strongest example of hospitality in mission in the Old Testament comes through the story of Boaz and Ruth. During the period of the judges, Ruth accompanies her mother-in-law, Naomi, back to Naomi's hometown of Bethlehem. Both women are vulnerable widows, and Ruth is barren. Though Naomi urges Ruth to remain in Moab among her people and gods, Ruth insists on migrating to Judah with her mother-in-law, declaring: "Where you go I will go, and where you stay I will stay. Your people will be my people and your God my God" (Ruth 1:16). More than simply being an immigrant, she expresses her intent to place her allegiance in the God of Israel.

Ruth was a Moabite, a people with a depraved history. On the heels of Sodom and Gomorrah's destruction, Lot's daughters got him drunk, slept with him, and bore children out of incest—Ammon and Moab (Gen 19:37). Sexual deviance continued to mark Moab's history, as Israelite men later had relations with Moabite women, resulting in Israel worshiping Moabite gods (Num 25). Throughout the Old Testament, Israelite relations with Moab were generally negative, leading Israel away from God. Given this background, Ruth, a poor widow from a gentile people with shameful origins, becomes a clear example of what the Old Testament means by a stranger.

Understanding Ruth's status as a gentile widow makes Boaz's hospitality and application of Israel's laws toward strangers even more significant. Naomi and Ruth return to Bethlehem at the time of the barley harvest, and Ruth volunteers to work in the fields to support them. She would have been motivated to glean in the fields because of this provision in the law: "And when you reap the harvest of your land, you shall not reap your field right up to its edge, nor shall you gather the gleanings after your harvest. You shall leave them for the poor and for the sojourner: I am the LORD your God" (Lev 23:22; see also 19:9–10; Deut 24:19–22).

Ruth happens to glean in a field owned by her distant relative Boaz. A man of "noble character" (Ruth 2:1), Boaz demonstrates the kindness of a benevolent landowner by stopping to greet those working in his fields. Taking notice of Ruth, Boaz addresses this stranger with familial language and offers her protection as well as refreshment:

> My daughter, listen to me. Don't go and glean in another field and don't go away from here. Stay here with the women who work for me. Watch the field where the men are harvesting, and follow along after the women. I have told the men not to lay a hand on you. And whenever you are thirsty, go and get a drink from the water jars the men have filled. (2:8–9)

Through his actions, he effectively obeys God's law: "When a foreigner resides among you in your lands, do not mistreat them" (Lev 19:33). Boaz also orders his men to treat her with kindness and cut down some stalks to make her labor easier (Ruth 2:15–16).

Though Ruth recognizes the protection afforded by Boaz's kindness, Boaz remarks that she is under God's care: "May you be richly rewarded by the LORD, the God of Israel, under whose wings you have come to take refuge" (2:12). By bringing a harvest to Bethlehem (which had experienced a severe famine) and by leading Ruth to Boaz's fields, God is ultimately showing Ruth hospitality.

In a further act of welcome and care, Boaz invites Ruth and others to sit at his table to receive refreshment and nourishment: "At mealtime Boaz said to her, 'Come over here. Have some bread and dip it in the wine vinegar.' When she sat down with the harvesters, he offered her some roasted grain. She ate all she wanted and had some left over" (2:14).

Following Ruth's successful day of work and favorable reception from Boaz, Naomi urges Ruth to meet Boaz on his threshing floor and request that

Boaz redeem her under the law, which includes marrying her (3:1–14). Once a closer relative declines the opportunity, Boaz accepts Ruth's proposal and redeems her (4:1–12). Her story closes with the redeemed widow bearing a child, Obed, who becomes the grandfather of King David. An amazing feature of the Davidic (and Messianic) line is the presence of a Moabite woman (Matt 1:1, 5). God's plan through Abraham's offspring—including the line of David and culminating in Christ—features a redeemed stranger.

In Ruth's story, we observe a faithful Jew, Boaz, upholding the law by welcoming the stranger.[26] In addition, Boaz seems motivated to demonstrate hospitality to the likes of Ruth because of the experience of his mother, Rahab, the gentile prostitute from Jericho who welcomed the Israelites and became a worshiper of Israel's God. Despite his settled, landed state, Boaz remembered his roots and took the posture of a sojourning Israelite. Finally, beginning with her confession to Naomi ("your people will be my people and your God my God"), Ruth receives God's hospitality and becomes a worshiper of Israel's God. Through her redemption, we see a further picture of how the future Messiah would welcome sinners, redeem them, and make them a part of God's family.

**Hospitality and Mission in the New Testament (John 2:1–11)**

The first account of Jesus's mission and hospitality in John's Gospel occurs at the wedding feast of Cana, where Jesus, his mother, and disciples are among the guests. Although John only mentions the wine-drinking portion of the banquet, the feast follows the pattern of a Greco-Roman banquet (symposium). Blomberg describes this as "a two-part banquet that began with an elaborate meal, followed by a 'drinking party' with various forms of entertainment . . . including discussions of themes ranging from the serious to the banal."[27]

The party organizers experience a crisis when they run out of wine for their guests. When Mary, the mother of Jesus, learns about the problem, she asks Jesus to do something. Though Jesus initially protests that his "hour has not yet come" (John 2:4)—the appointed time when he would reveal himself as the Messiah—he takes jars filled with water and miraculously turns them into wine. Unaware of what the Lord had done, the master of the banquet comments on the unusual practice of bringing out the best wine last.

26 See further Jipp, *Saved by Faith and Hospitality*, 139.

27 Blomberg, *Contagious Holiness*, 86.

For John, Jesus changing water to wine at the wedding feast was the "first of the signs through which he revealed his glory" (2:11)—a pattern of signs (*semeia*) that would continue through the Fourth Gospel. In performing the miracle, Jesus changes roles from guest to host—both a physical host who provides refreshment and a spiritual host who brings salvation. Joshua Jipp remarks: "The good wine that Jesus the Messiah provides at the wedding banquet then symbolizes the joy of God's saving presence with his people through Jesus the bridegroom and host of the messianic banquet."[28] John's vision of the wedding supper in Revelation 19 cannot be read apart from the context of the wedding feast at Cana.

John's wedding banquet miracle wonderfully illustrates Jesus's teaching in Mark's Gospel of pouring "new wine into new wineskins" (Mark 2:22). In revealing his glory and demonstrating the power of God, the Lord drew at least one group at the banquet to put their faith in him: "his disciples" (John 2:11).[29]

## Hospitality and Mission Today

As we look forward to the wedding supper of the Lamb as the outcome of God's mission and reflect upon hospitality in Scripture as a means for mission, how should these realities challenge the church on mission today?

First, since ingratitude and disordered loves characterize the fall and idolatry in the Scriptures, and because thanksgiving figures prominently in worship in Revelation and the wedding supper of the Lamb, the church should continually focus on giving thanks. Learning gratitude is the antidote for a complaining, self-centered, and even narcissistic attitude. In the life of the church, the clearest way to do this is to celebrate regularly the Eucharist or Lord's Supper—the celebration meal that Jesus inaugurated the night before he suffered. A means of grace, the Eucharist is a sacrament that allows the believer to remember the death, burial, and resurrection of Christ and to grow in the grace and knowledge of our Lord Jesus Christ. Given that our heavenly occupation will be communing with the Lord at his table where "the pure in heart . . . will see God" (Matt 5:8), we ought to prepare for this eternity by regularly celebrating Communion. During personal daily prayer and worship, believers should also focus on giving thanks—remembering God's blessings and provisions, both big and small.

---

28 Jipp, *Saved by Faith and Hospitality*, 83.

29 See further Blomberg, *Contagious Holiness*, 122–24.

Second, because of the future wedding feast, as the church, we should welcome others, including nonbelievers, into our worship gatherings. From the parking lot to the place of worship, we should be mindful of visitors (including those we have personally invited), extending them a warm welcome. In the worship service itself, seekers can hear the gospel through the reading and preaching of the Scriptures. Though nonbelievers cannot partake of the Lord's table in Communion, they can see the gospel dramatically retold through the Eucharistic liturgy and observe believers "feeding on Christ in their hearts through faith" by taking the bread and wine.[30] In short, visitors can observe the witness of the body of Christ at worship—praying, singing, giving, serving, and being the people of God. Finally, the church can invite visitors to its fellowship meals, potlucks, and picnics—a great space to build friendships and share the gospel.

Third, we must practice hospitality outside the walls of the church. Like Boaz, we need to invite nonbelievers and seekers to our tables (and into our homes and to our neighborhood barbecues). We can also practice "mobile hospitality" by inviting colleagues or friends out for coffee or a meal. Finally, like Jesus, we can be good guests and visit people in their homes. This is especially important for honoring immigrants, internationals, and refugees who come from hospitable cultures and enjoy welcoming visitors. In all these spaces we can build relationships and share the gospel hope within us as we look forward to the marriage supper of the Lamb.

Finally, the future hope of the wedding supper of the Lamb reminds us that God is a relational, hospitable, and missionary God, and we ought to imitate God in these ways. While mission work includes some important tasks and projects (e.g., distributing Bibles and literature, operating a medical clinic), participating in God's mission is fundamentally relational, not transactional. In mission, we are present; we build relationships, listen, and share our lives. As Paul conveyed to new believers in Thessalonica, "Because we loved you so much, we were delighted to share with you not only the gospel of God but our lives as well" (1 Thess 2:8).

30 See further Book of Common Prayer, 136.

## Bibliography

Aune, David E. *Revelation 17–22*. Word Biblical Commentary 52C. Nelson, 1998.

Beale, G. K. *The Book of Revelation: A Commentary on the Greek Text*. New International Greek Testament Commentary. Eerdmans, 1999.

Blomberg, Craig. *Contagious Holiness: Jesus' Meals with Sinners*. IVP Academic, 2005.

Blount, Brian K. *Revelation: A Commentary*. New Testament Library. Westminster John Knox, 2009.

*Book of Common Prayer*. Anglican Liturgy Press, 2019.

Fanning, Buist M. *Revelation*. Zondervan Exegetical Commentary on the New Testament. Zondervan Academic, 2020.

Jipp, Joshua W. *Saved by Faith and Hospitality*. Eerdmans, 2017.

Kistemaker, Simon J. *Exposition of the Book of Revelation*. New Testament Commentary. Baker Academic, 2001.

Köder, Siege. Misereor-Hungertuch "Hoffnung den Ausgegrenzten." MVG Medienproduktion, 1996.

McKnight, Scot. *Revelation for the Rest of Us: A Prophetic Call to Follow Jesus as a Dissident Disciple*. Zondervan, 2023.

Mounce, Robert H. *The Book of Revelation*. New International Commentary on the New Testament. Eerdmans, 1997.

Osborne, Grant R. *Revelation*. Baker Exegetical Commentary on the New Testament. Baker Academic, 2002.

Smither, Edward L. *Mission as Hospitality: Imitating the Hospitable God in Mission*. Cascade, 2021.

Smither, Edward L. *Mission in the Way of Daniel: Empowering Believers to Live into God's Plan*. William Carey Publishing, 2022.

Tabb, Brian J. *All Things New: Revelation as Canonical Capstone*. New Studies in Biblical Theology 48. IVP Academic, 2019.

# Chapter 13

# Worship and Witness

## The Missional Nature of the Worshiping Church in the Apocalypse

*Grant LeMarquand*

The Revelation to John[1] asserts that at the center of the universe is one who is seated on the throne—and the Lamb. In this chapter we will argue that, in the Apocalypse, the goal of mission is not merely the acknowledgment of God's lordship but the universal submission to, and adoration of, God and the Lamb.

This chapter will demonstrate, first of all, that "worship" is a central theme of the Revelation[2] and that worship is the goal, the purpose, not only of human beings but of the whole creation. Second, we will examine how the theme of worship is connected to mission. We will note that Revelation shows that *the mission of God* is to rescue and remake the world through "the blood of the Lamb" (7:14), and that *the mission of the church* is to witness—in word and in faithful suffering—to "follow the Lamb wherever he goes" (14:4).[3] Through the church's witness to God's redemptive action in Christ, people from "every tribe, people, tongue and nation" (5:9) turn and give "glory to the God of heaven" (11:13). Even former enemies are welcomed into the new Jerusalem (contrast 19:19 and 21:24).

## The Revelation and Worship

### The Revelation as a Christian Worship Text

It is instructive to begin with a brief glance at one way that Revelation has been used.[4] Although many encounter the Revelation as a confusing and

---

1 Unlike other apocalypses, the Revelation is not pseudonymous. It does not claim that the author is a hero from the long-distant past, but merely "John." However, John was a popular name, and several leaders with that name were active in the early church. A recent discussion can be found in Wright and Bird, *New Testament in Its World*, 812–14.

2 It is not necessary to argue here that "worship" is the central theme of the Revelation. Nigerian scholar Olutola Peters (*Mandate of the Church*) considers three themes—worship, witness, and repentance—asking which theme is dominant. He concludes that "faithful witness" is John's primary concern. Whether or not he is correct, we should note that his thesis has to do with what John considers to be most important for the church. The question of what God's primary concern might be is not in Peters's purview.

3 English biblical quotations are from the NRSV unless otherwise noted.

4 Traditionally, biblical scholarship has been interested in what texts originally meant. Recently, scholars have shown interest in the history of effects, *Wirkungsgeschichte* (impact history), and *Rezeptionsästhetik* (the art of reception), an approach that considers how texts have been used. For a recounting of many uses of the Revelation, see Kovacs and Rowland, *Revelation*.

frightening blueprint to the end times, liturgists and hymn writers have mined the Apocalypse for worship resources. In many liturgical churches, the Eucharistic Prayer includes the Sanctus: "Holy holy holy is the Lord God of power and might, heaven and earth are full of your glory," an adaptation of the song of the seraphim in Isaiah 6:3—and also of the four living creatures around the throne of God in Revelation 4:8.[5] Some liturgies include the following lines before the congregation receives Holy Communion: "Behold the Lamb of God, behold him who takes away the sin of the world. Blessed are those who are invited to the marriage supper of the Lamb," an adaptation of John 1:29 and Revelation 19:9.[6]

The Christian musical tradition does not shy away from the Apocalypse. Virtually every Christian denomination sings, or says, or exclaims the word "Hallelujah" during worship—but the only example that we have of that Hebrew word in the New Testament is in Revelation 19. The "Hallelujah Chorus" in George Frederick Handel's (1685–1759) *Messiah* is based on Revelation 11 and 19. The famous hymn "Holy, Holy, Holy" (Reginald Heber, 1783–1826) is largely a paraphrase of Revelation 4. Charles Wesley (1707–1788) acquired much of the language of his "Lo! He Comes with Clouds Descending" from Revelation 1 and a good portion of "Ye Servants of God" from Revelation 5 and 7. "Crown Him with Many Crowns" by Matthew Bridges and Godfrey Thring, written in 1851, is based on Revelation 19:12. African American gospel music employs images from the Apocalypse ("Oh, What a Beautiful City" is based on Revelation 21, and "John the Revelator," recorded by Blind Willie Johnson in 1930, is from Revelation 6). Newer "praise music" also looks to the Apocalypse: "Revelation Song" by Jennie Lee Riddle (1967–) employs various parts of the Revelation, but especially Revelation 4–5. Craig Koester sums up this subject well: "By translating the book into song, musicians have helped to give Revelation an integral place in a living faith tradition."[7] Many church people may be afraid to read the Revelation, but virtually all Christians sing it in the context of worship. If the Revelation has been such a rich resource for worship, surely it is because the book itself is a text *about worship*. So we turn now to discuss briefly how Revelation is *about worship*. Several kinds of evidence point to worship as a significant motif of the Revelation.[8]

---

5 See, for example, *Book of Common Prayer*, 115.

6 *Book of Common Prayer*, 120.

7 Koester, *Revelation and the End*, 38.

8 My list of evidence is not meant to be exhaustive but merely to provide some important examples.

### Worship in the Context and Structure of John's Vision

The first thing to notice is that John's vision seems to have been given to him in a worship context. The early church came to see the first day of the week, the day of resurrection, as the principal gathering time for the community. In 1 Corinthians 16:2, Paul instructs the church to take up a collection on "the first day of the week," presumably because that day had already become the Christian day of worship. In Acts, the Holy Spirit was poured out on the first day of the week (Acts 2:1). John the seer "was in the Spirit on the Lord's day" (Rev 1:10), the day of resurrection. Like Isaiah, who received his vision of the Lord in the temple (Isa 6), John seems to have been in a worship context when he received his vision.

### Worship as a Formal Feature in the Revelation

A second piece of evidence for the centrality of worship is a formal feature of the book itself. The Apocalypse has a bracketing structure that has as its subject John's action of falling down in worship. In Revelation 1:13, "one like the Son of Man" appears to John. John's response is to fall "at his feet as though dead," clearly an act of worship. Significantly, although Jesus tells John not to be afraid (1:17), he does not correct him—the physical act of obeisance is considered appropriate. Conversely, at the end of the book, John receives two angelic visitations. On both occasions John falls down to worship and is rebuked: "I fell down at his feet to worship him, but he said to me, 'You must not do that! I am a fellow-servant with you and your comrades who hold the testimony of Jesus. Worship God!'" (19:10); "I fell down to worship at the feet of the angel . . . but he said to me, 'You must not do that! I am a fellow-servant with you and your comrades the prophets, and with those who keep the words of this book. Worship God!'" (22:9). Jesus receives John's worship without objection at the start of the book, but at the end of the book, when John prostrates himself before angels, he is instructed to desist because only God deserves worship. The christological implications could not be more clear.[9] By using this bracketing structure, the Apocalypse reveals that Christ and God (and Christ as God) are both to receive worship.

9 On early high Christology, see Hurtado, *Lord Jesus Christ*; Bauckham, *God Crucified*; and Bauckham, *Climax of Prophecy*, 118–49.

**Revelation Condemns False Worship**

Third, the messages to the seven churches in Revelation 2–3 suggest that false worship, idolatry, is an essential subject in John's visions.[10] The churches in Asia Minor faced internal and external pressure to compromise both their public witness and their worship of God.[11] All the cities where the churches were situated included significant pagan worship sites dedicated to pagan gods. Shrines and temples were also dedicated to the worship of emperors and members of the imperial family—especially Julius Caesar and Domitian.[12] The presence and prominence of these sites presented Christians with significant social pressures. For example, "much of the meat in Pergamum and other places came from animals that were offered to Greco-Roman deities. . . . Christians had to decide whether they could legitimately eat meat from pagan sacrifices."[13] Christians were forced to ponder when and how they might be crossing the line into idolatry. The false teacher in Thyatira (2:18–29) is identified as Jezebel, because the original Jezebel, the wife of King Ahab, led Israel into the worship of false gods (see 1 Kgs 18–19; 2 Kgs 9).

Revelation 12 makes it clear that the primary enemy of God's people is the dragon, "that ancient serpent, who is called the devil and Satan, the deceiver of the whole world," but Revelation 13 tells us that the dragon works through a surrogate, a "beast" (13:1), who receives from the dragon "his power and his throne and great authority" (13:2). The beast, most agree, is the ruler of Rome itself, a religiopolitical leader who demands ultimate allegiance: "[The whole earth] worshiped the dragon, for he had given his authority to the beast, and they worshiped the beast, saying, 'Who is like the beast, and who can fight against it?'" (13:4). The beast is a parody, an imitation of the true God: God is "the Lord God, who is and who was and who is to come, the Almighty" (1:8; cf. 1:4; 4:8), but the beast is the one who "was and *is not* and is to come." The beast (and behind it, the dragon) is worshiped, but the authority of the beast and the dragon is temporary, and their destiny is "the lake of fire" (20:10). The

---

10 Although commonly called "letters" these messages do not exhibit typical Hellenistic epistolary features. Weima (*Sermons to the Seven Churches*) calls them "sermons," but they may not conform to those conventions either. The more neutral term "messages" is appropriate enough. On the social setting of these messages see Hemer, *Letters to the Seven Churches*.

11 See especially Friesen, *Imperial Cults and the Apocalypse of John*.

12 I am assuming that the Revelation dates to Domitian's reign. There are allusions to Nero in the Revelation, but this theme is built on the idea that Nero, who had died, might one day return. See Bauckham, *Climax of Prophecy*, 384–452.

13 Koester, *Revelation and the End*, 59.

beast is a fake god, appearing powerful but ultimately impotent. The beast demands worship, but that demand is blasphemous (13:5–6; 17:3). For the Christians in Asia Minor, worship was never a private experience. Refusing to worship the beast had social and economic implications: "No one can buy or sell who does not have the mark, that is, the name of the beast or the number of its name" (13:17). To worship the one on the throne and the Lamb was dangerous since the beast (and behind it, the dragon) demanded fidelity and obedience. A second beast (the beast from the land, also called the false prophet) could "cause those who would not worship the image of the beast to be killed" (13:15). Persecution may not yet have been widespread, but it certainly is a clear and present danger.[14]

### Worship Is Centered on the Throne

A fourth item to note is the presence of throne vision scenes in Revelation. We will focus on only one of these scenes, chapters 4–5.[15] It is significant that the final of the seven messages (the one to Laodicea, 3:14–22) concludes with an invitation to a meal: "Listen! I am standing at the door, knocking; if you hear my voice and open the door, I will come into you and eat with you, and you with me" (3:20). Jesus's appeal for entry is immediately followed by a vision in chapters 4–5, not of a simple house church meal but of a cosmic scene of heavenly worship. Eugene Peterson writes suggestively, "At the Lord's table, hymns were sung, the word read and preached, prayers offered, offerings made, the life of Christ received under the forms of bread and wine. The Lord's table, to which the Laodiceans were invited, was the place of worship."[16] The juxtaposition of the request in 3:20 and the heavenly scene of chapters 4–5 suggests that the readers should understand their small, seemingly insignificant services of breaking bread to be a participation in the worship of the saints and angels around the throne.

Revelation 4–5 is filled with images and insights into worship. The setting recalls the Old Testament tabernacle and temple with a throne, reminiscent of the mercy seat where the Lord was enthroned (4:2; e.g., 1 Sam 4:4; 2 Sam 6:2), a lampstand (4:5; e.g., 1 Kgs 7:49; 1 Chr 28:15; 2 Chr 4:7, 20; Zech 4:1–2), a sea (4:6; e.g., 2 Kgs 16:17; 25:13; Jer 52:17, 20), and priests (Rev 5:10).

---

14 According to Koester, "The messages in Rev 2–3 reflect a social setting in which persecution is a threat, but limited in scope" (*Revelation*, 98). Blount, although agreeing that persecution is not yet widespread, says that the suffering of the church is a major issue: "The Apocalypse is preoccupied with the idea that persecution will occur as a result of believers' testimony to the lordship of Christ" (*Revelation*, 236).

15 See Hurtado, *Ancient Jewish Monotheism*, 465–82.

16 Peterson, *Reversed Thunder*, 58.

Revelation 6:9 says that the throne room also contains an altar (cf. 8:3)—certainly the idea of sacrificial worship is present in the reference to blood in 5:9. As well as temple furniture and personnel, the throne room includes equipment used in worship such as bowls for incense (5:8; cf. 8:3). In John's vision, the Old Testament temple reflected the heavenly temple.

Chapters 4–5 also introduce a worship theme that is repeated throughout the book: The worship of God's creatures is musical. Harps accompany praise (5:8; cf. 2 Sam 6:5; 1 Kgs 10:12; Ps 150:3; Isa 5:12). Later visions in the book include trumpets (8:2–9:21; 11:15–19), instruments that could be used to summon people to battle and to worship (2 Chr 5:13; Pss 98:6; 150:3). As Isaiah's temple included winged angelic beings singing of God's holiness (Isa 6:2–3), so does John's vision (4:6–8). The theology of heaven is sung. The hymns of Revelation 4–5 contain a theological progression. God is praised, first of all, for who he is, the Holy One (4:8), then because he is the Creator (4:11), next (astonishingly for a Jewish text) *the Lamb* receives worship because of the work of redemption (5:9, 12). Finally, the one on the throne and the Lamb receive worship together (5:13). A glance through the rest of the book reveals that musical praise punctuates the narrative (7:15–17; 11:17–18; 15:3–4; 16:5–6; 19:1–3, 5, 6–8).

### The Universality of Worship

A fifth feature is that the praise of God is universal. The Old Testament restricted entry to tabernacle and temple worship to the nation of Israel, while anticipating that one day all nations would come to worship in God's presence (e.g., Ps 96; Isa 2:1–4; 19:24–25).[17] The New Testament proclaims that Israel has been remade as a worldwide people, consisting of both Jews and gentiles. Beginning in 5:9, the Revelation describes the nations of the world using four terms: "every tribe and language and people and nation." This list, although the terms vary in order and occasionally in wording, appears seven times. Richard Bauckham's comment is apt:

> In Revelation, four is the number of the world, seven is the number of completeness. The seven-fold use of this four-fold phrase indicates that reference is being made to all the nations of the world. In the symbolic world of Revelation, there could hardly be a more emphatic indication of universalism.[18]

---

17 On the pilgrimage of the nations to Zion, see Jeremias, *Jesus' Promise*. On Egypt as an anticipation of the conversion of the nations in Isaiah 19–20, see LeMarquand, "Blessed Be My People Egypt."

18 Bauckham, *Climax of Prophecy*, 326.

John's use of this device asserts that God's will for the nations, promised to Abraham in Genesis 12:3 ("in you all families of the earth will be blessed"), has been fulfilled in the work of the Lamb.

But the universality of praise is not restricted to human beings. In common with passages throughout the canon (e.g., Deut 32:43; Pss 97:6–7; 145:21; 148:1–10; 150:6; Isa 6:2–3; 55:12; Luke 19:40; Phil 2:10–11; Heb 1:6), Revelation proclaims that nonhuman creatures—earthly and heavenly—are also worshiping beings. The four living creatures who sing of God's holiness (Rev 4:6–9) represent domestic and wild animals, and birds, as well as humans. The living creatures and the twenty-four elders (representing the whole people of God) are joined in the adoration of God and the Lamb by the voices of "many angels . . . [numbering] myriads of myriads and thousands of thousands" (5:11) and by "every creature in heaven and on earth and under the earth and in the sea, and all that is in them" (5:13).[19] Worship is the proper vocation of all creation.

**The Culmination of Worship**

The concluding chapters of the Apocalypse present a sixth feature of the worship motif: the zenith of worship in the new Jerusalem. John uses the metaphor of the marriage of the Bride (the church) and the Lamb (the exalted Lord Jesus)—Jesus's invitation to the Laodiceans to join him in a meal (3:20) is brought to fruition in the marriage supper of the Lamb (19:6–9).[20]

The last scenes of the Apocalypse picture the new Jerusalem as a worship space. The city itself is a cube (21:15–17), the heavenly version of the holy of holies. It is made of jewels (21:18–21), reflecting the luminous and precious character of God himself (Ezek 1:26–28; Rev 4:3) and contrasting the great harlot of Revelation 17–18, whose jewelry, earned by unjust exploitation, is a blasphemous parody of the appearance of the one on the throne (17:4; 18:11–17).[21]

The evidence presented above is sufficient to make a cumulative argument that worship is a prominent theme in the Apocalypse. As we have examined this theme, we can also begin to see how worship is connected to missional themes. First, John declares that God has come in Christ as the Lamb whose blood has brought a multicultural people to worship around the

19 A "myriad" (μυριάς) is the Greek word for ten thousand, the largest number for which ancient Greek had a name. Danker, et al., *Greek-English Lexicon*, 661.

20 The Lord's Supper is an anticipation of the marriage supper of the Lamb.

21 LeMarquand, "Jewelry in the Apocalypse."

throne. Next, the universality of worship is not limited to human beings—the universe declares God's praise. Finally, the world in John's day was idolatrous, but John declares that the demonic powers behind pagan worship will finally come to an end.

## Mission and Worship in the Revelation

Having established the importance of worship in John's Revelation, we turn to the subject of mission and the question of how mission and worship are related. Mission has two important dimensions: first, the purpose of God to reverse the curse of evil, sin, and death and renew the fallen creation (the *missio Dei*); and second, the participation of God's people in God's mission (*missio ecclesiae*). It is crucial to acknowledge that the mission of the church follows and is dependent upon the mission of God.

### The Mission of God Through the Lamb

The Revelation asserts that the salvation of human beings and, indeed, the renewal of the whole creation flows from God's initiative. In the midst of the varied images of Revelation, the throne is prominent. No matter what chaos the world is in, God is in control. In common with other apocalypses, Revelation asks the question, "Who is Lord over the world?"[22] Bauckham adds:

> The righteous suffer, the wicked flourish: the world seems to be ruled by evil, not by God. Where is God's kingdom? . . . [John] sees God's rule over the world apparently contradicted by the rule of the Roman Empire, which arrogates divine rule over the world to itself and to all appearances does so successfully. He faces the question: who then is really Lord of this world?[23]

In Revelation 5, praise is given because redemption has come to the world. Christ the Lamb was "slain" (5:6). Some believe that the predominant background for "the slain lamb" is the Passover lamb (Exod 12:21); others contend that the "lamb led to the slaughter" is the lamb of the servant song of Isaiah 53:7. Gregory Beale is surely correct that "neither should be excluded, since both have in common . . . the central function and significance of the sacrifice of a lamb," the atoning significance of sacrificial death.[24] This violent death had a goal—this blood "purchases," "ransoms," humans for God "from

---

22 Bauckham, *Theology of the Book*, 8.

23 Bauckham, 8–9.

24 Beale, *Revelation*, 351. In his otherwise fine commentary (*Revelation*), Blount asserts that Christ's death is not expiatory but merely exemplary (e.g., p. 109).

every tribe and language and people and nation" (5:9). By his sacrifice, the Lamb accomplished God's intention declared from Genesis 12:3 onwards: Through Abram's offspring "all the families of the earth shall be blessed." An apparently defeated figure becomes the means of God's victory.

> A weak creature with no sign of triumph but the marks of his own slaughter . . . [turns] out to be the agent of God's purposes. . . . The Lamb becomes the means of bridging the gap between heaven and earth which injustice and disobedience have brought about.[25]

Positively, the work of God and the Lamb was to bring "salvation" (7:10) so those from every nation might wash their robes, making them white in the blood of the Lamb (7:14).[26] Negatively, this means that a battle must be fought against the demonic forces in which Christ is the victor. The Lamb is "standing" (5:6) because, although he had been slain (5:6), he now lives. He was crucified (11:8) but now is the victor who is able "to receive power and wealth and wisdom and might and honor and glory and blessing!" (5:12).[27] Because the Lamb has conquered death, he receives divine acclamation: "They [the worldly/demonic powers represented by the great prostitute and the beast] will make war on the Lamb, and the Lamb will conquer them, for he is Lord of lords and King of kings" (17:14). This victory will reach its climax in the final judgment, a judgment that results in worship because God has done away with evil:

> Hallelujah!
> Salvation and glory and power to our God,
> for his judgments are true and just;
> he has judged the great whore
> who corrupted the earth with her fornication,
> and he has avenged on her the blood of his servants (19:1–2)

Judgment against the powerful Roman Empire is based on God's nature as righteous and just in the face of an empire that was not simply idolatrous but unjust and oppressive. In judging Rome, God reveals himself to be on the side of all those who are oppressed—not just the Christian community but all who suffer from injustice. Revelation 18, for example, teaches that the

25 Rowland, *Revelation*, 75.

26 Beale notes, "This is not a redemption of all peoples without exception but of all without distinction (people from all races), as 14:3–4, 6 makes clear." *Book of Revelation*, 359.

27 That John lists seven words of praise is no accident. Seven is the number of completeness: The adoration directed to the Lamb is perfect praise (cf. 7:12).

glories of Rome (vv. 7, 14, 16–17) are the result of economic practices that took advantage of conquered peoples. The riches that flowed to the imperial capital were not the result of "fair trade" but of exploitation. The merchants and client kings who benefited from the empire (18:3) weep when Babylon/Rome falls—because their wealth is threatened by God's righteous judgment (18:9–19).[28] Idolatry, false worship, does more than rob God of the worship due only to him. Idolatry creates unjust and dehumanizing structures, as 18:13 reveals when it concludes the list of merchandise traded in the empire with the words σωμάτων, καὶ ψυχὰς ἀνθρώπων—literally, "bodies, that is human souls"[29]—false worship produces the fruit of enslaved lives.

But amazingly, even the kings of the earth who had been God's enemies through most of Revelation are, in the end, given access to the new Jerusalem.

> Taken as a whole, the nations seem to be constantly opposed to God and his people. They trample the holy city (11:2); they are angry with God (11:18); they were seduced by the great prostitute (14:8; 18:3) and deceived by the magical spells of her prosperity (18:23); they are deceived by Satan and make war with the Lamb . . . (19:15; 20:8). . . . The same is true of the *kings of the earth*.[30]

And yet, once Satan and his allies have been overthrown and cast into the lake of fire (20:14), the nations are no longer deceived. Because God has judged evil, the nations, and even the kings of the nations who used to bring "their gifts and treasures to demonstrate homage and fidelity to Rome, . . . now bring their glory into God's city instead."[31] The promise of a pilgrimage of the nations to Zion is fulfilled in Christ. The scenes of judgment in the Apocalypse are good news, because the mission of God makes the world right, resulting in the conversion of peoples to God.

Importantly, God's mission to save the world through the Lamb is not limited to the redemption of human beings. The whole cosmos is the object of God's mission. Early in Revelation we see the four living creatures (4:6–9), unnumbered angelic beings (5:11), and indeed "every creature in heaven and on earth and under the earth and in the sea and all that is in them" (5:13) praising God. Likewise, John's final vision is not merely about the marriage of Christ and his people (the Lamb and the Bride) but of heaven and *earth.*

---

28 On God's judgment against injustice in the Revelation, see especially Boesak, *Comfort and Protest*; and Richard, *Apocalypse.*

29 My translation. The *καί* is epexegetical.

30 Paul, *Revelation*, 356.

31 Blount, *Revelation*, 393.

Revelation does not depict a nonphysical ethereal heaven but a new heaven and a new earth. God's ultimate mission is not the world's destruction but its renewal. Although the demonic imperial powers are bent on destroying the earth, God's judgment is against those who cause harm to God's world: "The nations raged, but your wrath has come, and the time for destroying those who destroy the earth" (11:18).[32]

God's mission is to bring salvation to those from every race, tribe, people, and language who follow the Lamb and to renew the whole creation so that every creature will give God glory. But what is the place of the church in this mission of God?

**The Mission of the Church to Follow the Lamb**

In Asia Minor in the late first century, Christian witness was dangerous because there were rivals to the biblical claim that "Jesus is Lord." As we have noted, the Roman Empire was filled with gods and goddesses. In this pantheon, the clearest rival to the God of the Christians was the emperor himself. Domitian went beyond the claims of his predecessors. Past emperors were content to be *divi filius* (son of God) and to wait until their deaths to be formally divinized. Domitian, however, accepted being called "Lord and God" during his lifetime.[33] Christians, on the other hand, insisted that God rules and that Jesus, not Caesar, is "Lord." This reality marked Christians as potential enemies of the state.

As we have seen, Revelation depicts the emperor as the beast, and behind the emperor is the Satanic power of the dragon—and those who refused to worship the beast were in danger of social and economic marginalization. Because of this danger, the temptation to idolatry was a reality regularly faced by believers in Asia Minor. In the face of false worship, John calls his readers to radical obedience. Antipas, who was martyred in Pergamum (2:13), is an example of the kind of faithfulness to which the church in Asia Minor is called. Jesus commends Antipas as "my faithful witness" (ὁ μάρτυς μου, ὁ πιστός μου), with μάρτυς, of course, later becoming a technical term for a person put to death for the faith. Far from being privatized, the question of worship was public. Witnessing to Christ involved lifestyle choices—what and where and with whom to eat, what should or could be purchased in the marketplace. The pressure to

32 On this theme, see Wright, *Resurrection*.

33 Suetonius, *Domitian*, 13.2. Thanks to Mike Naylor for pointing out that Claudius was also addressed as a "deus" during his lifetime (see Scribonius Largus, *Compositiones*, Praef.; C60; C163), so this was not a completely unique development in the time of Domitian.

bow to Caesar was everywhere because imperial propaganda was pervasive: on coins, on pottery, on public inscriptions and announcements, at festivals, in graffiti.[34] How were believers—in John's language, "Lamb followers"—to witness in the face of constant socialization?

Revelation includes several metaphorical pictures of the church.[35] In a passage crucial for its missiological implications, John describes the church as "two witnesses." In Revelation 11, John tells the story of two figures who combine features of Moses (they can turn water into blood: 11:6; cf. Exod 4:9) and Elijah (fire pours from their mouths to consume their enemies, and they can inhibit rainfall: 11:5–6; cf. 1 Kgs 17:1; 18:38). Their witness, like that of other prophets (11:3, 6, 10), includes symbolic actions. But, also like other prophets, their actions did not stand uninterpreted—they *spoke* the word of the Lord. Their witness (11:3, 7) is not by deed alone. The career of the witnesses follows the pattern of their Lord, who was crucified (11:8). Like Jesus, they speak and act prophetically. Like him, they face opposition that finally leads to their death ("the beast . . . comes up from the bottomless pit . . . [to] make war on them and conquer them and kill them," 11:7). But also like Jesus, they are raised to life again after three days (11:9, 11) and then ascend to heaven (11:12). Their life follows the pattern of Jesus. In other words, the two witnesses are ideal disciples in that they "follow the Lamb wherever he goes" (14:4).

The story of the witnesses is placed within Revelation's larger narrative of three cycles of plagues: seven seals, seven trumpets, and seven bowls. In the midst of these (Exodus-like) plagues, humankind (like Pharaoh) does not repent but continues in worship of demons and idols (9:20–21; 16:9–11). But the response to the two witnesses differs from humankind's response to the plagues. After the death and resurrection of the witnesses, some people do repent.

> After the first six trumpets, many die and "the rest" persist in sin and false worship (9:20); but after God's witnesses have suffered faithfully and been raised, and judgment has fallen upon a part of humanity, "the rest" do what they have not done before by giving glory to God (11:13). Thus the interlude [between the sixth and seventh trumpets] culminates not with universal destruction, but with a lessening of

34 Friesen, *Imperial Cults and the Apocalypse of John*; Price, *Rituals and Power*. On numismatic evidence, see Kreitzer, *Striking New Images*.

35 They are lampstands (1:20), twenty-four elders (4:4), an innumerable multitude who are also 144,000 (7:1–9), the children of the woman clothed with the sun (12:1, 17), the bride (19:7).

> judgment and an occurrence of conversion. As inhabitants of the earth give glory to God, the seventh trumpet sounds and heavenly voices announce that "the kingdom of the world has become the kingdom of our Lord and of his Christ, and he shall reign forever and ever" (11:15).[36]

Mission—faithful witness following the Lamb—leads to the glorification of God. The prophetic suffering testimony of the church leads to repentance and conversion and results in worship.

## Conclusion

Revelation reveals a link between missiology and doxology. That link is double-sided: It is God's mission, his goal, to redeem creation through the Lamb; it is the church's mission to follow the Lamb, a following that will involve the church as a faithful witness to Christ in word and in suffering. In common with the believers in first-century Asia Minor, contemporary Christians who follow the Lamb will likewise find that their witness puts them in opposition to a hostile world that worships the beast. However, in the end, the whole creation will be redeemed and healed in the new creation, where all God's creatures will give him glory.

## Bibliography

Bauckham, Richard. *The Climax of Prophecy: Studies on the Book of Revelation.* T&T Clark, 1993.

Bauckham, Richard. *God Crucified: Monotheism and Christology in the New Testament.* Paternoster, 1998.

Bauckham, Richard. *The Theology of the Book of Revelation.* Cambridge University Press, 1993.

Beale, Gregory. *The Book of Revelation: A Commentary on the Greek Text.* New International Greek Testament Commentary. Eerdmans, 1999.

Blount, Brian K. *Revelation: A Commentary.* New Testament Library. Westminster John Knox, 2009.

Boesak, Allan A. *Comfort and Protest: The Apocalypse from a South African Perspective.* Westminster, 1987.

*The Book of Common Prayer.* Anglican House, 2019.

Danker, Frederick W., Walter Bauer, William F. Arndt, and F. Wilbur Gingrich. *Greek-English Lexicon of the New Testament and Other Early Christian Literature.* 3rd ed. University of Chicago Press, 2000.

36 Koester, *Revelation and the End*, 94.

Friesen, Steven J. *Imperial Cults and the Apocalypse of John: Reading Revelation in the Ruins*. Oxford University Press, 2001.

Gorman, Michael J. *Reading Revelation Responsibly: Uncivil Worship and Witness; Following the Lamb into the New Creation*. Cascade, 2011.

Hemer, Colin J. *The Letters to the Seven Churches of Asia in Their Local Setting*. Journal for the Study of the New Testament Supplement Series 11. JSOT Press, 1986.

Hurtado, Larry W. *Ancient Jewish Monotheism and Early Christian Jesus-Devotion: The Context and Character of Christological Faith*. Baylor University Press, 2017.

Hurtado, Larry W. *Lord Jesus Christ: Devotion to Jesus in Earliest Christianity*. Eerdmans, 2003.

Jeremias, Joachim. *Jesus' Promise to the Nations*. Studies in Biblical Theology 42. SCM, 1958.

Koester, Craig R. *Revelation: A New Translation with Introduction and Commentary*. Anchor Yale Bible 38A. Yale University Press, 2014.

Koester, Craig R. *Revelation and the End of All Things*. Eerdmans, 2001.

Kovacs, Judith, and Christopher Rowland (in collaboration with Rebekah Callow). *Revelation*. Blackwell Bible Commentaries. Blackwell, 2004.

Krietzer, Larry J. *Striking New Images: Roman Imperial Coinage and the New Testament World*. Journal for the Study of the New Testament Supplement Series 134. Sheffield Academic Press, 1996.

LeMarquand, Grant. "'Blessed Be My People Egypt': Isaiah 19–20 with Special Reference to Its Reception in the Coptic Church." In *Context Matters: Old Testament Essays from Africa and Beyond Honoring Knut Holter*, edited by Madipoane (ngwan'a mphahlele) Masenya, Marta Høyland Lavik, Ntozakhe Simon Cesula, and Tina Dykesteen Nilsen. International Voices in Biblical Studies. SBL, 2023.

LeMarquand, Grant. "Jewelry in the Apocalypse." In *A Sort for Homecoming: Essays Honoring the Academic and Community Work of Brian Walsh*, edited by Marcia Boniferro, Amanda Jagt, and Andrew Stephens-Rennie. Wipf & Stock, 2019.

LeMarquand, Grant. "'Worship' in the Apocalypse Against the Background of the Emperor Cult." In *Bible and Religious Plurality: Proceedings of the Nineteenth Congress of the Panafrican Association of Catholic Exegetes; Abuja, Nigeria, 1st to 8th September 2019; In Honour of John Olorunfemi Cardinal Onaiyekan on the Occasion of His 75th Birthday and Priestly Golden Jubilee*, edited by Moïse Adekambi, Chris Ukachukwu Manus, Paulin Poucouta, Margaret Aringo, and Paulin Degni. Presses de l'ITCHI, 2021.

Paul, Ian. *Revelation*. Tyndale New Testament Commentaries 20. IVP Academic, 2018.

Peters, Olutola K. *The Mandate of the Church in the Apocalypse of John*. Studies in Biblical Literature 77. Peter Lang, 2005.

Peterson, Eugene H. *Reversed Thunder: The Revelation of John and the Praying Imagination*. Harper & Row, 1988.

Price, S. R. F. *Rituals and Power: The Roman Imperial Cult in Asia Minor.* Cambridge University Press, 1984.

Richard, Pablo. *Apocalypse: A People's Commentary on the Book of Revelation.* Orbis Books, 2003.

Rowland, Christopher. *Revelation.* Epworth Commentaries. Epworth, 1993.

Suetonius. *The Twelve Caesars.* Translated by Robert Graves. Penguin, 1979.

Weima, Jeff A. D. *Sermons to the Seven Churches of Revelation: A Commentary and Guide.* Baker Academic, 2021.

Wright, N. T. *The Resurrection of the Son of God.* Christian Origins and the Question of God 3. Fortress, 2003.

Wright, N. T., and Michael Bird. *The New Testament in Its World: An Introduction to the History, Literature, and Theology of the First Christians.* Zondervan Academic, 2019.

# Chapter 14

# The Missional Implications of the All-Inclusive Worship of God in Revelation 5:9–10

*Michel Kenmogne*

Revelation provides the ultimate perspective on the biblical story that began in the garden of Eden. It depicts a reversal of the tragedy that resulted from the fall of the first created human beings in Genesis 3. The scene transitions from a garden to a city where all things are made new, and life has triumphed over death and suffering. God restores his dwelling among his people. "I heard a loud shout from the throne, saying, 'Look, God's home is now among his people! He will live with them, and they will be his people. God himself will be with them.'" (Rev 21:3)[1]

There is no longer any barrier to the fullest communion and fellowship with God, with fellow humans, and with the rest of creation that unites around the worship of the one who sits upon the throne (21:5). The Holy City does not need lighting because the radiance of God's glory illuminates every nook and corner (21:23).

A central feature of this picture is the multicultural worship of the Lamb of God by a multitude from all nations, tribes, and tongues.

> After this I saw a vast crowd, too great to count, from every nation and tribe and people and language, standing in front of the throne and before the Lamb. They were clothed in white robes and held palm branches in their hands. (Rev 7:9)

> And they sang a new song with these words:
> "You are worthy to take the scroll
> and break its seals and open it.
> For you were slaughtered, and your blood has ransomed people for God
> from every tribe and language and people and nation.
> And you have caused them to become
> a Kingdom of priests for our God.
> And they will reign on the earth." (Rev 5:9–10)

1 All Scripture quotations are from the NLT unless otherwise noted.

The gathering of the restored and redeemed community represents the end purpose of God's plan for his creation. This chapter argues that the all-inclusive and multilingual worship of God has significant implications for the mission of the church. It claims that developing the languages of the peoples of the world and translating God's word therein foreshadows the advent of God's multicultural and multilingual kingdom. In other words, the development of languages and the translation of the Bible equip, transform, and qualify the speakers of these languages for the worship of the eternal God. More specifically, this chapter briefly explores the place and role of language in what God does to fulfill his purposes in the world. In this regard, Bible translation appears as a way for God's incarnate presence to be manifested among each language community that receives the eternal word of God in the categories that speak to their daily realities. This incarnate presence restores the recipients' dignity as beings created in the image of God and furthers unity in the church and in our broken world while allowing for the cross-cultural transmission of the Gospel and the worship of the only one Creator God by all the peoples of the earth.

## Language and the Mission of God

Whenever we use language to communicate with someone, we are using one of the most fascinating gifts God has given us. Many species can communicate in some way, but human language is unique in its almost limitless possibilities for interaction and relationship with others and with God himself. We communicate because we were created by a God who communicates. In creation, God spoke, and the universe, with everything in it, came into existence. Then God created Adam and spoke to him. One of Adam's first tasks in the newly created world was to name the animals. Adam spoke and their names were given (Gen 2:19).

In Psalm 19:1 we read that the "heavens declare the glory of God; the skies proclaim the work of his hands" (NIV). Paul wrote in Romans 1:20, "Since the creation of the world God's invisible qualities—his eternal power and divine nature—have been clearly seen" (NIV). But this is only part of how God makes himself known. When he wanted to communicate with Adam and Eve in the garden, he used language—human language. Indeed, ever since then God has been making himself known, establishing covenants, and disclosing the mystery that was hidden for ages and generations (Col 1:26–28) through language—the languages we use every day!

The triune God who communicates created humans to live in loving relationship with him. Language is one of the things that enables that relationship. As such, language is not only the means through which God created the universe, but additionally, the diversity of the world's languages expresses his infinite power and unmatched glory. What's more, language is manifested through the whole plan of redemption as God speaks through prophets and ultimately through his incarnate Son (Heb 1:1–2). Yet, the perception of language diversity has been ambivalent through the biblical narrative and in the world today.

**Language Diversity: Curse or Blessing?**

Approximately more than 7,100 languages, including sign languages, are in use around the world today.[2] Genesis 11 states that God allowed language diversity to prevent the success of the people's project to build a tower that reaches into the sky to make themselves famous and to avoid being scattered over all the world (v. 4).[3] Language diversity aimed to "confuse the people" so that they would not be able to understand each other (v. 7). In this regard, language diversity appears as a curse or a problem. However, in hindsight we recall that God created Adam and Eve, blessed them, and said, "Be fruitful and multiply. Fill the earth and govern it" (1:28). Understood from this perspective, what could be seen as a curse was indeed the means by which God allowed people to pursue his creational intent for them. Put differently, building the tower had distracted people from multiplying and filling the earth. But the diversity of languages obliged them to pursue this very purpose, even if unconsciously. For these reasons, most commentaries concur that the confusion of tongues and the geographic dissemination is a judgment on people's rebellion and disobedience, not a condemnation of languages per se.[4]

The event of the coming of the Spirit in Acts 2 confirms that God did not dismiss language diversity as a problem. All the people who were present in Jerusalem on the day of Pentecost heard the mysteries of God, each in their own tongue.

---

2 Eberhard et al., *Ethnologue*.

3 Language diversity is already mentioned in Genesis 10:25–31. Yet Genesis 11:1 says, "At one time all the people of the world spoke the same language and used the same words." In this chapter, we see that language diversity returned by God's initiative.

4 Guzik, *Genesis*.

> When they heard the loud noise, everyone came running, and they were bewildered to hear their own languages being spoken by the believers. They were completely amazed. "How can this be?" they exclaimed. "These people are all from Galilee, and yet we hear them speaking in our own native languages!" (Acts 2:6–8)

God indicated through this that he despises no language; instead, each is valuable, for behind every language are the people who use it and identify with it. Since God created all human beings to be his image bearers irrespective of their race or socioeconomic condition, God values all languages because all people have equal dignity in his sight. Yet, the essence of language diversity and the fall of humanity often cause people to use language as a means of exclusion; language is the main means through which people assert their identity and ethnic belonging. Ethnicity and identity are not inherently negative. However, the corruption of humanity that resulted from the fall led to conflictual relationships as each ethnic group sought to exercise dominion over others.

**Language and Identity**

As indicated earlier, the ability to use language as a set of sounds and symbols to convey meaning among human beings is the manifestation of our being created in the image of the triune God who speaks. As an expression of that ability, each specific language shapes the identity of the people who have it as their mother tongue. By this, I refer to the language that we each have acquired—almost unconsciously—as we grew up. The mother tongue provides each of us with a set of concepts that express the experiences, stories, and realities that inform our relationship to the rest of the world. As such, it conveys our worldview, our deepest beliefs and values. These, in turn, inform our visible attitudes and behaviors. The shared value systems and assumptions among those who use the same language cause them to form a community in which they find their sense of being and belonging. The sinful condition of humanity often causes people to assert their identity by excluding those who are not like them. In Judges, we see how language was used to identify the people of Ephraim, resulting in persecution.

> Whenever a fugitive from Ephraim tried to go back across, the men of Gilead would challenge him. "Are you a member of the tribe of Ephraim?" they would ask. If the man said, "No, I'm not," they would tell him to say "Shibboleth." If he was from Ephraim, he would say "Sibboleth," because people from Ephraim cannot pronounce the

word correctly. Then they would take him and kill him at the shallow crossings of the Jordan. In all, 42,000 Ephraimites were killed at that time. (Judg 12:5–6)

The sinful nature of people and the resulting tendency toward exclusion have turned this beautiful ethnic diversity that glorifies God into the ugly problem of ethnicism. The result of this is conflict, strife, hatred, and even wars among peoples. Such realities have led leaders of nations and organizations to view language diversity as a problem that should be resolved by furthering the use of a single language spoken by everyone. But, as Hounkpati Capo points out, referencing Lowenfeld, it is important to note that "language can be used to flatter, to irritate, to excite, to soothe, to stimulate, to intimidate, to invigorate, to deceive, to create, to destroy, to murder or to immortalize."[5] In its essence, language is neutral. The purpose for which people choose to use it determines the way language tends to be perceived. The biblical narrative offers many examples of how language can be used to allow for effective communication and appropriation of the message.

**Language and Effective Communication**

The book of Esther tells us that during a royal feast, Queen Vashti dishonored her husband, King Xerxes, by refusing to appear before the king's guests to exhibit her beauty. The queen thus fell into disgrace, and the king sent her away. In his effort to ensure that such behavior would be banished from his kingdom, the king issued a decree to be sent "to each province in its own script and to each people in its own language, proclaiming in each people's tongue that every man should be ruler over his own household" (1:22 NIV). His choice for this painstaking strategy to translate the message into the many languages and scripts of the people points to the effectiveness of the mother tongue to convey a message.

Another illustration is seen in 2 Kings 18. During the reign of King Ahaziah, God's people came under attack by the Assyrians. Ahaziah encouraged his people to have confidence in the Lord, to wait on him to protect and defend them. But the king of Assyria decided to shake the faith of God's people by claiming that their hope in God was nothing but an illusion. It is instructive to note that the envoys of the Assyrian king chose to convey that message in Hebrew, although the people also understood the language of the Assyrians.

5 Capo, *Langues africaines*.

> Then Eliakim, son of Hilkiah, Shebna, and Joah said to the Assyrian chief of staff, "Please speak to us in Aramaic, for we understand it well. Don't speak in Hebrew, for the people on the wall will hear." But Sennacherib's chief of staff replied, "Do you think my master sent this message only to you and your master? He wants all the people to hear it, for when we put this city under siege, they will suffer along with you. They will be so hungry and thirsty that they will eat their own dung and drink their own urine." Then the chief of staff stood and shouted in Hebrew to the people on the wall, "Listen to this message from the great king of Assyria! This is what the king says: Don't let Hezekiah deceive you. He will never be able to rescue you from my power. Don't let him fool you into trusting in the LORD by saying, 'The LORD will surely rescue us. This city will never fall into the hands of the Assyrian king!'" (vv. 26–30)

In Acts 21:37–40 we see a similar illustration of how Paul uses different languages in light of the audiences he is addressing. In each case, we note that each language used triggers the desired response, that is, the sympathy of the Greek commander and the silence and attention of the Jewish crowd.

In conclusion, each language has an important symbolic and identity value for those who use it. Although language is neutral in itself, pressures are often exerted on it because of what its use can allow or prevent. This is why the colonial enterprise, for example, set out to spread European languages while annihilating the indigenous and vernacular ones. However, we must never lose sight of the fact that each language represents somebody's mother tongue. Therefore, it has value, at least for its native speakers. It is rarely possible to effectively engage a people group with a message and obtain the desired deep response if their language is not considered in the communication process. For this reason, God did not choose to draw people to himself through an abstract and confusing message in a foreign or elite language. He instead chose to become flesh and blood through his Son, to live with human beings, to speak their language, so that they could rightly understand who God truly is and respond to him accordingly. Bible translation remains the best metaphor of God's incarnation[6] and the central means of enabling the cross-cultural transmission of the gospel.[7]

---

6 Walls, *Missionary Movement*, 27.

7 Sanneh, *Translating the Message*.

## Bible Translation Foreshadows Revelation 5:9-10

Through the Scriptures we learn that God has revealed the splendor of his glory to human beings. As Paul puts it, "Through everything God made, they can clearly see his invisible qualities—his eternal power and nature. So they have no excuse for not knowing God" (Rom 1:20). But his inspired word is the means through which people can come into an intimate relationship with him. He disclosed and modeled it through his own Son Jesus Christ, who adopted the human condition and "made his dwelling among us" (John 1:14 NIV) to reveal God's love, compassion, justice, and mercy. God did not choose to flash this message from a distance but used the coming of his own Son into this world to ensure the effective transmission of the message. As Andrew Walls notes,

> The translation of God into humanity, whereby the sense and meaning of God was transferred, was effected under very culture-specific conditions. . . . Christ [became] visible within the very things which constitute nationality. The first divine act of translation into humanity thus gives rise to a constant succession of new translations.[8]

The incarnation of Jesus Christ is the translation of the divine message into the language and categories that human beings are able to understand and make their own. In the same manner, Bible translation is the best way to follow Jesus Christ in his incarnation and allow him to be at home in the various languages and cultural groups of the world.[9]

### Bible Translation and the Cross-Cultural Advance of the Gospel

Historians of the church and missiologists have sufficiently defended the irreplaceable role of Bible translation for the cross-cultural transmission and effective reception of God's message.[10] As Philip Jenkins copiously illustrated, the church of North Africa, which grew and blossomed over the early centuries, had a fundamental flaw. It spread with the use of Latin as the dominant and colonial language, despising and disregarding the languages that people used in their homes.[11] It is no surprise that, though this church produced many of the eminent theologians who became some of the fathers of

---

8 Walls, *Missionary Movement*, 27.

9 Kwame Bediako, "Bible Translation and African Theology," paper presented at the Forum of Bible Agencies of Cameroon Conference, Yaoundé, July 1, 2004.

10 Johnstone, *Bible Translation*.

11 Jenkins, *Next Christendom*, 25.

the Christian faith, the common people did not truly appropriate the message of Christianity. When Islam rose in the seventh century and conquered them, the people of Libya, Tunisia, Algeria, and Morocco had no strong arguments to withstand the new religion. In the meantime, the Coptic believers in Egypt and Geʿez speakers of Ethiopia, who had the Scriptures in their vernacular tongues in the early centuries, were able to defend and preserve their faith.[12] In the same way, though the whole continent of Europe was Christian, the failure to have access to Scriptures in the peoples' languages led to grave doctrinal abuses in the medieval church. However, when the availability of Scriptures in German, English, French, and other European languages grew, a spiritual revival known as the Reformation brought the faith home to the people. Whenever the church neglects Bible translation and the use of the vernacular, it creates fertile ground for heresy or sows the seeds of its own decline and death. Christianity, in its essence, is a translatable religion; "Christians do not possess the Scripture in the language of the founder of their religion."[13] Put differently, our Christian faith relies on a translation of the original words of Jesus Christ. Whenever the Bible is translated into a language, it allows its new recipients to experience a relationship with the same triune God.

Analyzing the modern missionary movement of the past two centuries, Ralph D. Winter noted three phases that were each marked and undergirded by Scripture translation.[14] In the first phase, the gospel reached the coastlands of Asia and Africa, with William Carey as the representative of this era. The second phase was that of inland missions, when the gospel moved further into the continents, adopting major languages for outreach. Hudson Taylor, who worked in China, is the most prominent figure of this wave, followed by the Sudan Interior and Africa Inland Mission, among others. In the third phase, Cameron Townsend, founder of SIL and Wycliffe Bible Translators, is representative of efforts to reach the ethnolinguistic minorities, or "hidden people" in the words of Ralph Winter.[15] The more recent spread of the gospel in the Southern Hemisphere and in the East has, to a large extent, been

12 Milkre-Sellassie, *Early Translation into Ethiopic/Geez*, 302.

13 Sanneh, *Whose Religion*, 110.

14 Ralph D. Winter, "Three Mission Eras: And the Loss and Recovery of Kingdom Mission," 263–78.

15 Ralph D. Winter, "The Highest Priority: Cross-Cultural Evangelism," paper presented at the International Congress on World Evangelization, Lausanne, Switzerland, July 16–25, 1974, https://lausanne.org/content/the-highest-priority-cross-cultural-evangelism.

attributed to people receiving the gospel in their own languages. As Lamin Sanneh puts it,

> One thing that is absolutely clear is that the Christian impact overlapped almost exactly with the incidence of translation of Scripture into vernacular languages, almost everywhere. In other words, there were very few places, if any, where Christian awakening had taken root where people didn't have Scriptures in their mother-tongue. In fact, I couldn't think of any.[16]

Bible translation allows Christianity to remain a vibrant movement unrestricted by any form of establishment. Put differently, no language has the primacy or monopoly of conveying God's message. Additionally, Christianity is not weakened by translation because the breadth of translation furthers a deeper organic unity, despite the various expressions of the Christian faith.

### Bible Translation Strengthens the Church

Contrary to other religions, Christianity does not have one single language or culture. This could lend itself to division along linguistic and cultural lines, driven by Bible translation, which incarnates the Christian message into ever more languages and cultures. However, linguistic and cultural diversity promotes local agency and empowerment for those who adopt Christianity and even furthers the acknowledgment of other linguistic groups and their right to also enjoy the benefits of full access to God's word. In this way, all the peoples who have fellowship with God, each in their own language, can be respectful of one another and coexist harmoniously. Just as we see in Revelation 7:10, the vast crowd, too numerous to be counted, can shout together in praise: "Salvation comes from our God who sits on the throne and from the Lamb!" Despite the multitude and differences of tongues and nations, all can claim God as "our" God. The possessive in English lacks the specificity that many other languages, such as my own mother tongue Ghomala', normally have. In Ghomala', there is a generic possessive *yok* ("our"). It entails the possession of something by a group that clearly excludes others. There is also a possessive for two people at the exclusion of all others: *yok pu*. Finally, there is a possessive that indicates possession by all involved: *yok pa*. It is this inclusive possessiveness that is referenced in Revelation 7:10. It entails the recognition of the universality of God's salvation but also the

---

16 Lamin Sanneh, "Bible Translation and the Birth of Christianity," paper presented at the Andrew Walls Lectures, Scripture Use Conference, Wycliffe European Training Programme, Horsleys Green, UK, 2006.

acknowledgment of others as co-beneficiaries of the same salvation. Though the Greek itself does not distinguish the inclusive and exclusive possessives, the Ghomala' translation provides a nuance that enriches the meaning. In this way, true worship of the same God takes place together with deep and mutually valuing relationships among all the worshipers.

When the effect of Bible translation is understood in this way, the church can dispel the superficial discomfort that multilingualism can create and promote the ability for all to have access to God's word in the languages most valuable to them. Bible translation strengthens and deepens the faith of people as they achieve a better understanding of God's word. Recently, a lady receiving God's word in her Bakoko language in Cameroon expressed this special feeling, saying,

> It is like we are closer to God because he understands even our sighs. He understands when we don't want to talk in French or in English. We can speak in our language. And we can talk about the gospel to everyone. We can talk to grandmothers. We can address everyone. The gospel has become accessible to everyone. There is no one who can say that they are not going to understand the Bible in French or in English. Really, it gives a lot of joy.[17]

Bible translation also restores dignity and empowers people who have been pushed to the outer margins of their societies by more dominant groups. "When we go to the politicians, they don't know us. But now God knows us. Now we are counted among the children of God," said the Chief of Kpandai Wura as he tearfully evoked the marginalization of the Nawuri people of Ghana.[18] This was a call for the Nawuri people to look beyond their current sociopolitical marginalization and develop the confidence that comes from the knowledge of being "children of God." In this regard, Bible translation and the empowerment it brings become a critical organizing principle and a practical tool for transformation. For a vulnerable and marginalized group like the Nawuris, being "counted as children of God" is more than spiritual transformation. It transforms their perception of themselves and unleashes their potential to flourish in all regards as people created in the image of God.

---

17 Personal conversation, July 25, 2024.

18 Kenmogne, "Bible Translation as Justice," 125.

Beyond or even prior to the effect of the translation of Scriptures on people, the process of Bible translation has strengthened the church that is easily fragmented along doctrinal, liturgical, cultural, and historical traditions. The process of Bible translation among the Bagwere people of Uganda was instrumental in ushering in a new beginning for the entire community and church. Today, all the church denominations in that language community work together for the translation of the Old Testament while enjoying the benefits of the use of the New Testament in their Lugwere language. The Anglican bishop who heads this interchurch Bible translation project stated the following:

> Bugwere had an obscure past, an uncertain history and a controversial heritage. Bugwere was guilty of having never before given serious undertaking to foster unity. However . . . the arrival of the Lugwere Bible ushered a new beginning, a new era of self-belief and self-determination, an opportunity to unite for a common purpose, to pursue a common goal for a common good.[19]

The research and testimonies presented here clearly indicate that Bible translation foreshadows the new earth and community depicted in Revelation. The well-known writer Stephen Covey is credited with the saying "begin with the end in mind."[20] If we apply this leadership and management principle to the field of mission, it means that the picture of the end that God desires should inform and prescribe the priorities of the church in the world today. For this reason, the church that understands Revelation missiologically should pay special attention to Bible translation and vernacular language use.

**Bible Translation and the Renewal of Worship**

One of the features of Revelation is the abundance of exuberant worship it contains (4:1–8; 5:9–14; 7:9–17; 11:15–18; 15:3–4; 16:5–7; 19:1–8). The praise and worship of the living God and the Lamb are the primary privilege of the redeemed community in heaven. A missiological understanding of Revelation, therefore, describes worship as a core function of the church. Not only does the church need to worship God now, but it also needs to prepare the redeemed for the diverse, multicultural, and multilingual concert of worship that will ring through the corridors of heaven for eternity. Bible translation harvests the rich expressions of worship from around the world and prepares God's people for eternal kingdom life.

---

19 Bishop Vincent Watolia, personal conversation, May 2022. Bugwere refers to the land and ethnic group of the Bagwere people who speak Lugwere.

20 Covey, *7 Habits*, 2020.

Over the past two centuries, one of the merits of Bible translation has been the ability to adopt the names of God that were in use in the various ethnolinguistic communities of the world. This choice has been motivated by a need for critical contextualization that follows the example laid out by Paul in Acts 17, where he identified the shrine to "an unknown God" as pointing to the true God about whom he was preaching. The wisdom that undergirds this choice is that names, as linguistic signs, are two-sided, comprising a "signifier" and a "signified."[21] Look at these names of God: *Si* (Ghomala'), *Zamba* (Ewondo), *Loba* (Duala), *Mungu* (Swahili), *Allah* (Arabic), *Theos* (Greek), *Dieu* (French), and *Dios* (Spanish). These names have been loaded with the attributes of the triune God as revealed in the Scriptures. For example, the Ghomala' people knew God the eternal, Creator, and almighty God as *Si*. However, they did not experience him as a personal God but as a distant one who required ancestral mediators. Moreover, the mythologies that made sense of how he created and ordered the world have given way to the biblical notion of God. In this way, though the signifier remains the same, the signified has been completely changed and reoriented toward the Creator and all-eternal God as revealed in the Scriptures. In the same way, through the process of translation and the theological formation of the church, the former meanings that were attached to those names, as well as the stories and legends, are constantly sifted and modified to align with Scriptures. It has been observed that, when an ethnolinguistic community engages in this theological formation, transformation occurs over a few decades; the new generations no longer recall the stories and attributes used to relate to the names of God.

As an illustration, the hymn "Yeso Kristo ba Fo Yokpa" is a recent creation of NACAM[22] in the Ghomala' community of West Cameroon.[23] It employs a rhythm from a well-known traditional musical genre. The song is participatory: A leader sings couplets, and people respond with a refrain.

21 When we use language, we express each reality through a sequence of sounds. This is called the signifier. Through a sort of agreement among those who have the language in common, this signifier refers to or points them to the same representation of the reality in their minds (signified).

22 Nouvelle Alliance du Cameroun (NACAM) is a choral group of l'Eglise Evangélique du Cameroun (Evangelical Church of Cameroon). It was formed during the 1960s to fight the domination of the Medumba language in the church and to give its speakers the chance to praise and worship God in their mother tongues. They primarily use the Ghomala' language and its expressive forms and musical rhythms indigenous to this cultural region in their songs and performances.

23 Kenmogne, "Theologising in Context."

Specifically, when the leader declares, *Cyepo Yeso ba Fo yokpa* (The Lord Jesus is our King), the people and the chorus respond in unison, *E ba Fo* (He is indeed King). In this hymn we can observe how the various attributes of God are derived from people's daily experience and from Scriptures. In the process, the concept of *fo*, which historically applied to an earthly king, is redirected to become an attribute of God. Meanwhile, the new meanings of *fo* that are derived from the new understandings of the attributes of God allow the people to reappraise human leadership, which is often marked by corruption and abuse.

**Table 14.1. Yeso Kristo ba Fo Yokpa**

| Couplet | Ghomala' | English |
|---|---|---|
| **1-7: Jesus in Relation to People's Experiences of Reality** | | |
| 1 | Yeso Kristo bə fo yɔkpa | Jesus Christ is our king |
| Refrain | E bə fo | He is truly king |
| 2 | Bə fo bə dɔkta yɔkpa | A king who is our doctor |
| 3 | Bə fo bə də ŋkəkuɔ gə ŋkam | A king who raises the lowly into elites |
| 4 | Bə fo bə tá gwɔ̀ŋ pǒmcyə | A king who is the father of all orphans |
| 5 | Bə fo bə dé mpfɔk pənjẅi | A king who takes care of widows |
| 6 | Bə fo nɔmtəma' fo a jo | The king of the paramount ruler of Bandjoun high chief of the Jo |
| 7 | Bə fo bə nyap gwuŋ yok e | A king who is the creator of our world |
| **8-15: Biblical Basis for Statements About Jesus** | | |
| 8 | Mo lǎ m jɔ gó' pâ' Yeso a | No one has suffered like Jesus |
| 9 | Pu lə kwe é thə nta' mbu | He was nailed to pieces of wood |
| 10 | Eloi Lama Sabaktani | My God, my God why have you abandoned me? |
| 11 | Si a Si a O tak a bi wa | My God, my God why have you abandoned me? |
| 12 | E lə yɔ go tə mpfǘ | He suffered until he died |
| 13 | Yɔsep sɔ' kwa e ŋgɔ təŋ | Joseph carried him to be buried |
| 14 | Nga mo la' bin si pa' Yosep a | May everyone have Joseph's faith in God |
| 15 | Nga gɔm yɔsep mu e Arimathé a | I'm speaking of Joseph of Arimathea |

| **16-21: Jesus in Relation to People's Experiences of Reality** | | |
|---|---|---|
| 16 | Yeso bə fo mu' fo tə wə a | Jesus is a king without equal |
| 17 | Yeso Kristo bə fo yɔkpə | Jesus Christ is our king |
| 18 | Bə fo tə pə də mo jɔ ŋgó' | He is a king who doesn't torture his subjects |
| 19 | Bə fo tə pə ncó' la' mo | He is a king who doesn't banish anyone from his kingdom |
| 20 | Bə fo tə pa niŋ mo cɛ | He is a king who doesn't imprison his subjects |
| 21 | Bə fo tə pə gɔm biŋ fɛ | He is a king who doesn't go back on his word |
| **22-30: Biblical Basis for Statements About Jesus** | | |
| 22 | A lə cyə dzʉ́ tyə̌' tá | When three days had passed |
| 23 | Yeso piŋ jam nə vʉ̌ | Jesus rose from the dead |
| 24 | Nga ga mo la yɔ mo lə yu' e | I say that people saw and listened to him |
| 25 | Tomasi gə ndě yɔ ndə piŋ a | Thomas said that he couldn't believe without seeing |
| 26 | Yeso sɔ' ntɛ po pyə | Jesus appeared in the midst of his disciples |
| 27 | Nga po le mbu mǎ mɔ njɔ | He said to them: Look at my hands and see! |
| 28 | Po piŋ de mkwə mǎ mɔ njɔ́ | Then look at my feet and see! |
| 29 | Siŋ pú o njap nə be a | Stretch out your hand and touch my side |
| 30 | Nwɛnyə bi mo yə e piŋ tə yɔ a | Happy is the one who believes without seeing |

## Conclusion

Revelation picks up on Daniel 7:13–14 and displays frequent references to the themes of tribe, people, and language (Rev 5:9–10; 7:9–10; 11:9; 13:7; 14:6). These verses emphasize the universal reach of God's salvation, the inclusivity of worship, and the diversity of those who come to faith. While differences and diversity are often perceived as a problem, they are to be treasured in God's economy because they reflect the nature of God as Creator of all. The beauty of the scenery of 5:9–10 is like a multifaceted diamond with a variety of shining lights and colors. The multilingual and multicultural crowd that stands before the throne of God sings a harmonious, polyphonic anthem of praise and worship to the Lamb, whose blood redeemed them from all corners of the earth. This is the full manifestation of God's reign that we all long for. In turn, it sets God's expectation for the committed participation of his redeemed people to the advent of that kingdom.

In conclusion, it appears that engaging the ordinary languages of people and translating God's word into those languages constitutes the foundational step to orient people toward worship of the triune God, and it fulfills the goal as stated in 7:9–10. The fall of humanity resulted in the alienation of human beings from God and in the corruption of creation. The cultures of peoples and the languages that best convey them are all marked by this corruption. Hence, beyond restoration into fellowship with God, this missional activity allows for the redemption of the languages and cultures as they allow God's eternal word to "make its dwelling" (John 1:14 NIV) in them. Through ongoing interaction with the word, the worldviews, values, and beliefs of people are reappraised and redirected toward their Creator. The result is that people turn their cultural artifacts into instruments of worship of the Lamb of God. In the meantime, they rediscover their true identity as people created in the image of God. This discovery relieves them of the idolatry of their ethnic identity and enables them to appreciate God's hospitality as he welcomes into his kingdom all peoples, irrespective of their nations, tribes, and tongues. Rather than competing, each nation or ethnic group brings its uniqueness to the worship of the eternal God. There is no better way to prepare for the advent of the all-inclusive worship around the throne and the Lamb of God than to intentionally align more with our Christian identity than our ethnic identity. In this, the diversity of languages and cultures becomes a diamond that shines and radiates a diversity of colors, thereby expressing the glory of the almighty, all-knowing, and triune God.

## Bibliography

Capo, Hounkpati. "Langues africaines pour le développement durable et la culture de la paix en Afrique." In *Actes du 3e Congrès Mondial de Linguistique Africaine*, edited by Kézié K. Lebikaza. Rüdiger Köpper, 2000.

Covey, Stephen R. *The 7 Habits of Highly Effective People: Powerful Lessons in Personal Change*. Simon & Schuster, 2020.

Eberhard, David M., Gary F. Simons, and Charles D. Fennig, eds. *Ethnologue: Languages of the World*. 27th ed. SIL International, 2024. https://www.ethnologue.com/insights/how-many-languages/.

Guzik, David. *Genesis: Verse by Verse Commentary*. Enduring Word Media, 2018.

Jenkins, Philip. *The Next Christendom: The Coming of Global Christianity*. Oxford University Press, 2011.

Johnstone, Patrick. "Bible Translation and the Cross-Cultural DNA of the Church." Wycliffe Global Alliance, 2025. https://www.wycliffe.net/what-we-do/articles-for-further-reflection/bible-translation-and-the-cross-cultural-dna-of-the-church/.

Kenmogne, Michel. "Bible Translation as Justice." *Journal of Translation* 20, no. 1 (2024): 119–27. https://www.sil.org/system/files/reapdata/80/02/92/80029292755258210350131875986503806468/siljot2024_1_05.pdf.

Kenmogne, Michel. "Theologising in Context: An Example of the Study of a Ghomala' Christian Hymn." *Ethnodoxology* 6 (2018): A14–26.

Milkre-Sellassie, G. A. "The Early Translation of the Bible into Ethiopic/Geez." *The Bible Translator* 51, no. 3 (2020): 302–16.

Sanneh, Lamin. *Whose Religion Is Christianity? The Gospel Beyond the West.* Eerdmans, 2003.

Sanneh, Lamin. *Translating the Message: The Missionary Impact on Culture*. Rev. ed. Orbis Books, 2015.

Walls, Andrew. *Missionary Movement in Christian History: Studies in the Transmission of Faith*. Orbis Books, 1996.

Winter, Ralph D. "Three Mission Eras: And the Loss and Recovery of Kingdom Mission." In *Perspectives on the World Christian Movement: A Reader*, 4th ed., edited by Ralph D. Winter and Steven C. Hawthorne. Pasadena: William Carey Library, 2009.

# About the Contributors

**Cornelia van Deventer** (PhD, Stellenbosch University) is the academic dean of the South African Theological Seminary (SATS). Her research focus centers on the literary dimensions of Johannine literature (John's Gospel, John's Letters, Revelation) and the intended rhetorical effect on the reader or hearer. Previously, she served as the head of faculty research at SATS and as the editor-in-chief of the seminary's journal, *Conspectus*.

**Sigurd Grindheim** (PhD, Trinity Evangelical Divinity School) is professor of New Testament at Mekane Yesus Seminary, Addis Ababa, Ethiopia. His publications span a wide range of topics in New Testament studies, biblical theology, and missiology. His most recent book is *The Letter to the Hebrews* (Eerdmans, 2023).

**John D. Harvey** (ThD, Wycliffe College, University of Toronto) is professor of New Testament and director of the PhD program at Columbia Biblical Seminary of Columbia International University, where he has served since 1991. He has taught in Germany, the Netherlands, Moldova, the Republic of South Africa, Zimbabwe, and Zambia. His books include *Acts: A Commentary for Biblical Preaching and Teaching* (Kregel, 2023), *Romans* (B&H Academic, 2017), and *Interpreting the Pauline Letters* (Kregel Academic, 2012).

**Jessica Janvier** (PhD, Columbia International University) is a writer and academic whose focus crosses the intersections of African American religious history, church history, and theology. She currently lectures at Meachum School of Haymanot, which focuses on contextualized theological education for Black communities around the nation. She is an associate pastor in the United Methodist Church and worked as a transition leader for the Global Methodist Church.

**Michel Kenmogne** (PhD, University of Buea, Cameroon) is the executive director/CEO of SIL Global and has lived in Germany since 2016. Previously, he served for about twenty years in the field of Bible translation and language development in Cameroon and Francophone Africa. His publications intersect linguistics, Bible translation, and missiology, including "Translation in the 21st Century: Who Needs Scripture?" (2020).

**Kwa Kiem-Kiok** (PhD, Asbury Theological Seminary) is associate professor in Intercultural Studies at Singapore Bible College. She coedited *Missions in Southeast Asia: Diversity and Unity in God's Design* (Langham, 2022) and has published on a wide range of subjects, including human dignity, urban ministry, and justice. A lawyer by training, she also sits on several medical ethics boards in Singapore.

**Grant LeMarquand** (ThD, Wycliffe College, University of Toronto) is emeritus professor of biblical studies at Trinity School for Ministry and retired Anglican Bishop for the Horn of Africa (Ethiopia, Eritrea, Djibouti, Somalia). He has written and edited numerous articles and books in biblical studies, missiology, and Anglicanism, including *An Issue of Relevance: A Comparative Study of the Story of the Bleeding Woman in North Atlantic and African Contexts* (Peter Lang, 2004). He and his wife, Wendy, a retired medical doctor, are Canadians. They have two grown children and one grandchild.

**Sarah Lunsford** (PhD, Columbia International University) is an instructor of global studies for Liberty University and book review editor for *Evangelical Missions Quarterly*. She has served as an international church planter in Asia and is the author of *Missiological Triage: A Framework for Integrating Theology and Social Sciences in Missiological Methods* (Pickwick, 2023).

**Michael Naylor** (PhD, University of Edinburgh) is professor of New Testament at Columbia International University. He is the New Testament book review editor for the *Journal of the Evangelical Theological Society* and author of *Complexity and Creativity: John's Presentation of Jesus in the Book of Revelation* (Gorgias, 2018). He has also served as a guest lecturer at ministry training centers in Tasmania and Albania.

**Andrea L. Robinson** (PhD, New Orleans Baptist Theological Seminary) serves on the doctoral faculty of Huntsville Bible College, where she teaches biblical languages and strategic inclusive ministry. She is an interdenominational speaker and author whose work centers on ethics, ecotheology, and eschatology. Her previous books include *Heaven or Halakah: Walking with Jesus in John 14* (Wipf & Stock, 2024) and *Temple of Presence: The Christological Fulfillment of Ezekiel 40–48 in Revelation 21:1–22:5* (Wipf & Stock, 2019).

**Narry F. Santos** (PhD, Dallas Theological Seminary; PhD, University of the Philippines) is associate professor of Christian ministry and intercultural leadership at the seminary of Tyndale University in Toronto, part-time senior pastor of Greenhills Christian Fellowship (GCF) Peel and GCF York in Canada, and vice president of the Evangelical Missiological Society Canada. He has written *Family Relations in the Gospel of Mark* (Peter Lang, 2021) and *Slave of All* (Bloomsbury, 2003), coedited *Mission and Evangelism in a Secularizing World* (Wipf & Stock, 2019) and *Mission amid Global Crises* (Tyndale Academic, 2020), and contributed to many other books and academic journals.

**Edward L. Smither** (PhD, University of Wales Trinity Saint David; PhD, University of Pretoria) is dean of the School of Missions and Intercultural Ministry and professor of history of global Christianity at Columbia International University. Previously, he served for fourteen years in intercultural ministry in North Africa, France, and the USA. His previous books include *Christian Mission: A Concise Global History* (Lexham, 2019) and *Mission as Hospitality* (Cascade, 2021).

**Alexander E. Stewart** (PhD, Southeastern Baptist Theological Seminary) is vice president of academic services and professor of New Testament studies at Gateway Seminary in Ontario, California. Previously, he served for nine years with European Christian Mission in the Netherlands. He is the author of *Reading the Book of Revelation* (Lexham, 2021) and *Revelation* (B&H, 2024), among other books and articles.

**Abeneazer G. Urga** (PhD, Columbia International University) has served as the department head for the MA in biblical studies, lectures in biblical studies at the Evangelical Theological College in Addis Ababa, Ethiopia, and is an adjunct professor at Columbia International University and Ethiopian Graduate School of Theology. He is a member of Equip International, SIL Ethiopia/International, and an associate member of Studiorum Novi Testamenti Societas (SNTS). He is the author of *Intercession of Jesus in Hebrews* (Mohr Siebeck, 2023). He coedited *Reading Hebrews Missiologically* (William Carey Publishing, 2023), *Reading 1 Peter Missiologically* (William Carey Publishing, 2024), *Reading James Missiologically* (William Carey Publishing, 2025), and *Reading Hebrews and 1 Peter from Majority World Perspectives* (T&T Clark, 2024).

**Alistair I. Wilson** (PhD, University of Aberdeen) is a lecturer in mission and New Testament at Edinburgh Theological Seminary, Scotland. He is a minister of the Free Church of Scotland. He served in theological education in South Africa from 2005 to 2014. Alistair has published several books and articles, including commentaries on Colossians and Philemon in the ESV Expository Commentary.

# Scripture Index

## Revelation

www.ingramcontent.com/pod-product-compliance
Ingram Content Group UK Ltd.
Pitfield, Milton Keynes, MK11 3LW, UK
UKHW041636190726
13854UKWH00006B/2529

9 781645 086802